PETS, PEOPLE, AND PRAGMATISM

AMERICAN PHILOSOPHY

Douglas R. Anderson and Jude Jones, series editors

PETS, PEOPLE, AND PRAGMATISM

ERIN McKENNA

FORDHAM UNIVERSITY PRESS   NEW YORK   2013

Fordham University Press has no responsibility for the persistence
or accuracy of URLs for external or third-party Internet websites
referred to in this publication and does not guarantee that any
content on such websites is, or will remain, accurate or appropriate.

Fordham University Press also publishes its books in a variety of
electronic formats. Some content that appears in print may not
be available in electronic books.

Library of Congress Cataloging-in-Publication Data

McKenna, Erin, 1965–
Pets, people, and pragmatism / Erin McKenna. — First edition.
pages cm
Includes bibliographical references and index.
ISBN 978-0-8232-5114-8 (cloth : alk. paper) —
ISBN 978-0-8232-5115-5 (pbk. : alk. paper)
1. Animals (Philosophy) 2. Human-animal relationships. I. Title.
B105.A55M38 2013
179'.3—dc23
2012043865

Printed in the United States of America
15 14 13 5 4 3 2 1
First edition

*To my mom—Barbara W. McKenna—for those early
lessons on living respectfully with other animal beings*

Contents

Acknowledgments

I would like to thank all the instructors in my life—especially philosophical, riding, and herding—who helped me gain experience and perspective. I would like to thank the philosophical community of the Society for the Advancement of American Philosophy for listening and responding to my work over the years. In particular I would like to thank Paul Thompson, Lisa Heldke, Lee McBride, Larry Cahoone, Judith Green, Scott L. Pratt, and David Vessey for valuable conversations and insight about my work on other animal beings. I would also like to thank Philip McReynolds, Kelly Booth, Steven Fesmire, Brian Henning, and Tadd Ruetenik for joining me on panels related to these issues at several meetings of the association. I learned much from these sessions. A special thanks goes again to Paul Thompson and Lisa Heldke for their careful reading of earlier drafts of this manuscript. While the three of us disagree on much surrounding these issues, the exchanges we had did much to improve the thinking I present here and reminded me again why I value such a philosophical community.

For riding and horse related experience I would like to thank Arlene Benshoof, my first riding instructor, who made sure the first lesson was one of respect and love. I want to thank Dan and Julie Williams of Williams' Training Stable for the gift of keeping Donald in my life and for introducing me to Hank. They have also shown me what transformations love and patience can bring to a horse's life. For my continued riding education I thank Sandy Dossett and Marilynn Dammon who helped me make the transition to dressage, along with Jerry Schwartz and Max Gahwyler. I would like to thank Carole Gallert who arranged clinics and then gave me the privilege of instruction on her own horse, William. I would like thank the instructors who have pushed me and prepared me for competition: Charles DeKunffy, Kim VonHopffgarten, Jeremy Steinberg, Jeremy Beale, and Joanna Herrinstad. I would also like to thank the countless people who have helped me care for, transport, and show my horses over the years: Carla and Phil Collett, the Halls, Rebecca Larson, Polly Kranick, Michelle Hoedeman, Helen Greenwell, Tanja Oliver, and Diane Winters. And for the dogs I again thank Arlene Benshoof for first introducing me to Australian Shepherds. I thank the obedience class instructors, whose names I've forgotten—Tuffy and Pandora loved those classes. I thank Alice Kapelos and Linda DeJong for helping me learn to herd sheep with Nemesis, always keeping the welfare of the sheep in mind.

I would like to thank Pacific Lutheran University for supporting my scholarship over the years. I specifically thank them for monetary support that enabled me to spend time at the Center for John Dewey Studies. I would also like to thank my Spring 2010 Writing 101 class on Pets and my Spring 2012 Pragmatism and American Philosophy class. Our discussions were enlightening. I would like to thank my department colleagues for their support. I thank Chris James (Senior Office Assistant in the Division of Humanities) for her help with the manuscript and Leann Evey (Senior Administrative Associate in the Office of the Provost) for her assistance and insight. I would also like to thank various colleagues in the Department of English for useful conversations about other animal beings over the years: James Albrecht, Charles Bergman, and Barbara Temple-Thurston in particular.

I would like to thank *The Pluralist* for permission to reprint a modified version of some of what appeared in an article titled "We Are Hers" (Vol. 6, No. 3, Fall 2011). Similarly I would like to thank Routledge for permission for some material from my chapter, "Charlotte Perkins Gilman: Women, Animals and Oppression," in *Contemporary Feminist Pragmatism* (Routledge, 2012).

I would like to thank Nemesis, Tao, Maeve, and Kira—the dogs who had to live with me while I worked on this project. Their patience was admirable; their insistence on taking breaks to play invaluable. Of course I would like to thank the many horses, dogs, and cats who have shared so much with me over the years.

PETS, PEOPLE, AND PRAGMATISM

INTRODUCTION

The Problem with Pets

[T]he use of animals for our purposes without consideration of their interests is so pervasive and our dependence up on it so great, it becomes invisible to us, in much the same way that exploitation of women and minorities was invisible for too long.

—Bernard E. Rollins, *The Unheeded Cry*

How does a vegetarian animal advocate justify "owning" three dogs, two horses, and living with two indoor cats? Worse yet, how does she justify training the dogs, herding sheep with the dogs, and training and competing with the horses? How does she object to factory farming but participate in stabling horses? Isn't it just a difference in degree of confinement? How does she object to eating meat (including lamb) for reasons of environmental harm and animal suffering, yet pay a stock fee so she can train her dogs to herd sheep?[1] The sheep are used so her dogs can have some work to do (have fun). If the confinement of livestock for meat production causes suffering and so is wrong, doesn't this apply to the confinement of animals for pleasure uses, even if the level of confinement and the conditions differ?

---

1. The keeping of these animals also has repercussions for the environment and the potential for feeding more humans. These will not discussed here, though they are very important. For instance, if the feed consumption of livestock raised for meat is wasteful and harmful to the environment, doesn't this apply to sheep used for herding and horses used for riding? What about manure disposal?

Many animal advocates would like to end the practice of keeping animals in captivity in zoos, aquariums, marine parks, circuses, biomedical labs, farms, and homes. Many animal advocates object to domestication and would like to end the practice of people "owning pets" or living with "companion animals." Such advocates, People for the Ethical Treatment of Animals (PETA) and philosophers Tom Regan and Gary Francione among them, believe that we should return to some idealized condition or time when we humans just left other animal beings alone to be animals.

I agree that many, if not most, of human beings' current practices with regard to other animal beings are morally problematic. I have my own arguments critiquing zoos, animal experimentation, factory farming, and many instances of pet ownership. None of these arguments, however, is based on a "non-interference" goal nor on a sense that human beings should be separate from all other animal beings. *The idea that human beings are ontologically different from other animal beings is a problematic view and, ironically, one often shared by animal rights/welfare people as well as by those who support the idea that the rest of nature exists simply for humans to use in any way they see fit—a dominance and use view.* Both positions rest on a belief in human exceptionalism, though with different outcomes.

To challenge these views, we need to realize that human beings are animals and we are part of nature. Our interactions with other living beings are not by definition non-natural and so to be avoided. Such interactions are natural and can be mutually beneficial. What we need to do is examine and improve such interactions, as we have historically done with many human-human relationships. We do not need to end these interactions or abandon the relationships. We couldn't abandon them even if we wanted to. Our lives are intertwined with the lives of other animal beings—especially domesticated animal beings. This book examines whether there can be morally satisfactory relationships with horses, dogs, and cats that include some level of confinement, training, and control. Given that "more Americans (63 percent, or 71 million households) live with a companion animal than have children of their own," this is a pressing issue (E. Williams 231).[2]

---

2. Most books on animal rights, animal welfare, animal liberation, or animal ethics focus on discussions of human obligations to, and treatment of, other animal beings in the wild, in food production, in research settings, in zoos, and in the entertainment industry. The position developed here has something to say about all of these, but here I start with the relationships *most* human beings

A Brief History of Some Views

When people find out I live and work with horses, dogs, and cats, all sorts of preconceptions about what that means start to emerge. They are sure they know what I think about many issues. For instance, since I ride horses I must agree with the recent US ban on the slaughter of horses for human consumption. Given recent tragedies on the racetrack, I must be against horse racing as well. Since I live with multiple dogs, I must want to meet all dogs, want dogs to be off leash as much as possible, oppose all physical and behavioral modifications, and oppose buying purebred dogs. If I like cats, I must always oppose de-clawing. There is the split between those who insist cats should be kept indoors and those who insist they should have access to the outdoors, but both sides assume I agree with them completely. If one is not willing to endorse an absolutistic position, one ends up walking a tight rope stretched between the extreme positions on these issues. But extreme positions unnecessarily divide people who could work cooperatively to improve the lives of various animal beings.

For example there are legal action committees within the Cat Fancier's Association (CFA) and the American Kennel Club (AKC). One of their main tasks is to keep abreast of "unreasonable animal control legislation" (cfa.org). The CFA warns about the "coercive legislation" being pushed by "animal activists." They point out that "cat and dog groups can and do contribute to rescue and other solutions when they are not alienated by organizations insensitive to their contributions." Instead of these groups working together, however, the CFA regularly posts "Legislative Alerts" to urge its members to oppose legislation backed by various animal rights groups, and some of these same animal rights groups (PETA for example) attack the idea of purebred cats and dogs and argue that "no breeding can be considered 'responsible'" (peta.org). On the other hand, the American Society for the Prevention of Cruelty to Animals (ASPCA) does promote adoption, but they also believe there are "responsible breeders" and that such breeders are well-positioned to help educate those who buy and adopt these animal beings and so improve the lives of these animal beings (aspca.org). The Humane Society of the United

---

have with other animal beings. That is with their relationships with pets—the animal beings with whom they live and share their lives.

States (HSUS) endorses adoptions as a good way to bring a dog or cat into one's home, but does not say it is the *only* responsible way. But given the fear that exists, many breeders are as suspicious of groups like the ASPCA and HSUS as they are of PETA. They are all seen as interchangeable and equally dangerous. These misperceptions create divisions that distract from the potential of focusing on the common ground that exists among these groups.

A clear example of this is the subgroup of animal rights advocates, animal welfare workers, and animal liberation people who think that if I care about other animal beings, and if I am concerned about treating them morally, I shouldn't "own" any animal beings and certainly shouldn't keep them in confinement or compete with them. Moreover, I shouldn't refer to them as "pets." This view is most closely identified with the animal rights position of philosopher Tom Regan and the work of Gary Francione. Francione says, "If we took animals seriously and recognized our obligation not to treat them as things, then we would stop producing and facilitating the production of domestic animals altogether. We would care for the ones whom we have here now, but we would stop breeding more for human consumption. And with respect to nondomesticated nonhumans, we would simply leave them alone" (13). This kind of view translates into much division and suspicion among groups who could be allies in improving the relationships between human and other animal beings.

An instance of this in action can be seen in the campaigns to replace the term "owner" with "guardian." The ASPCA, which does believe "that the keeping of appropriate, carefully maintained pets is fully justified," supports this change as it "is intended to better reflect humans' relationship with and responsibility toward companion animals, and to recognize animals as separate and unique entities deserving of protection and respect." They argue that this shift helps humans see themselves as caretakers who protect and nurture rather than owners who have "title and dominion over the animal . . ." (aspca.org). The HSUS refers to "human companions" in their policy and belief statements, but appears to have no official stance on this issue. On the other hand the American Veterinary Medical Association (AVMA) "recognizes the role of responsible owners in providing for their animals' care. Any change in terminology describing the relationship between animals and owners, including 'guardian,' does not strengthen this relationship and may, in fact, harm it" (avma.org). These two opposing views represent the more balanced discourse on this topic. Others who weigh in take more extreme views and further divide potential allies. For instance, In Defense of Animals (IDA) ties this "Guardian Campaign" to commitments to spay and neuter all animal companions (and so stop all breeding), and to only adopt animals—never buy or sell (idausa.org). This places them in opposition to all breeders who respond with the concern that such a change will limit their ability to care for the animal beings. "While the term 'guardian' may generate warm and fuzzy feelings to pet advocates, there is little beyond this intentional misguided softness that can be considered positive. The term 'guardian' is based on the desire of certain animal rights groups to eliminate pet ownership" (defendingdog.com). This concern gains support from statements from PETA:

> We at PETA very much love the animal companions who share our homes, but we believe that it would have been in the animals' best interests if the institution of "pet keeping"—i.e., breeding animals to be kept and regarded as "pets"—never existed. . . . This selfish desire to possess animals and receive love from them causes immeasurable suffering, which results from manipulating their breeding, selling or giving them away casually, and depriving them of the opportunity to engage in their natural behavior.

Reactions to statements like this result not just in opposition to PETA, but to all the groups concerned with the welfare of animal beings. Efforts by the HSUS to pass the Puppy Uniform Protection and Safety Act are seen as "intended to destroy the dog breeding industry and pure bred dog sales nationwide: (24thstate.com). Even as the AKC works to enforce responsible breeding practices, they argue that "the American public has adopted a negative focus and has absorbed a lot of misinformation and half-truths about breeding and purebred dogs from groups that in some cases oppose breeding altogether" (High Volume Breeders Committee Report, 20). As a result the AKC sees itself as an advocate for those who breed dogs, and is committed to the rights and interests of dog owners.

I do not wish to vilify or praise any of these groups, only to set the landscape. All of these views tend to oversimplify the situations we face. They often rely on willful misreading and misinterpretation of what people say. They tend to push people to extreme and often contradictory positions. This results in unnecessary opposition and commitment to rigid positions. This makes work for real change in the relationships among humans and other animal beings difficult.

Human beings' many and varied relationships with other animal beings are not so simple, though. I think that the key to resolving specific issues, and to examining the ethics of how human beings interact with other animal beings, is to be found in examining the various relationships we have with each other. Is there respect and regard for the particular animal or animal beings in particular situations? While potentially it might be easier to ban the slaughter of horses, without taking other actions to ensure the well being of horses such a ban won't do much to improve the lives of horses and may, in fact, make it worse. And why ban the slaughter of horses but not address the slaughter of cattle, pigs, or sheep? It might be easier to have veterinarians simply stop doing cosmetic surgeries such as cropping ears, docking tails, or de-clawing, but such sweeping action lumps a variety of issues and concerns together and probably addresses none of them well. For instance, how does one sort out opposition to branding and tattooing (since they cause pain) from the endorsement of microchips? With microchips there is still pain (though briefer) and the animal is still "numbered." Similarly, those who want to ban certain breeds of dogs, shut down off-leash areas, or remove all horses from work on the streets are failing to consider the individual variations in circumstances and beings. *All or nothing kinds of changes may be easier to support and enact, but they often do as much harm as good. This may sound like common sense to some. However, the debates among animal advocates, and between animal advocates and others interested in relationships with other animal beings, have not generally been guided by informed contextual thinking. Instead, principles have been applied in absolute and universal ways.*

For instance, many people who love other animal beings, and are concerned about ethics, take cues from wildlife issues and seek some kind of non-interference approach to life with other animal beings.[3] On this view human beings are just caretakers, and the other animal beings should be left to express their natures as they will. This view, ironically, often is

---

3. It's another question as to whether this is a good approach to living with "wild" animals. The ideas of wildness and wilderness are very complicated, but such concepts cannot reasonably mean no human contact or no influence from or by humans. Our influence, as that of other natural creatures, is present everywhere on the planet.

found in people who also have little to no information about what that particular "nature" might be. On the other extreme, there are many who treat the other animal beings in their lives as dependent humans. They often project their own interests and desires onto them as well. They must want more food, dessert in particular. They must hate being told what to do. The human assumes the other animal beings must want to have offspring and won't be fulfilled if they don't have them. *Both of these approaches, hands-off and overly anthropomorphic, often lead to unhappy relationships in which both human beings and other animal beings suffer and have their interests thwarted.*

A whole different problem, of course, is the abuse and neglect of animals. This can be outright cruelty, it can be neglect, it can be harsh use, or it can be disregard for the individuals' well being. Discussions of ethics don't always differentiate between these circumstances or the issues that arise in these different situations. If there is abuse or neglect on race tracks—dog or horse—many jump to the position that racing is cruel. Since cruelty is wrong it follows, for them, that racing must be stopped. If some exhibitors engage in cruel practices in the pursuit of competitive titles with other animal beings, many jump to the position that showing and competition with animals is always wrong. If training other animal beings to perform certain tasks or tricks is sometimes done in ways that harm the other animal beings, training in general comes to be seen as something that is always an unwarranted and cruel manipulation of the other animal beings and so something to be stopped.

None of these issues is so simple, nor does this logic work. Our relationships with other animal beings are long and complicated. This is especially true of our relationships with domesticated animal beings. That is the focus of this book. While I will discuss domestication in general, and ethical issues connected with many domesticated animal beings, my primary focus will be on those animal beings who are commonly considered to be pets in the twenty-first century in the United States.[4] I am concerned about "the inevitable social tendency, reflected all across society, to see animal life as cheap and expendable, and to see animals as tools whose lives may be taken freely, especially if this is done

---

4. Later projects will take up the concerns with those domesticated animal beings commonly considered farm or meat animals and then move to the issues confronting our relationships with non-domesticated animal beings.

painlessly" (Rollins, *Unheeded Cry* 173). I will argue that animal life has value and animal beings have interests beyond avoiding pain. We need to learn about and begin to respect these interests, but we do not need to abandon our relationships with the other animal beings who are in our lives.

To examine the ethics of the relationships we have with domesticated animal beings, we need to take a step back and examine our understanding of the nature of these relationships. In philosophical terms, this calls on us to examine the metaphysical views and assumptions that operate when we consider the human relationship with the rest of nature. That is, what is entailed in being human, being a horse, being a dog, being a cat? How are the natures of these various beings impacted by interactions with other beings? While humans have a long history of understanding themselves as somehow superior to other creatures, an entirely different picture emerges if we understand that while we are not the same as any other animal beings with whom we have relationships, we do co-constitute each other. What it means to be human is influenced by our historical and current relations with other animal beings, especially the domesticated animal beings we call pets with whom our lives are intertwined. What it means to be a horse, a dog, or a cat is also influenced by these relationships.

Given that, we might want to spend less time trying to see how other animal beings can be "like us" (and so be deserving of ethical treatment), and more time trying to understand them as they are and examine how we interact with each other. If we think about other animal beings one way we make ourselves into "owners, eaters, wearers, vivisectors, trainers, users, hunters." If we understand them differently, we can become "lovers, protectors, communicators, observers, pupils" (Fudge 165). A whole range of relationships are available. I will suggest it is not completely an either/or choice. However, in order to avoid slipping into unreflective and disrespectful relationships of use, humans need to see and think differently. "[W]hen we turn to look another way, when we reverse the normal order that sees us attempting to assess the animal's capacity to be like us, and ask to learn from animals, we find something different. We find, in fact, a limitation to our own sense of power and dominion" (157). This shift in perspective is what is needed if we are going to be able to build and sustain respectful relationships between ourselves and other animal beings.

Pets and Anthropomorphism

To get started, we need to examine the term "pet" and we need to examine the tendency to attribute human traits and motivations to other animal beings—anthropomorphism. As mentioned, many animal advocates want us to stop using the term "pet." It is assumed to be demeaning, to imply ownership and dependence, and to anthropomorphize the other animal beings. That is, it understands them in human terms. I will defend the use of the term "pet" and I will, as many others are now doing, defend limited anthropomorphism.

First, anthropomorphism. Attributing human traits to other animal beings came to be seen as problematic as western science sought objectivity in the study of the behavior of other animal beings. Carried to its extreme, the avoidance of anthropomorphism results in seeing other animal beings as lacking emotions, intelligence, and interests. On the other hand, over-indulgence in anthropomorphism results in humans ignoring how the needs, interests, and intelligences of various other animal beings differ from those of human beings. This can lead to treating them as a kind of defective human—doted on but dependent. People with such views often indulge in dressing or blanketing animals even when it negatively affects their health and well-being; feeding them human food even when it negatively effects their health and well-being; and turning up the heat or shutting doors and windows to keep them warm even when it negatively affects their health and well-being. It can also lead to human beings being disappointed with the non-humanlike behavior of other animal beings. This disappointment often results in the humans abandoning and discarding the animal beings in their lives (Serpell, "People in Disguise" 131).[5]

However, without some amount of anthropomorphism, human beings would not have been able to interact with other animal beings as successfully as we have. We would not have been successful hunters or trappers, we would not have been able to domesticate livestock, nor would we have been able to live with pets. Some amount of anthropomorphism allows us to understand other animal beings because we do share a lot in common (more on this in Chapter 1). Our success can be

---

5. Anthropocentrism—human centeredness—can also enter here as human beings breed other animal beings to meet our aesthetic desires or for our preferred use.

seen in the fact that pets outnumber their wild relatives. "According to recent figures from the United States alone, there may be as many as 58 million dogs in American and nearly 73 million pet cats. . . ." (Serpell, "People in Disguise" 128). The relationship also works for the human beings. One study showed that people readily

> interpreted and evaluated the various behavioral signals of social sup-
> port they received from their pets as if they were coming from fellow
> human beings. In other words, anthropomorphism—the ability, in
> this case, to attribute human social motivations to nonhumans—
> is what ultimately enables people to benefit socially, emotionally,
> and physically from their relationships with companion animals.
> Most pet owners believe that their animals genuinely "love" or
> "admire" them, "miss" them when they are away, feel "joy" at their
> return, and are "jealous" when they show affection for a third party. . . .
> Anthropomorphism rules because, for most people, any other inter-
> pretation of the animals' behavior—any suggestions that it might be
> motivated by other than human feelings and desires—would instantly
> devalue those relationships. . . . (127–28)

So some amount of anthropomorphism has been necessary for these inter-species relations to exist at all. It is also necessary for such relationships to thrive. What is needed, then, is a view between the rejection of, and the over indulgence in, anthropomorphism. Human beings need to learn new and different ways of relating with other animal beings as well. "It is not, of course, impossible for a person to identify with and appreciate the 'dog-ness' of dogs or the 'cat-ness' of cats, but in most cases these are special skills that need to be learned. Anthropomorphism, in contrast, tends to come naturally" (128).

And what about the term "pet"? Alternatives have been proposed: companion species, companion animal, significant other. There are similar issues with the word animal. Using the terms "human" and "animal" comes with a history of views that see human beings as superior to animals and the rest of nature. Using "human animal" and "nonhuman animal," helps to show the animal aspects of being human, but still sets up the human as the measure. Both of these usages also lump all nonhuman animals together. I want to emphasize that humans are animals and that "other animals" are not some homogeneous or undifferentiated group. I am using *human beings* and *other animal beings* for general discussion, though I prefer to discuss horse beings, dog beings, cat beings, and so on. We are all animal beings, though, and I don't want to lose sight of this as we examine our various relationships.

So why call some animal beings "pets"? Alan Beck and Aaron Katcher tell us that "the word 'pet' is derived from an agricultural term for an animal reared or mothered by hand, implying that a pet is a child within the family. The use of the word as a verb meaning 'to stroke, touch gently, or fondle' reflects the belief that touch necessarily accompanies any mothering" (84). As we will see in the next chapter, touch probably played a key role in the very possibility of domestication. For my purposes here, "pet" applies to those animal beings with whom human beings have especially intimate relationships that are not primarily focused on use value, but are heavily focused on companionship. These relationships allow for mutual benefit and engagement. Mutual benefit and engagement are not guaranteed, however. There are serious issues related to the status of pets.

"Is a pet an animal? . . . A pet . . . is an animal who enters our (human) domestic space. . . . [T]hey are both human and animal; they live with us, but are not us; they have names like us, but cannot call us by our names." The category of pets emerged in the sixteenth century as livestock were being removed from the home. The term "pet" applied to animal beings with no utilitarian function. The lap dog is an extreme version of this. They are in our lap and in our bed. They are pretty or cute, but they generally provide no services beyond companionship (Fudge 27–28). Are such relationships beneficent or exploitative?

Some believe pets are positioned as slaves. We own them, can buy and sell them at will. We control their breeding and decide if they will live or die. Francione writes,

> Slave welfare laws, like animal welfare laws, generally required that slave owners merely act as rational property owners but did not recognize the inherent value of the slaves. Slave owners were, of course free to treat their slaves, or particular slaves, better. But as far as the law was concerned, slaves were merely economic commodities with only extrinsic or conditional value, and slave owners were essentially free to value their slaves' interests as they chose, just as we are free to value the interest of our dogs and cats and treat them as members of our families or abandon them at a shelter or have them killed because we no longer want them. (9)

Those who argue that slavery best describes the current status of pets argue that we shouldn't use animals as resources, but should accept them as persons (11, 23).

While human beings give pets homes, give them names, feed them human food, have birthday parties for them, dress them, put them in daycare, take them to specialists, pay for expensive surgeries for them, we still often see them as things. These same animals may have their ears cropped, their tails docked, or their claws removed. When they don't act the way we want them to, or they become inconvenient, many humans just get rid of them. In the United States about six to eight million dogs and cats are abandoned or relinquished each year and over half of those end up being killed (humanesociety.org).

The legal and ethical status of pets is still much in question. It is legal, however, to kill one's pet, for any reason, as long as it is done humanely. Pets are generally seen as property, even when humans attempt to protect them. For instance, in the United Kingdom, the 1911 Protection of Animals Act allowed one to prosecute a driver for causing unnecessary suffering to an animal being. But their 1972 Road Traffic Act requires that one report hitting a dog with one's car, but does not require one to report hitting a cat. In the United States, pets who are injured or killed in a traffic accident are considered property. An owner may receive money based on the estimated value of the pet, but not compensation for medical care that results from the accident or for pain and suffering.[6] The Cat Fancier's Association actually defends this property status as they think it helps people protect and provide for the animal beings in their lives.

> The Cat Fanciers' Association, Inc. strongly supports caring and responsible pet ownership. CFA upholds the traditional property rights of animal owners that provide the basis for their ability to make decisions about their animals' well-being, including health, reproduction and transfer to a new owner. Owned cats are valued family members. As legal property, they cannot be taken away from us except by constitutional due process. The term "guardian", whether inserted

---

6. There is reason to be cautious here. If we begin compensating for pain and suffering there is a risk that lawsuits will drive up health care and insurance costs for pets as it has done for humans. This problem may require reform of how we treat human loss and suffering as well if it is to be a rational reform.

into animal laws or in common usage, contradicts this critical protective and personal relationship. CFA rejects the concept of animal "guardianship", which can be challenged or revoked, because of the potential legal and social ramifications that would negatively impact veterinarians, animal rescuers, breeders and sellers of animals as well as pet owners. (cfa.org)

Regardless of the ambiguity and disagreement about the legal status of pets, most human beings love the pets in their lives. This does not necessarily mean treating them well or respecting their "rights," though. Further, while loving pets does not frequently transfer to seeing other animal beings similarly, there are some places of overlap. For instance, many human beings love dog beings at the same time that they eat pig beings. There is no transfer from the relationship with the dog to the relationship with the pig. But there is generally some transfer for rabbit beings. Many human beings in the United States do not want to eat rabbits, even if they do not keep a rabbit as a pet themselves (Fudge 29–34). To ask what is the proper way to view other animal beings is to ask a very complex question. Are other animal beings seen as kin, as objects of use, or as citizens? Human beings seem to mix all three analogies (Fudge 11–12). Domestication tends to be tied to concepts of property and money, and so domesticated animal beings are owned and seen as being for the exclusive use of their owners. They keep all profit the animal beings earn, have the right to kill them, and they can be taken in payment of debt. Today, for instance, it is quite common in a horse boarding or training agreement for there to be a clause that says if the owner of the horse gets behind in paying their bill, the horse may be taken and used or sold as payment. "Animals are commodities that we own and they have no value other than that which we, as property owners, choose to give them" (Francione 37).

That we do value pets can be seen in the fact that we persist in keeping them, despite some heavy costs. In the United States we spend about $11.6 billion on food and another $11 billion on healthcare for pets. Another estimate says that in 2006 we spent $40.8 billion on food, toys, and clothing. We also spent $2.1 billion buying 382 million animals. We pick up and dispose of waste. This results in an annual cost to the taxpayer of $2 billion (E. Williams 231–33, 250). There are other costs as well. About 800,000 people are treated for dog bites each year in the United States (Serpell, "People in Disguise" 124).

Some consider pets to be social parasites, others see pets as substitute humans for those who are unable to have normal human relations. However, humans benefit from these relationships of companionship. As James Serpell points out, "Pet owners, for instance, have been shown to possess fewer physiological risk factors . . . for cardiovascular disease than nonowners, and they also exhibit improved survival and longevity following heart attacks. They also appear to be more resistant to the stressful effects of negative life events, resulting in fewer health problems and fewer visits to doctors for treatment" ("People in Disguise" 125). These relationships also seem to function as a form of social support. For most people the emotional bond with other animal beings is more important than any economic utility (131). Serpell notes that "The anthropomorphic tendency to attribute human feelings and motivations to nonhuman animals has given rise to a unique set of interspecies relationships that have no precedent elsewhere in the animal kingdom. These human-pet relationships are unique because they are based primarily on the transfer or exchange of social rather than economic or utilitarian provisions between people and animals" (131). Using the term "pet" helps to distinguish these kinds of social relationships from the many other kinds of human being/other animal being relationships while at the same time allowing for comparisons of these various relationships.

According to Serpell, "pet keeping is no different, and probably no worse, than other ways of using animals for human ends, including farming and biomedical research" ("People in Disguise" 132). There are ethical limits and costs to all of these relationships. However, these relationships *can* improve if we think about other animal beings differently. While we prefer to deny any personality to farm animals, we tend to think of pets as people in disguise. "[I]nstead of accepting and appreciating companion animals for what they are, we seem more inclined to abduct them across the animal-human divide, render them in our own 'image' . . ." (132).

Not seeing these other animal beings for who they are can also allow human beings to see them as property, and their status as property is used to justify our dominion and control of them. This is especially true of domesticated animals. With the increasing industrialization of society in the nineteenth and twentieth centuries full exploitation of animals as profit-producing objects emerged. The extreme of this can be seen in livestock production. Pets are less subject to this kind of use by the average "owner," but breeding and showing dogs, cats, and horses *can* exhibit some of the same tendencies. And other beings have market prices whether they are sold at auction, by breeders, or in stores. Their "value" is determined by our use or interest.

Further, there are common abuses. In breeding, these include the increased presence of congenital diseases and defects, over-breeding, confinement, and early weaning. In the realm of showing we have confinement, the use of drugs, abusive training techniques, and cosmetic surgeries. Pets often experience neglect, long confinement, verbal and physical abuse. In extreme cases they may be shot or burned. Of the high-profile abuse cases reported in the United States, 57 percent are cases of cruelty and 43 percent are cases of neglect (E. Williams 255).

While there are limits on ownership rights—one must provide food and shelter—the property status of other animal beings does not generally prohibit keeping them tied, hitting them, having them put to sleep for any reason, or killing them oneself (as long as it is done humanely. There is great latitude since they are seen as property (Francione 99, 163). This is what makes many people concerned with animal welfare, animal rights, and/or animal liberation see domestication as "a story of domination." "Our relationships with companion animals are born of submission and control. The bond we have with them is powerful, but so is our dominion over the animals with whom we bond. Worse, we betray and break the bond constantly" (E. Anderson 199).

At one extreme, some will argue that domesticated animals are "living artifacts" (Callicott, "Animal Liberation: A Triangular Affair" 52–53). They are not natural creatures so no natural behaviors are being frustrated by the conditions in which they exist. There is nothing to liberate and it's practically impossible to liberate animals, especially domesticated animal beings. At another extreme, some say that concern for other animal beings is required only when "they become participants in a scheme of cooperation with humans." Cows participate in milk production; cats, dogs, and horses serve as pets; primates participate in language experiments. The ideal is to make such activities virtually voluntary. On this view we are positively obligated to nurture and to support pets, and some other animal beings, when we regularly use them (Franklin 62, 105). A more extreme version of this view makes an exception of the animal beings we use and suggests that our moral obligations to other animal beings stop with pets: "Pets, for example, are . . . surrogate family members and merit treatment not owed either to less intimately related animals, for example to barnyard animals, *or*, for that matter, to less intimately related human beings" (Callicott, "Animal Liberation and Environmental Ethics" 256).

At another extreme is the position that all animals are persons and no use, confinement, or alteration of their being can be justified. We should stop breeding and keeping any domesticated animals. As Gary Francione says, "Although we express disapproval of the unnecessary suffering of animals, nearly all of our animal use can be justified *only* by habit, convention, amusement, convenience, or pleasure" (36). We do not need to hunt, wear fur, test cosmetics, or eat meat. None of these are necessary, the argument goes, so any suffering that accompanies these activities is unnecessary and should be stopped. There is "no moral justification for treating animals as replaceable resources—as our property—however 'humanely' we may treat them or kill them." When we do offer to protect animals, we almost always do so based on a desire for achieving some economic gain (xiii). From this position, to focus on our *treatment* of other animal beings is to miss the fundamental moral error of our *use* of other animal beings. So we must "stop producing and facilitating the production of domestic animals altogether. We would care for the ones whom we have here now, but we would stop breeding more for human consumption" (13). As mentioned before, the upshot of this approach is a call to see and treat animals as persons. This does not mean treating them as human persons, but it "does require that we accept that we have a moral obligation to stop using them for food, biomedical experiments, entertainment, or clothing, or any other uses that assume that animals are merely resources, and that we prohibit the ownership of animals" (62).

I reject all of these extremes. The idea that domesticated animal beings are not natural and therefore that no natural behaviors are being frustrated by the conditions in which they are kept relies on a sense of nature that puts humans outside of nature. It also assumes that anything that results from human action is not natural. Finally, it assumes that if something is not natural it has less or no value. The philosophical views of American Pragmatism challenge all of these assumptions.[7] The idea that *all* human relationships with other animal beings must end—because they violate the interests of the other animal beings and they fail to respect any intrinsic value of the other animal beings—is also a flawed idea. Equally flawed are the assumptions that humans are ontologically privileged, that any interaction with humans is harmful to the rest of nature, and that all relations are relationships of use and all use is a form of exploitation.

I use the resources of American Pragmatism, and some aspects of ecofeminism, to develop a middle ground. Many (if not most) of the human relationships with other animal beings in the United States are very problematic. However, the solution is neither to explain away the problems nor to prohibit all relationships. We cannot extricate ourselves from relations with other animal beings, nor would it be wise to try. Further, many of us are in special social relationships with those other animal beings commonly considered to be pets. While the term "pets" may be problematic, I use it here to describe the intimate and mutually transformative relationships experienced by many human and other animal beings. Rather than try to find a new term, I am interested in finding ways to develop more respectful relationships between other animal beings and their humans. For respectful relationships to be a real possibility, though, humans must make the effort to understand the beings with whom they live, work, and play. This requires that we begin with a look at the history of domestication.

7. I will be using "Pragmatism" as shorthand for some of the general views attributed to classical American Pragmatism. I am capitalizing Pragmatism to distinguish the philosophical ideas from the ordinary use of the term pragmatism, which means to treat things practically. There is more to the philosophical idea. Further, some use pragmatic as a disparaging term that implies a willingness to take up any position that will get them what they want. I think this is opposed to the spirit of Pragmatism.

UNDERSTANDING DOMESTICATION AND VARIOUS PHILOSOPHICAL VIEWS

The Legacy with Which We Live

We live with animals, we recognize them, we even name some of them, but at the same time we use them as if they were inanimate, as if they were objects.

—Erica Fudge, *Animal*

As philosopher Mary Midgley says, "Man does not naturally exist in species isolation." Human beings live in multiple-species communities and one of our special powers "is to draw in, domesticate and live with a great variety of other creatures" ("The Significance of Species" 135). This may even be a need. She says, "The point is not just that most human beings have in fact been acquainted with other creatures early in life, and have therefore received some non-human imprinting. It is also that children who are not offered this experience often actively seek it. Animals, like song and dance, are an innate taste" ("The Mixed Community" 218). This can be seen in the ubiquitous presence of animals in human lives: "All human communities have involved animals." Dogs were the first domesticated species. For domestication to succeed, human beings had to be able to understand the dog beings' social signals and form individual bonds. It doesn't work to rely on force or to treat other animal beings as machines; they must be recognized as social beings. Our successful cross-species relationships often rely on the fact that we each respond to the need for love and play. As Midgley puts it, "There is real individual affection, rather than mere exploitation, which arises between animals and people" (211–217).

Human beings and other animal beings are, and always have been, in relationships. We have evolved together. These relationships are not all the same; they vary. As Donna Haraway notes, "Through their reaching into each other, through their "prehensions" or grasping, beings constitute each other and themselves. Beings do not preexist their relating" (*Companion Species* 6). While many see the ways humans beings have constituted and transformed other animal beings, many miss the ways human beings have been constituted and transformed by their various relations with other animal beings. "Co-constitutive companion species and co-evolution are the rule, not the exception." Domestication has been a two-way street. Humans have been altered as much as they have done some altering of others. Relations with other animal beings altered human options for food, clothing, and travel. They may also have increased human empathy and sociality. Sharing environments and genetics has linked us from the start; our sharing of our lives has involved us in an increasingly complex and transformative set of relationships. For Haraway, "Domestication is an emergent process of cohabiting, involving agencies of many sorts and stories that do not lend themselves to yet one more version of the Fall or to an assured outcome for any-body" (*Companion Species* 30–32). Not all influences have been beneficial (on either side), but neither have they all been evil and so to be avoided. *To try to withdraw from relationships with domesticated animal beings would be to deny something central about who and what human beings, and other animal beings, are.*

Since no particular outcome is assured, we need to consider these relationships carefully and include in our considerations how the other animal beings are affected. "[I]nsofar as domesticated animals enter human systems of cooperation, concern for their well-being and (ascribed) interest in cooperating with humans will be obligatory on their human custodians and partners." With respectful attention, we can build on and improve these relationships. At the very least we need to make sure that any "use" we make of other animal beings can provide them with some benefit. "Domesticated animals . . . can surely share in the end for which they are used if they are adequately compensated for their efforts." This means not using them merely as a means nor keeping and discarding them as mere thoughtless instruments (Franklin 60, 41).

It means paying attention to the interests and needs of all the animal beings involved. This applies to our relationships with all domesticated animal beings, but especially to our relationships with those animal beings we consider pets.

In this book I focus on a subset of domesticated animal beings because our relationships with domesticated animal beings in general are complicated. We love and cherish some of these animal beings, we neglect and abuse others. Some are full members of our homes and families, others are made invisible until they appear on our plate as food. Here I focus on those other animal beings most often loved and cherished as part of our homes and families. However, understanding these pet relationships differently will have implications for our relationships with other domesticated animal beings as well as other non-domesticated species.

A Little Philosophy

I use the philosophical perspective of American Pragmatism to explore these relationships. The philosophical perspective of Pragmatism is not just about what is practical or expedient, though this is how the word is commonly understood. Rather, it is a view that understands humans as natural creatures already in interactive and transactive (mutually transforming) developmental relationships with the environment and the other creatures in it. Recognizing that humans are limited in perspective and prone to error (fallible), Pragmatism calls for a pluralist and experimental approach to living that focuses on trying to improve conditions (ameliorate). This is a perspective that has been largely missing from the discussion of how human beings and other animal beings can enter into respectful relationships, though it is well positioned to be part of that conversation. Most of the work in philosophy on animal issues has focused on a few approaches. The utilitarian perspective is most often represented by Peter Singer, and the deontological perspective is most often represented by Tom Regan. This has meant the debate has mostly been one between the utilitarian focus on reducing suffering—animal welfare—and the deontological focus on justice—animal rights.

Peter Singer's views may be the best known outside of philosophical circles and he has done much to influence the public debate about animal issues and efforts of reform. Focused on extending consideration of pain and suffering to all beings who can experience pleasure and pain, Singer's main point is that we are not morally justified in ignoring pain and pleasure in beings of another species just because they are not human. In his work he calls for improving or ending the use of other animal beings in agriculture and research. However, he does think that human pleasure and pain often trump the pleasure and pain of many other animal beings because humans have a higher degree of self-awareness and more capacity for meaningful relationships. Tom Regan takes issue with the utilitarians' focus on overall pleasure and pain rather than respecting the interests of individuals. He argues that, at least for most one-year old mammals, we have an obligation to respect the rights of these individuals who are the "subject of a life." As a result he calls for the abolition of farming, research, and sport hunting.

More recently other views have been given voice in these debates. Virtue ethics has emerged to ask us what kind of person we become when we treat other animal beings in particular ways and to suggest that in order to achieve human flourishing we need to alter our relationships with the rest of nature. Martha Nussbaum is a prominent voice here. Calling generally for providing the conditions that make it possible for all living beings to flourish, she includes attention to other animal beings. "[N]o sentient animal should be cut off from the choice for a flourishing life, a life with the type of dignity relevant to that species, and . . . all sentient animals should enjoy certain possible opportunities to flourish" (351).

Donna Haraway, among others, has brought the insights of Continental philosophy to these issues, helping us see the importance of "seeing" companion animals and companion species. She looks at the "myriad of entangled, coshaping species of the earth" and "contemporary human beings' meetings with other critters, and, especially, but not only, with those called 'domestic' . . ." (*When Species Meet* 5). Kelly Oliver has also both critiqued and used the resources of Continental philosophy to examine respectful understandings among human and other animal beings. This allows her to note the limits of the basic approach of Singer and Regan when they try to extend humanist ethics to other animal beings, even though those ethics depend on separating human and other animal beings. "Considering animals takes us to the limits of assimilationist politics and ethics based on sameness. . . . In the future, the extension of rights might begin to shift who belongs to what group, but it does not address the conceptual hierarchy of human and animal" (32).

Ecofeminism has also emerged as an alternative perspective. Early on, however, ecofemininsts did not take up animal issues as a central focus. Carol Adams, Josephine Donovan, and Val Plumwood (among others) have done much to change that. Some apply an extended ethics of care. Adams and Donovan write, "The feminist ethic of care regards animals as individuals who do have feelings, who can communicate those feelings, and to whom therefore humans have moral obligations. An ethic of care also recognizes the diversity of animals—one size doesn't fit all; each has a particular history" (2–3). Others point to how human women and other animal beings are often conceived of in similar ways—as objects of use and desire. This status is usually justified by denying woman and other animal beings the full capacity to reason. That some states are now including pets in protection orders that are issued in cases of domestic violence is a result of the work done by ecofeminists to combat such views. Similarly challenging the focus on reason alone, Plumwood notes: "Our failure to situate dominant forms of human society ecologically is matched by our failure to situate non-humans ethically, as the plight of non-human species continues to worsen" (2).

Given that the field seems crowded, why add another player? I think that, with the exception of some of the ecofeminist positions, these other philosophical perspectives start with some assumptions that limit the possibilities for understanding the relationships between human beings and other animal beings. The utilitarian, deontological, and virtue ethics perspectives were all developed before Darwin and the ideas of evolution. While current proponents take the changes in science into account when they discuss the nature and needs of other animal beings, they often smuggle in remnants of the view of humans as separate from the rest of nature. They also often fall into the trap of seeing certain relations as static and unchanging. The Continental approach improves on this, but often turns real animal beings into ideas or reflections of ourselves. Haraway offers a corrective to much of this, but her writing still tends in this direction and puts language and concepts in front of actual relations. Oliver, too, tends to focus on what other animal beings can teach us about being human rather than actually looking at the lives of the other animal beings. Ecofeminism does much to overcome this, but it sometimes unnecessarily limits who has connections with nature and how these are formed.

Regan notes the growing variety of perspectives in the call for reconsidering how humans interact with the rest of nature.

> [T]here is a variety of contenders each at war with the others, each vying for widespread acceptance, each having to face the hard fact that theirs is but one voice among many—and that a voice which more often than not speaks to (and is heard by) 'the converted'. Deep ecology, Feminism, Animal rights. These are among the voices in the insistent choir of dissent, and the message of one is seldom the same as that of the others.
>
>   Usually, that is. But not always. Dissonant though their demands often are, one main theme is the same: traditional moral anthropocentrism is dead. This is the faith shared by deep ecologists, feminists, proponents of animal rights, and other critics of the intellectual status quo. Their common task is to bury Protagoras once and for all. Humans are not the measure of all things. ("Foreword" x)

But anthropocentrism is not dead, even in these contending views of animal rights, animal welfare, and animal liberation. Singer prioritizes human interests. "[I]t is worse to kill a normal adult human, with a capacity for self-awareness and the ability to plan for the future and have meaningful relations with others, than it is to kill a mouse, which presumably does not share all of these characteristics; or we might appeal to the close family and other personal ties that humans have but mice do not have to the same degree; . . ." (19). Regan uses traits that have given humans' special status to measure which animals are "subjects of a life." "[T]he basic similarity is simply this: we are each of us the experiencing subject of a life, a conscious creature having an individual welfare that has importance to us whatever our usefulness to others. We want and prefer things, believe and feel things, recall and expect things. And all these dimensions of our life, including our pleasure and pain, our enjoyment and suffering, our satisfaction and frustration, our continued existence or our untimely death—all make a difference to the quality of life as lived, as experienced, by us as individuals" ("Justice, Rights and Obligation" 185). Nussbaum's list of capabilities also privileges sentience and self-consciousness. Haraway and Oliver seek to contest the divide, but still end up focusing on characteristics like language and consciousness. Oliver especially fails to see animal beings as animals and instead sees them merely as beings who can teach us about ourselves. While the roots of American Pragmatism also suffer from some of the same biases (and this will be discussed), its method moves us to some new possibilities. *It is a new approach, not just an extension of moral theories that were built on the assumption of human separation and superiority.*

I think American Pragmatism can help move us to a new way of relating with other animal beings. In exploring the view of Pragmatism I will use some of the ecofeminist insights to develop a Pragmatist feminist account of the possibilities for relationships between human beings and other animal beings that will help us all re-think how we live together.

Specifically, I want to counter the view that domesticated animal beings (especially pets) constitute a kind of unnatural being whom we use as a substitute for human companionship or for replacing our lost connection to the "wild." An example of this position can be found in Paul Shephard's *The Others: How Animals Made Us Human.* He says, "Pets are not part of human evolution or the biological context out of which our ecology comes" (150). I disagree and will use the views of American Pragmatism to argue otherwise. He also says, "What is wrong at the heart of the keeping of pets is that they are deficient animals . . . . They are monsters of the order invented by Frankenstein except that they are engineered to conform to our wishes, biological slaves who cringe and fawn or perform or whatever we wish. As embodiments of trust, dependence, companionship, esthetic beauty, vicarious power, innocence, or action by command, they are wholly unlike the wild world" (151). Again, I disagree and will argue that this kind of view fails to understand the continuum of life that undergirds the Pragmatist position.

Shephard says pets are "compensations for something desperately missing, minimal replacement for friendship in all of its meanings." If not used that way they are sought as a way to connect to the "wild." But, he says, "Pets, being our own creations, do not replace that wild universe" (151). The view of pets as replacements for human relationships is not supported by current research and fails to acknowledge how deeply embedded humans are in their environments. From the Pragmatist view we will see that *all creatures* interact and transform each other. Humans are no exception to this. To believe otherwise is to fall prey to yet another version of human exceptionalism. Similarly to think that there are some "wild" animal beings who are not affected by relations with humans is equally naïve and misguided. I will use American Pragmatism to argue against these views and to argue for the natural development of the relationships between human beings and various pet beings. To do this, though, we have to look at the physical and social evolution of the animal beings we now commonly consider pets in the United States.

Some Thoughts on Domestication

To begin, let us examine what it means to be a domesticated animal being, what characteristics allow for domestication, and what effects result from domestication.[1] According to Juliet Clutton-Brock, in *A Natural History of Domesticated Mammals*, a domesticated animal is "one that has been bred in captivity for purposes of economic profit to a human community that maintains total control over its breeding, organization of territory, and food supply" (32). Although Clutton-Brock is mainly focusing on domesticated livestock, the characteristics are useful

---

1. There are a number of different definitions of domestication. In an interesting book considering whether zoo animals might be semi-domesticated, Keekok Lee offers some of the possibilities. First, Price:

> that process by which a population of animals becomes adapted to man and to the captive environment by genetic changes occurring over generations and environmentally induced development events occurring during each generation.

Next Clutton-Brock:

> One that has been bred in captivity for the purposes of economic profit to a human community that maintains total control over its breeding, organization of territory, and food supply.

Then Bokanyi:

> The essence of domestication is the capture and taming by man of animals of a species with particular behavioural characteristics, their removal from their natural living area and breeding community, and their maintenance under controlled breeding conditions for mutual benefits.

Finally Issac:

> 1. The animal is valued and there are clear purposes for which it is kept.
> 2. The animal's breeding is subject to human control.
> 3. The animal's survival depends, whether voluntary or not, upon man.
> 4. The animal's behavior (i.e., psychology) is changed in domestication.
> 5. Morphological characteristics have appeared in the individuals of the domestic species which occur rarely if at all in the wild. (Lee, 60–61)

While there are interesting differences in these definitions, for my purposes here there is sufficient overlap for me to proceed by focusing on the definition offered by Clutton-Brock, though the others will enter the discussion along the way. I would like to note that while I am intrigued by Lee's basic premise, I do not completely agree with her view of domestication as an artificial state for the animal. It is a state *different* than being "wild." Human intervention is not, by definition, unnatural. I do agree with her, though, that the needs and desires of "wild," semi-domesticated, and domesticated animals differ.

here. Horses, dogs, and cats have served, and still do serve, as meat animals. But they have also become something more for most in the United States.

Candidates for domestication must be hardy—"the young animal has to survive removal from its own mother, probably before weaning, and adapt to a new diet, new environment, and new conditions of temperature, humidity, infection and parasitic infestation." To be become domesticated, animal beings must like humans and have behavioral patterns "based on a dominance hierarchy so that it will accept a human leader." They must not be overly prone to flight, so that they can be kept in pens and herds—this is described as "comfort loving." They must be useful—that is they are "an easily-maintained source of food, an itinerant larder that can provide meat when required." And finally, they must breed readily and be easy to tend—"be reasonably placid, versatile in their feeding habits and yet gregarious so that a herd or flock will keep together . . . ." (Clutton-Brock, *Natural History* 9). These many and varied requirements mean that only a small fraction of the earth's animals have proven suitable for domestication. What has this meant for these "chosen" few?

In general, domestication results in a reduced body size, a curled and larger tail, more white hair, lopped and lengthened ears, extra fat, smaller cranial capacity and smaller brain, shortened jaw, and smaller teeth (33–37). Behaviorally, however, most agree there are fewer obvious changes. With the possible exception of the cat, all domesticated animal beings come from social mammals (and it is not clear that free-living and domesticated cats are as anti-social as once thought). For most animal beings, the length of gestation, blood group, chromosome number, and the structure of their social behavior remain little changed with domestication (38). Many can interbreed with their wild cousins. They still have many of the instincts and much of the intelligence required by free living animal beings to negotiate their environments successfully. While these same instincts and intelligence sometimes frustrate the human beings who live with domesticated animal beings, it is these very characteristics that make the living together possible in the first place. This is an important point to keep in mind if human beings are to live with these other creatures in ways that respect and honor who they are. It can also help us to approach, and adapt to, the wide variety found in individuals.

Human beings have manipulated and changed the ways of life for a subset of mammals for at least 10,000 years. Clutton-Brock writes, "Human history has been inexorably linked with the exploitation and often very cruel treatment of animals. In today's society attitudes to animal welfare have improved, and it is beginning to be recognized that an understanding of the ecology and behavioral patterns of the wild species is necessary in ensuring the well-being and correct husbandry of their domesticated descendants" (*Natural History* iii). "Enfoldment" within human society is a done deal for domesticated animals. There is no going back—no return to a so called natural condition. *From a Pragmatist perspective domestication is a natural event and condition.* Improving our future treatment of these domesticated animal beings depends on our evolving understanding of who they are and who we are, not on denying the ways we have and continue to constitute each other. Humans bear an increased responsibility for domesticated animal beings because their very existence is the result of human beings separating groups from their "wild" counterparts and selectively breeding these animals. Why was this done in the first place? There are many competing answers to this question and they have different implications for our relationships with other animal beings.

To start, in the case of livestock, many assume it was to provide a "walking larder" (19). About 9,000 years ago, humans moved from following herds, to enfolding them within human society (19). It is argued by some that this was done in large part out of necessity. Ten thousand years ago all humans were hunter/gatherers; 5000 years ago most were farmers (63). One theory is that a decrease in habitable land, combined with a decrease in prey (due to overhunting), resulted in a move toward cultivation. Meat was hard to store before canning and refrigeration, so it needed to be stored "on the hoof." By 7000 BC there was evidence of changes in morphology in goats and sheep, and probably in cattle and pigs as well (66).

When we speak of domestication in this way, as intervening in nature, we often unconsciously presuppose human transcendence over nature (Manning and Serpell 4). We see domestication as a feat of engineering that is deliberate and planned (5). We see it as requiring compliance and domination (16). We then see that to be domesticated is to be second class (10). But for the Pragmatists this is false—there is no nature-human dichotomy or hierarchy. Further, this common story of domestication does not help us as much with pets.

With the animals we in the United States now commonly consider pets, the story is less clear. Horses, domesticated around 5,000 years ago, allowed for advances in transportation and pulling power. Dogs predate all other mammals, living with humans some 14,000 years ago. Dogs may have aided humans in hunting, pulling, and providing meat, but it seems that companionship may have been the main reason for the start of domestication: "[T]here is as much reason to believe that man's psychological needs were the primary cause for domestication of animals as that man needed to use animals for such material purposes as the saving of human labor and the satisfaction of a hunger for food" (Levinson in Beck and Katcher 167). Companionship and pest control probably best explain the domestication of cats. Cats don't technically qualify as domesticated on this account. But, cats are found living with humans 9,000 years ago, and control of their breeding may have been present by 4,000 years ago.

Other ways of looking at the story of domestication may make more sense out of the history of pets. In *Hunters, Herders, and Hamburgers,* Richard Bulliet questions the received wisdom on domestication. Specifically, he questions the common assumptions that "(1) domestication was a process, (2) that it was a process that involved purposeful human activity, and (3) that it was roughly the same process for all species" (80). Rather, he believes "domestication came about as an unintended, unremembered, and unduplicatable, consequence of human activities intended to serve other purposes" (46). In other words, rather than humans intentionally selecting and breeding for tameness, tameness was likely inherent or was a by-product of an activity engaged in for some other purpose. Ten thousand years ago humans would not have known enough about selective breeding to be so deliberate. Further, the farming story doesn't work for him. First, it would have taken too long to get enough other animal beings bred in captivity to supply meat or other products, and it would not have been worth the work and resources if the other animal beings served no other purpose along the way. Further, dogs were domesticated before humans settled down to farm and those animals most associated with providing labor (horses, donkeys, camels, water buffalos, yaks) were not domesticated until well after humans had been farming (81).

Instead, he conjectures, different animal beings came to be associated with human beings in different ways, at different times, in different places, for different reasons. For dogs and cats he suggests a process of self-domestication. Tame animals have smaller adrenal glands and so are less prone to the flight or fight response of most "wild" animals. Such animals would tend to survive only in small numbers in the wild as they would be eaten. But such animals would naturally be less flighty and might start hanging around humans in order to eat their garbage and/or to hunt the other small animal beings such as rodents who would feed on human garbage. The humans, over time, would see the advantage of having these animals around and offer protection. These animal beings, would then have more breeding success than they would have had in the wild (89). Specific breeds could emerge in particular areas due to limited breeding populations. Then, moving with the humans, the different populations might be mated in an effort to achieve certain behaviors or looks.

So, the beginning of domestication could have been unintentional and not conscious. Rather it was rooted in natural contact. When seen in the biological environment, the habits of other animal beings can make domestication seem almost inevitable. The whole process presupposes a social medium (Zeuner 15, 36–37). The relationships can be relationships of symbiosis, scavenging, social parasitism, taming, or systematic domestication (Zeuner 37–55).[2]

Similarly with pigs Bulliet argues for seeing domestication "as a naturally arising symbiotic relationship, rather than an extraordinary discovery . . ." (90). Rather than one event, domestication can arise differently in different societies. He notes that

> The wild porcine species *sus scrofa*, from which all domestic pigs are believed to descend, is widely spread geographically in Eurasia and

---

2. In all of this it is important to remember that domestication is a *process*—a long and complicated process. Lee quotes Bokonyi again,

> Since domestication is a complex interaction between man and animal, its consequences are influenced by society, economy, ideology, environment, way of life, etc. Any successful definition of domestication must reflect all these possible aspects of the evolutionary process. The result of domestication is the domesticated animal that first culturally and later morphologically differs from its wild form.

Then Price,

> Animal domestication is best viewed as a process, more specifically, the process by which captive animals adapt to man and the environment he provides. Since domestication implies change, it is expected that the phenotype of the domesticated animal will differ from the phenotype of its wild counterparts. Adaptation to the captive environment is achieved through genetic changes occurring over generations and environmental stimulation and experiences during an animal's lifetime . . . . In this sense, domestication can be viewed as both an evolutionary process and a developmental phenomenon. (Lee, 75)

North Africa. Over this vast territory, several patterns of pig domestication came into being. Some societies grazed pigs in forests where
they could eat acorns and hazelnuts and root for tubers. Other societies kept them close to human settlements and fed them on kitchen
waste or shared with them the roots and tubers eaten by the people
themselves. Some societies involved pigs in their religious rituals and
observed rigid restrictions on eating them. Others regarded pig meat
as a staple food. Some treated piglets as pets, even to the extent of
women letting them suckle at their breasts. Others considered them
embodiments of filth. . . ." (90)

He argues that the vast territory and the diversity in views argues for
multiple and local domestication events that arise out of "naturally
arising symbiotic relationships, rather than an extraordinary discovery
made by one group of humans who figured out how to achieve domestication" (90).[3]

A third story, or at least another factor to consider when trying to
understand domestication, involves the role of our body chemistry.
It turns out that relationships with other animal beings make us feel
good. Just being in the presence of other animal beings releases oxytocin.
It does the same in those beings now considered domesticated. In her
book, *Made For Each Other*, Meg Daley Olmert writes: "Oxytocin,
whether it's released by friendly human contact or various chemical
agents, can make us smarter, calmer, friendlier, healthier, even more
attractive. But our pets may do this best, since they seem to be particularly good at filling us with oxytocin. For this reason—and countless
others—we simply couldn't have a better friend" (191–192). There is feed-
back loop. As oxytocin makes social interactions possible, the social
interactions themselves produce more oxytocin.

> The receptive state of mind created during the approach phase pro-
> motes all kinds of positive interactions from fruitful conversation to
> casual touch to sexual intimacy. When the interactions involve
> welcome touch, pressure-sensitive nerves in our skin convey signals

3. It is also important to note that such relationships don't always result in domestication.
Elephants, for instance, perhaps because they have so few natural predators, are "tame" in the wild.
Humans engage in use relationships with them but, probably due to their size and appetite, have not
domesticated them.

to the oxytocin-producing nerves in the brain that lower heart rate, blood pressure, and our stress chemistry. They also cause a rise in the feel-good chemicals, dopamine, serotonin, and beta endorphin, that mark the occasion as enjoyable. The end result is a social encounter that produces a rewarding sense of relaxation and satiety. This also creates a fond memory that in the future, will whet our appetite for more. (50)

So, domestication was made possible by shared body chemistry and, because of that shared chemistry, our relationships with domesticated animal beings are continuously reinforced. These relationships generally make us, and the other animal beings, happier and healthier.

Why exactly some animals are domesticated and some are not is complicated and may ultimately be inexplicable. These relationships go too far back in history to be sure of their origins. Bulliet offers the possibility of humans originally using particular animals in religious sacrifice to conclude his narrative. He argues that as we lost our spiritual connections with nonhuman animals we moved to seeing them purely as a product. One does not have to agree with his whole argument to see that today, in western industrialized countries (particularly the United States) the view of animals as product dominates our mindset. This is particularly true for those animals classified as livestock and/or research animals.[4] I believe it is also often true of those animal beings we claim to love—our pets.

For my purposes here it doesn't matter if any particular explanation for the emergence of domesticated animals is entirely true or complete. In fact, the competing explanations demonstrate the complexity of human history and speak against any single, essentializing account of domestication or our relationship with pets. All the accounts mentioned here are likely incomplete and express particular biases of the academic fields of the authors (Clutton Brock—archaeozoology, Bulliett—history, and Olmert—documentarian for nature shows). However, all acknowledge the longevity of intimate relationships between human beings and other animal beings. Human beings and other animal beings were interacting and co-constituting each other even *before* the emergence of

---

4. I have addressed this in other places.

domestication. But something does seem to change as we enter the more intimate relationship of domestication—whatever the multiple reasons for that development. To successfully domesticate other animal beings, human beings had to be able to read, understand, and provide for the physical, intellectual, social, and emotional needs of the other animal beings—at least to a large degree.

At some point it was less costly in evolutionary terms for humans to learn to communicate with animals than it was for them to get bigger and so be able to dominate them by force (Morton 114). Humans had to be able to express intentions and read the intentions of others (other human beings and other animal beings). This put a premium on a complex brain and capacity for memory and learning. These connect with complex social systems and behavior. Early humans probably did not try to put animal communication in terms of human language, as our scientific approach does today, but accepted that animals communicated and learned to enter into their communication. This was necessary in order to eat and in order to not be eaten (Morton xviii, xxv).

Other animal beings have done the same with human beings. Domesticated animal beings have had increased opportunity for such learning due to their long proximity with humans. Despite our close genetic relationship with chimpanzees, dogs are generally better than chimpanzees at reading our communication cues.[5] Dogs are more likely than chimpanzees to find hidden food when a human points to where it is hidden. "Dogs also perform better in food-finding tests than wolves who were reared like puppies by humans. Even puppies, as young as nine weeks of age, some with rare human contact, tested well. Ancient dogs possibly mastered their ability to find food by reading human cues as part of their successful collaboration with humans" (E. Anderson 25). Dogs and humans have been training each other for over 10,000 years (Morton xii–xiii). While we have modified dogs, dogs have also modified us. So have the other animal beings we now consider pets.

---

5. An exception to this may be found in chimpanzees who have been "cross-fostered." In the case of Washoe, Moja, Tatu, and Dar—four chimpanzees who were cross-fostered and acquired the signs of American Sign Language (ASL)—there is an evident capacity to read the intentions and desires of their caregivers. These chimpanzees were raised as if they were deaf human children and "enfolded" into a human community. This further supports the idea that contact with humans, not innate capacity, is what is most influential.

Domestication and Pets

James Serpell provides important insights into the various views of the importance of human-pet relationships. He suggests that those human beings who do not like the idea of being influenced by other animal beings often hold pets and pet keeping in contempt. They see pet keeping as either wasteful—seeing no purpose in it—or as pathological—substituting for human relations (*Company of Animals* 119). Another motivation to keep pets at bay results from our conflicted relationships with other animal beings—do we kill or care (Rodberseck et al. 297–300)? Humans and other animal beings are intertwined in complex ways. We have important social relationships with each other, and these relationships help make us who we are. In some cases we are actually interdependent—socially and ecologically. There is great diversity in these relations as well, and so they require individualized research and examination. However, many try not to face the contradictions of personalizing pets and depersonalizing the animal beings we eat (Benton 68, 73). As Serpell notes, some disparage pet keeping in order not to face contradictions this practice presents for other forms of use. To do this we often focus on the extreme cases of pet keeping. It is easier to dismiss those who see pets as human substitutes or engage in extreme practices (*Company of Animals* 16–19). Thirty nine percent of pets have human names. We spend more on pets than we do on candy. Eighty percent of dog owners and sixty three percent of cat owners buy these animal beings gifts. The average gift costs $17. We spend billions on their food and toys (E. Anderson 82–85). There are the birthday parties with fire hydrant birthday cakes, day care opportunities, and pet hotels with fully furnished rooms. The Ritz-Carlton hotel offers aromatherapy, Burberry raincoats, and gold plated identification tags. Some see these kinds of products and services as patronizing and condescending to the other animal beings (Serpell, *Company of Animals* 41).

Clearly some do see pets as playthings (even if loved), but not all do. There is dependency, but inequality does not always entail domination or lack of understanding (Serpell, *Company of Animals* 41–42). Generally there is mutual liking and mutual trust. Pets don't substitute for human relations. They augment and complement these relationships (103, 116). Pets help with loneliness and social isolation by their presence, and they often act as a social lubricant for other human relations. Human-pet relations help human beings become more empathetic and help them learn to think about others.

Serpell, interestingly, notes that pet keeping increased as anthropocentrism decreased and an egalitarian view developed (*Company of Animals* 135). However, pet keeping also moved humans toward the domestication of other animal beings (livestock) and that has led to some of our current problematic views and practices, which are rooted in unreflective relationships of use. But now pets may help us alter our view again by increasing our empathy (187). We are ready to move to new forms of relationships. If domestication was rooted in hunting and furthered with the development of agriculture, it was not an intentional process (Zeuner 15, 30). It resulted from being together, and the socialization went both ways. The process continues and it is not just cognitive, but is enacted and experienced (Sabloff 67).

When we try to deny our past or continued interconnectedness with most of nature, we try to mute the animal in pets and the animal in humans. We disguise the needs and behaviors of other animal beings by making them seem human. In doing this we have gone from being just a "master of nature" to being an unnatural species that denies its connectedness (Sabloff 72, 75, 78). Both views—unreflective relations of use and making other animal beings seem human—enable us to see other animal beings, pets in particular, as being here primarily for our pleasure. This has the potential to make them seem discardable insofar as we do not see them as connected with us in any way. So, ironically, the very animal beings we most see as "being human" are still denied entrance into the moral community (Sabloff 92).

The root of the problem is an outmoded metaphysics. We need to reject the myth of human superiority and centrality (Serpell, *Company of Animals* 122–128). We need to stop seeing other animal beings as inferior beasts who have the potential to de-humanize us. Some try to replace this outmoded ontology with the metaphor of kinship (Sabloff 69). Animal welfare focuses on shared suffering. Animal rights offers the idea of citizenship (Sabloff 114). Ecofeminists offer the ideas of co-earthlings (Plumwood) and companion species for pets (Haraway).

American Pragmatism can take up pieces of all of these approaches, but it uniquely offers a *naturalistic* (sees humans as part of natural order), *pluralistic* (noting that we each have only a partial take on the world and so we need many viewpoints), *developmental* (sees the world and the creatures in it as being in process, not finished or static), *experimental* (does not seek final solutions but better working hypotheses), *and falli-bilist* (noting that we are possibly mistaken about what we think we "know") approach to understanding the human relationships with other animal beings. It also focuses on the *amelioration* of problems—that is to make things better. Pragmatism encourages an approach to ethics that differs from the more dominant moral theories in general, and those used to address animal issues in particular.

Many see the role of the ethicist as developing abstract, universal principles that can be applied to a variety of contexts. The ethicist pro-vides the principle and then guides others in the application of these principles to general and specific situations. Pragmatism shifts the role of the ethicist. Rather than absolute principles or answers, ethics is about framing the discussion of ethical issues. *The Pragmatist ethicist keeps the conversation and the deliberation open and informed.* On this account ethicists need to engage with relevant practitioners, and be informed by an array of disciplines. Other approaches to ethics can reach "answers" too quickly and apply them too universally. The Pragmatist approach does not result in absolute guidelines for practice or law. Nor does it define such relationships once and for all. Instead, it takes into account the general histories of various species, seeks to understand how various species have developed and continue to develop, and then comments on how various forms of human treatment do or do not match well with the pluralistic needs and desires of these other beings. This understanding allows us to improve human relations with other animal beings.

In the next chapter (Chapter 2) I will use this general Pragmatist approach to examine human relations with horses. In this chapter I briefly situate the *natural* history of the horse and the shared experience with human beings. I trace some of the *developments* in the horse and humans that result from this relationship. I argue that there are a variety of approaches (*pluralism*) to respectful relations, but that some have proved harmful. I then point to some *experiments* with ways to improve those relations, and call for an attitude of humility, as we continue to work on these relationships based on the *fallible* nature of our knowl-edge. I will discuss issues of abuse and neglect, use in research, use in entertainment, use in competition, use in work, and approaches to death—all in a Pragmatist context that seeks to make ethics about the framing of the ethical issues in a way that is informed by an array of disciplines and experiences.

Having demonstrated this general approach with horses, in Chapter 3 I provide a brief overview of some of the basic views of American Pragmatism. I will briefly sketch how the views of Charles S. Peirce, William James, John Dewey, Charlotte Perkins Gilman, and Alain Locke impact our views of our relationships with other animal beings. This discussion should deepen the understanding of the theoretical underpinnings of the approach. Then, in Chapters 4 and 5, I will again use this general framework of American Pragmatism to discuss human relationships with dogs and cats respectively. Each of these chapters involves a brief history of the relationship between humans and the specific animal beings, and employs American Pragmatism to examine issues of abuse and neglect, research, entertainment, competition, work, and death. The final chapter offers some suggestions for how, in general, to approach the most problematic aspects of our relationships with those animals we consider pets. I will draw on the work of Jane Addams (Pragmatist) and Val Plumwood (ecofeminist) to argue for an approach of humility, caution, and respect in order to build coalitions of individuals and groups that can work to improve (*ameliorate*) human-pet relations.

A Little More Philosophy

To help frame the discussion of horses in the next chapter, here are a few points to keep in mind. As I have said, generally, Pragmatism is a philosophy that is *naturalistic, developmental, pluralistic, experimental, fallibilistic,* and *ameliorative*. It is *naturalistic* in that it sees humans as part of the natural order, subject to the same processes of evolution as the rest of nature. Human beings are not a radically different kind of being. Pragmatism is *developmental* in that it sees the world and the creatures in it as being in process—not finished or static. As Darwin argued, we are all still in the making and relationships among various beings are also always in the making. The *naturalism* and *developmentalism* of Pragmatism shows us that in this "making" other animal beings both adapt to various environments and adapt the environment to their needs and desires. The relationships among humans and other animal beings include mutual modification. Thus, human beings are not so different from other animal beings and all of us—human and other animal beings alike—are who and how we are as a result of interacting and transacting with each other over time. This view is also supported by contemporary science:

> We share with other species a common relationship with the Earth. In accepting the biocentric outlook we take the fact of our being an animal species to be a fundamental feature of our existence. We consider it an essential aspect of "the human condition." We do not deny the differences between ourselves and other species, but we keep in the forefront of our consciousness the fact that in relation to our planet's natural ecosystems we are but one species population among many. (Taylor, 106)

This does not mean there are no differences to consider. There are. We must take into account both cuts and continuity. Philosopher John McDermott notes:

> We do not fit into the world as a Lego piece or a Lincoln Log. In fact, I believe that we have no special place in the organic constituency of nature. Our consciousness—so different, so extraordinary, so bizarre, especially in its dream state—is a marvelous and pockmarked perturbation of the eonic history of DNA. Following Dewey, we are in, of, and about nature. We are nature's creature, its consciousness, its conscience, however aberrant and quixotic; its organizer, namer, definer, and defiler; a transient in search of an implacable, probably unrealizable, final consummation. The human organism is surrounded, permeated, and contexted by both the natural and social environments. (373)

We are both continuous and distinct. It is important for some purposes to recognize the differences and for other purposes to focus on the similarities. For instance, we divide beings into species and focus on similarities within a species. Of course there are ambiguities in all species distinctions, and there is wide variation (difference) within any defined species. Nonetheless, the species distinction is useful and informative. Technically, "The species is the correct boundary for this degree of similarity because it is the potentially interbreeding population that is the receptacle for the consequences of natural selection" (Mitchell 109). Further, as we study beings within species, we notice regular patterns that help us understand and interact with them. Midgley notes that "Race in humans is not a significant grouping at all, but species in animals certainly is. . . . [W]ith an animal, to know the species is absolutely essential. . . . Even members of quite similar and closely related species can have entirely different needs about temperature and water-supply, bedding, exercise-space, solitude, company and many other things. Their vision and experience of the world must therefore be profoundly different . . ." ("Significance of Species" 122). Noting the differences helps us negotiate respectful and successful relationships with other animal beings.

However, evolution also entails continuity. It does not make evolutionary sense to suppose consciousness emerged only in humans, especially since other creatures have brains and similar neural-chemistry. As philosopher Bernard Rollins, in *The Unheeded Cry*, points out,

> Evolution entails continuity, and molecular biology has elegantly underscored that continuity at the cellular, subcellular, and biochemical levels. In so far as humans represent a step in the evolution of life, they share with other creatures enzymes, proteins, functions, and structures. It would be evolutionarily odd if consciousness had emerged solely in humans, especially in light of the presence in other creature of brains, nervous systems, sense-organs, learning, pain, behavior, problem-solving, and so on. Continuity and small variation constitute the rule of living things. (32)

As evidence of this Rollins notes that continuity can be found in the use of signs. He uses Pragmatism (specifically Peirce) to understand the continuity and so help us understand our relationship with other animal beings.

> [I]n the final analysis, much of sign interpretation involves being carried from what is present to what is not. Furthermore, as Peirce pointed out, all sign cognition is triadic, involving sign, what is signified, and some interpretation in the mind of the subject. Thus, even the ability to respond to natural signs bespeaks the presence of mind. And in so far as animals, even insects, interpret the world, perceive objects and events as signs of food, shelter, egg-laying space, or whatever, they must be said to have some subjective mental experience. (220)

Given this continuity, we need a non-reductive naturalism that can take both nature and culture into account as we seek ethical and fulfilling relationships with other beings. In *Being Human*, Anna Peterson notes that "we do not need to choose between biology and culture in making sense of human nature" (184, 192). Humans, as natural beings, are part of the natural order. So, our cultures—language, arts, tools—are natural as well. This is a naturalist position—a non-reductive realism (73–75). The non-reductive part is key, as we need to avoid the idea of fixed and unchanging natures. At the same time, however, we need to not deny the tendencies we observe.

Further, we can't simply dismiss evolution and naturalism as bad resources for ethics. As Peterson suggests, "[I]f humans are not outside its compass, then evolution must bear on philosophical anthropology and on ethics. . . . This means we cannot dismiss evolutionary naturalism as an irremedial fallacious resource for ethics. We need to find ways to move from evolutionary theory, as a general description of how the world works, to ethical reasoning and judgment. We must step cautiously, hedging our bets and taking the long way around, but we must look for a way" (173). To get started on this Midgley notes that evolution tells us we *are* animals, not just that we are *like* animals. This is an important insight. Equally important, though, is Peterson's insight that, "We cannot differ from animals in general anymore than a squirrel or a salmon can. This does not mean that we do not differ from other animals, just as squirrels and salmon differ from each other, and both from dragonflies. However, opponents of evolutionary interpretations of human nature often seem to prefer binary opposition—human or animal—to the continuum (or series of overlapping continua) suggested by evolution" (174). We do differ, but the difference does not set us completely apart. "Continuity, relationships of interdependence, and similarity . . . do not deny particularity. They do deny that a certain kind of natural object, and only that kind, stands absolutely apart from and above all the rest" (215). Humans have wanted to "stand absolutely apart from and above all the rest." This has been done through religion and the idea that humans alone are created in the image of the divine, and it has been done in science and philosophy with the supposedly unique ability of humans to reason and have language. Most animal-focused philosophers—be they Singer's utilitarianism, Regan's deontological approach, Nussbaum's capabilities approach— also tend to fall into one kind of human exceptionalism or another. However, human beings do not stand apart. Humans, for instance, cannot completely escape the role of biology in shaping what and who we are. Peterson notes that

> Humans are natural and cultural animals, created both as individuals and as a species out of the interactions between these features. The interactions of nature and culture in humans have parallels and continuities with the interactions of biology and environment experienced by other species. . . . Many species shape their environments even as those environments shape them, and humans do this to a greater extent than other animals. In this sense we construct ourselves, as any understanding of humanness must acknowledge. However, this constructionism must include the recognition that we do not create ourselves ex nihilo, or in isolation, or just as we please. . . . Biology and culture help determine each other, and neither one alone can explain what it means to be human. (196)

So, while we need to be careful about using biology to justify cultural or social constructions and biases (using biological determinism to support sexist, racist, classist, or speciesist prejudices), we also need to be careful about appealing to social and cultural practices as if there were no biological roots to, or influences on, how we understand and organize ourselves. The interface of culture and biology can help us examine our relationship with other animal beings. For instance, we should note that "We are bond forming creatures, not abstract intellects." Our bonds with our family are a reason why we often put their interests before those of other people. Yet we have social and cultural rules and practices that often extend our consideration. As Midgley notes, "The question which people who want to use the notion of speciesism have to decide is, does the species barrier also give some ground for such a preference or not?" (Midgley, "Significance of Species" 125). Species bonds are real. "All social creatures attend mostly to members of their own species, and usually ignore others" (129–130). However, cross-species bonds are real too. "For we have to notice next that species-loyalty in social animals, strong though it is, is not necessarily exclusive. At an ordinary social level, creatures of different species are certainly often aware of each other, and are probably interacting quietly far more than we realize." These relationships often form when an animal of one species has none of their own around. But sometimes there is a preference for a cross-species relationship. "More remarkable still, an outsider may be cherished even when one's own species is present. A clear instance is the well-established

tendency of race-horses to become attached to some apparently unim-
pressive stable-companion, such as a goat or even a cat, and to pine if
they are separated from it" (132–133). So, while recognizing a biological
tendency to prefer one's own species helps us understand certain behavior, it does not justify ignoring the variations in behavioral possibilities.
Nor does it justify rigid rules or boundaries. What we see is variation and
plasticity. This, in part, is why Pragmatism is *pluralistic.*

Pragmatism is *pluralistic* in that it notes that we each have only a
partial take on the world and so it seeks to incorporate as many viewpoints as possible. As Julian H. Franklin suggests, "The life of a particular
individual in a given species will vary with its circumstances" (101). Not
only do we have to consider the specific perspectives of a given species,
we need to consider the individual—the individual's age, health, and
personality. We need to go beyond simply accepting plurality to *see with*
other species and individual beings (Peterson 237).

Related to the recognition of pluralism, Pragmatism is also *experimental* in that it does not seek final solutions but seeks better working
hypotheses to help us cope with (*ameliorate*) the plurality we encounter
in our lives. We work to organize our experience in ways that are satisfactory, but we must always be open to revision. We must learn and develop
if we are to survive and grow. Given that, denying our *fallibility* is problematic, as are actions that close off future possibilities and revisions of
our action. One of the most important points of Pragmatism is to be able
to learn and grow in applying intelligence to our relations. To do this
Pragmatism must embrace *fallibilism*—the idea that we are usually mistaken is some way about what we think we "know." We must learn from
past experience and be open to revising our understanding of things. Just
because we treat other animal beings in a certain way, or have done so in
the past, does not mean this cannot and should not change.

Fallibilism opens up the possibility of new understandings and new
ways of acting. "The history of many of the ways in which we currently
live with animals offers some sobering reminders that those ways have a
source . . . . It is also included to remind us that many of our apparently
friendly gestures towards other species are grounded in a firm belief in
human superiority rather than a concept of animal 'worth'" (Fudge 10).
Because our understanding of the continuity of human beings with other
animal beings and our ability to see the world from a plurality of perspectives constantly challenge notions of human superiority, we must also

revise our practices. Practices rooted in notions of superiority may no longer serve human beings now (if they ever did). We must realize that, "Every organism, species population, and community of life has a good of its own which moral agents can intentionally further or damage by their actions.... One can act in its overall interest or contrary to its overall interest, and environmental conditions can be good for it (advantageous to it) or bad for it (disadvantageous to it). What is good for an entity is what "does it good" in the sense of enhancing or preserving its life and well-being" (Taylor, 97).

Pluralism and *fallibilism* should help us see that to do good for our own species, or for other species, we need to do more than protect other animal beings just in order to use them. We need to not ignore or trade their good just for human benefit. We need to recognize "that nonhumans have interests that are not tradable or able to be ignored merely because humans will benefit from doing so" (Francione 114). Given our continuity, our well-being overlaps with the well-being of other animal beings. We need to begin to *experiment* with different ways to live with other animal beings in more satisfactory and respectful ways.

The very emergence of human beings is connected to the evolutionary history of all mammals. The history of all mammals is connected to the evolutionary history of reptiles, insects, plants, and so on. The very possibility of humans emerged from past conditions and the continuing pressure and process of human evolution influenced the conditions in which all the life we know exists.[6] To get to a working philosophy that can help guide the various relationships among human beings and other animal beings, we need an understanding of ourselves that acknowledges the evolutionary realities while understanding that the evolutionary histories do not fully determine or constrain the present or future possibilities. Pragmatism is well suited to do this work. Moreover it suggests new possibilities for value. Let's begin the discussion with horses.

---

6. There are obvious connections between this kind of work and the work of those using Pragmatism in environmental ethics. I leave that work to others for now.

TWO

HORSES

Respecting Power and Personality

A good rider can hear his horse speak to him, a great rider can hear his horse whisper, but a bad rider won't hear his horse even if it screams at him.

—Anonymous

While not the most common pet in the United States (only 4 percent of the population owns a horse), horses play an important role in how human beings understand themselves and their relationships with other animal beings. Long used as a source of power and transportation, the domesticated horse very literally transformed human society and transformed the human sense of place, purpose, and power. Mounted societies were considered fierce, bold, aggressive, proud, defiant, and possessed an increased sense of self-worth. Cavalries have long intimidated foes (Lawrence 97–99, 102). Horses have also been (and are) sources of food in many times and places—literally sustaining the lives of humans. Various cultures have revered horses as spirit beings who have mystical qualities. A personal relationship with a horse can be a very magical experience. I start with the horse because, despite the fact that people keep horses as pets less frequently than they do dogs and cats, many humans have some dream of knowing a horse being and feel some investment in the well-being of horses—wild and domesticated.

Horses have been part of my life since before I can remember. Pictures of me on my brother's pony (Pokey) when I was two years old provide evidence of an early start. When I was five years old, Chula (my mother's Quarter horse) and I were riding through orange groves. I rode bareback because I couldn't fit in or lift my sister's saddle. I learned very clearly what it meant to be responsible for and care for the life of another being when Chula coliced. Being very small, I found it difficult to get her hay up into her feeder. I had to climb a fence while holding the hay and throw it over the top of the fence into the feeder. Sometimes my aim failed and I'd have to start the whole process again. This process was not only frustrating but, being allergic to hay, I usually wound up with red and itching eyes and arms. Once in a while I'd be tired or frustrated and just leave the hay on the ground—not always a bad practice, but not a good choice with this paddock and this horse.[1] Horses colic for many reasons, so I'll never know for sure, but when Chula coliced I was sure that it was because I had not always put the hay in the feeder. She had to have a tube put up her nose so oil could be administered and she had to be hand walked all night and day (a practice no longer recommended, but seen as necessary at the time). I had never felt the suffering of another being so acutely, nor felt so responsible for it. From that point on, I have done everything I can think of to provide the best possible conditions for the other animal beings in my life. Though none of us is perfect, because domesticated animal beings depend on us, we must make every effort to put their needs and interests first.

My mother always made it clear that the other animal beings were the responsibility of the child to whom they belonged. She also made it clear that they had to be taken care of before we could eat, go to school, or play. They were never an afterthought, but a central part of our lives and a major responsibility. This attitude does not govern all, or even the majority of relationships between human beings and other animal beings. But, I will argue, it should—especially with domesticated animal beings.

As we've seen, the domestication of other animal beings goes way back and is an integral part of the development of human beings.

---

1. While it can be fine, and even beneficial, for horses to eat off the ground, this is not the case if the ground is sandy or silty. Under these conditions a horse can ingest too much dirt and end up colicing—a blockage of the intestine that often kills horses.

Figure 1. Chula, the horse who helped me learn the important lesson of respecting the nature and needs of other animal beings. Caring for Chula at a very young age made some things, like getting her hay into her feeder, difficult. The importance of living up to the responsibilities of caring for a horse became clear when Chula developed a life threatening condition that may have resulted from eating her hay off the ground instead of from her feeder.

These interactions have been, and continue to be, transformative for both humans and other animal beings—a kind of co-evolution. In John Dewey's terms they were (and are) transactional relationships (see Chapter 3). For instance, humans who lived in the same area as free living horses were always already in relations with horses and the rest of nature. As this relationship changed, and the process of domestication began, both the human and the horse were, and continue to be, transformed. This altered the possibilities of human mobility, strength, and food. It also altered the horse.

While we are still not sure when horses were domesticated, most think that this happened around 3000–2500 BC. There is evidence that humans were riding horses about five thousand years ago (Borchardt 14). But things started long before then. Horses were used in the most recent Ice Age—about 20,000 years ago. That means they were tamed and controlled long before they were domesticated (Lawrence 96). In the late

Pleistocene wild herds were common in Europe, Asia, and North America. Hunting during the Ice Age and the spread of forests decreased their numbers. They were extinct in North America between five thousand and eight thousand years ago, and in Europe they were pushed to the edge of the Asian deserts (101). Even the famous Przesalski horse of the Mongolian steppes is only around now due to breeding in captivity (102). Many say they were saved by domestication (40).[2]

Some estimates suggest that horses have now been domesticated for as long as six thousand years (Budiansky, *Nature of Horses* 2). It is commonly believed that the first horses were domesticated in the late Neolithic age in order to be used for food, to be bearers of loads, and to be ridden and driven. We have evidence of such use in the first millennium BC in Russia and Asia and in the second millennium in Europe (100).

Horses meet many of the conditions of domestication.[3] Even though they are not considered great meat animals, their ability to survive in tough conditions made them desirable for this purpose in some areas (Budiansky, *Nature of Horses* 47). They are social and hierarchical—led by a dominant mare. There is also a hierarchy among stallions—leading to the practice of castrating most males to be better able to keep them together in captivity.[4] Horses are less territorial and more social than non-domesticated equids. This social nature enables them to read and relate to humans (107, 82, 93); we are able to tap into the horse's social structure and behavior to form bonds and modify behavior. Grooming helps in the process of building individual relationships, and in training, as it mimics the process of horse to horse bonding. In horse society, the more dominant usually leads, and humans need to keep this in mind when working with horses (81–86, 94). More dominant does not, however, mean abuse nor require the use of physical force.

Horses themselves have been altered through training and breeding, though they are considered one of the least manipulated and specialized of the domesticated mammals. We use and exploit their inherent characteristics, so there has been less change in morphology among horses than

---

2. This is not meant to justify keeping domesticated horses, but rather to explain the history.

3. Other forms of Equid have not proven suitable to domestication—zebra and onager.

4. Castration in horses, as in dogs, is generally done at a young age and with anesthetic. The level of care is much greater than seen with other livestock. Most people and barns are not well equipped to handle the needs of stallions. There are, nonetheless, obvious ethical questions related to the practice.

Figure 2. Horse history.

among many other domesticated mammals. Nonetheless, mules and hybrids were common by 2500 BC, showing greater human control of breeding. By 1500 BC there was a distinction between northern ponies and Arabian types (100, 106, 126). Today we have hundreds of recognized breeds in the United States.

Talk with horse people and they will tell you that the breed matters. When thinking about entering a relationship with a horse being, you should consider how various breeds fit with your intended activities. Not all horses are equally suited to pulling a cart—physically or mentally. Not all horses want to look a steer in the eyes. Not all horses have the suspended gaits desired for dressage. Not all horses have the temperament to enjoy parades, or the desire to jump, or the drive to run. There are also differences in personality by breed as well as by individual. Some breeds are more clownish, some are more serious, some are more absent minded, some are intent on learning. A brief on-line search of a few breed stereotypes reveals descriptions such as:

Morgan: A good solid student and a fast learner, the Morgan gives you his full attention even if you haven't earned it. Rarely has to be told twice. A willing, diligent hard worker that's reported to look forward to his job every day. It has been said that you can't wear a Morgan out. The Morgan is easy-going, spirited but easily managed. Courageous and not easily frightened. When he does get frightened, his flight impulse is low; he controls his fear and looks for your guidance. When asked to do something he doesn't want to do he is adaptable and compliant. Eager to please and accommodating. His self-protection impulse is low. If you apply a painful treatment, he tends to tolerate it without lashing out.

Arabian: The Arabian is an extremely fast learner. They are very energetic, generally not lazy. . . . The Arabian is easily bored. Likely to be playing with toys, people or other horses. Highly impressionable, with mood sensitivity. For example: If you tend to be a high-strung, anxious handler, your Arabian may be skittish. If you are laid-back and reasonable, he may be the same way. Some have been described as loving and spiritual. When asked to do something he doesn't want to do, he is eager to please but also smart and opinionated. Unlike the Appaloosa, the Arabian would rather die than act dumb. If he thinks your request to walk through a puddle is ill-advised, he may find a clever way to avoid it without technically defying you. He'll give to the bit, for example, then sidepass around the obstacle. . . . When subjected to pain, he may be fiercely self-protective or exceptionally tolerant.

Quarter Horse: A fast learner and reasonably solid student. The Quarter horse acts as though the standard Western-type activities are just what he was bred for, which they are. They are generally adaptable, patient and compliant. When asked to do something he doesn't want to do, he generally figures out quickly that it's easier to switch than fight. The Quarter horse is not particularly reactive to scary stimuli and not particularly prone to overreact when something does scare him. He has a low flight impulse and an average to slightly below average self-protection impulse. He is likely to bear painful treatments as well. (white_arabian.tripod.com)

Much of the frustration one finds in the horse world is due to a mismatch between horses and the activities they are engaged in, or a mismatch between the horse being and the human being. To do the best for domesticated horses, we should do our best to match horses with the appropriate person and activity. This comes with an understanding of their histories. Even with such understanding, though, things are not perfect.

Most domesticated horses live with some level of confinement that frustrates many natural behaviors and causes health and behavioral problems. Many domesticated horses will live in multiple homes and be ridden by a variety of people with various levels of skill. They may well be asked to perform activities they do not understand or are not well suited to perform. Many will face overwork and uninformed or intentionally cruel training practices. When money and/or reputation are involved, many horses will be pushed beyond their limits and face physical and mental breakdown.

I will explore these, and other, issues faced by horses who live with humans. I will use Pragmatism to help diagnose the problems and suggest alternative practices and attitudes that can improve the lives of horse beings and improve the quality of the human-horse relationship. While some would like humans to leave horses alone, domesticated horses cannot be returned to the wild; they do not have the physical toughness to survive nor is there space for them. We cull wild horse herds now. They exist because humans and horses have been in mutually transformative relationships for thousands of years and humans need to respect the aspects of horses that enable us to bond so powerfully.

Abuse and Neglect

Today's horses both benefit and suffer from their relationships with humans.[5] It is easy to list the ways in which they suffer. First, there are the obvious cases of abuse and neglect.

STARVATION OR UNDERNOURISHMENT

Feeding and caring for a horse can become an expensive affair. When feed prices go up, the number of underfed or starving horses increases, as does the number of abandoned horses. This happens when the financial circumstances of individual people change as well—the loss of a job or a divorce can be common catalysts. It is not an uncommon situation for someone to turn horses out in a field, offer no supplemental feed, and provide only limited access to clean water. Horses can survive, but may be undernourished. Horses confined to a stall or paddock are completely dependent on humans to provide food and water, remove manure, and trim feet. Neglected horses often end up standing in manure. Without care, their feet grow out and curl making it hard to stand or walk. They starve and become dehydrated. There are, of course, highly publicized cases that make the evening news. Our hearts are touched and we wonder how anyone could treat such a majestic being in this way. But what about what other, well cared for, horses regularly face? Many of the horses who receive the best care are competition and working horses. Nonetheless, they may face forms of abuse and neglect as they are "encouraged" to perform their job or win a competition.

BEATING AND PERFORMANCE/ENHANCEMENT TECHNIQUES

Even well cared for horses are asked to perform various activities and/or are "encouraged" to perform through techniques that cause pain or

---

5. It is also important to note that many other animal beings are involved in human's relationships with horses. Many creatures are killed in the harvesting and baling of hay and grain (not to mention the pesticides used). Mice, rats, and pigeons frequent barns, so cats, traps, and poisons are used to limit their numbers. For some sports like fox hunting, kennels of hounds are kept confined and animals chased and stressed during the hunt. Foxes are kept in cages so we can collect their urine to drag for scent on some hunts. Trail riding can damage flora and fauna. Horses trample the ground, disturb wildlife, and their droppings can spread seeds—increasing the range of invasive plants and animals.

physical harm. There is the cart horse, the cavalry mount, the race horse; there are those who are asked to perform artificial gaits. There are the wild horses who are "tamed" (Lawrence 106–108).

Some horses are overworked or worked in unsafe conditions. The recent breakdowns of race horses provide a good example of this, as I will discuss later. Others are the victims of banned training practices such as spiking (hitting a horse's back legs with spikes as they go over a jump to teach them to kick up to clear the jump), tendon firing or injecting irritants into the horses legs (so they will exaggerate their gait), deadening tails (so they won't move them), breaking tails (so they can wear tail wigs and appear to have an arching tail), the artificial weighting of their feet (to get the desired leg action), and the use of banned drugs (to calm horses down or give them more energy). As are human athletes, high-end competition horses are regularly tested for drugs. Nonetheless, drug use is not uncommon. Some drugs calm horses down, some give them excess energy. The United States Equestrian Federation's list of examples of forbidden substances includes over two hundred substances. The fact that cocaine, LSD, and morphine (among many others) are on that list gives you some idea of what people have done to horses to get the desired performance. Steroids and hormones are also used to alter physical appearance and ability. If not drugged, horses may be worked until they are exhausted so they will not spook or be too "hot." Some riders and trainers school the same movements over and over—leading to physical stress and boredom.

Some horses are harmed in training by the abusive use of spurs, whips, or bits, though what precisely "abuse" means is contested. The International Equestrian Federation (FEI) guidelines say that

> No person may abuse a Horse during an Event or at any other time. "Abuse" means an action or omission which causes or is likely to cause pain or unnecessary discomfort to a Horse, including without limitation any of the following:
>
> To whip or beat a Horse excessively;
> To subject a Horse to any kind of electric shock device;
> To use spurs excessively or persistently;
> To jab the Horse in the mouth with the bit or any other device;
> To compete using an exhausted, lame or injured Horse;
> To "rap" a Horse;

To abnormally sensitise or desensitise any part of a Horse;

To leave a Horse without adequate food, drink or exercise;

To use any device or equipment which causes excessive pain to the Horse upon knocking down an obstacle. (General Regulations, 23rd edition, Chapter VI, 2009)

Used properly, aids such as whips and spurs encourage more speed, greater bend, and help indicate direction of movement. They are extensions of the natural aids of the leg or arm. However, they can be applied too strongly and result in physical injury. Excessive or improper use can also result in fearful or angry horses, or cause horses to tune out and ignore the humans altogether. Activities involving profit and prestige for human beings increase the risk of human beings using and abusing other animal beings. Racing is an obvious example, but as we will see in the sections on entertainment and competition, it is not the only venue in which horses are abused. Something as prevalent as breeding for specific characteristics also causes pain and suffering.

BREEDING

Intentional breeding has resulted in some breeds being too big for their structure—joint problems in warmblood foals are an example. Warmbloods are genetically predisposed to a variety of forms of Developmental Orthopedic Disease. Wobblers syndrome and osteochondrosis dissecans (OCD) are two common examples. These can often be managed with diet and exercise, but the genetic predisposition is prevalent. In Quarter horses, breeding for heavy muscles lead many to breed to one sire (Impressive) who happened to have a genetic defect— Hyperkalemic Periodic Paralysis (HYPP). This is an inherited disease of the muscles. The American Quarter Horse Association (AQHA) requires that offspring of affected lines have this noted on their papers, but there is no prohibition against breeding animals with the inherited disease. It is simply labeled an undesirable characteristic. Quarter horses are also prone to hereditary equine regional dermal asthenia (HERDA)— a genetic skin disease predominantly found in lines of cutting horses (vgl.ucdavis.edu).

Less obvious are breeding programs that, while selecting for speed or action, result in horses with very fine bones that cannot hold up to athletic demands—this happens in thoroughbreds, Morgans, Saddlebreds, and

Arabians to name a few. With thoroughbreds we know that, "Virtually all 500,000 of the world's thoroughbred racehorses are descended from 28 ancestors, born in the eighteenth and nineteenth centuries, according to a new genetic study. And up to 95% of male thoroughbreds can be traced back to just one stallion. . . . One tenth of thoroughbreds suffer orthopaedic problems and fractures, 10% have low fertility, 5% have abnormally small hearts and the majority suffer bleeding in the lungs . . ." (newscientist.com). Breeding for color has many potential pitfalls as well, no matter the breed. We have the knowledge to address these problems, but it is not clear that we have the will. As long as titles are won and money is made, the long-term health of the horse does not take priority. We further show our disregard for the horse's wellbeing when we breed for color. Examples of people breeding for color can be found in the world of paints—seeking striking coat patterns. It also occurs when people want to match pairs or teams of horses for driving.

No matter the reason, breeding for color can result in breeding horses with conformation and temperament problems; such breeding can result in the propagation of congenital conditions. Pragmatism would caution us about this level of manipulation. *Experimentation* with breeding, over many years, has demonstrated many of the dangers of highly selective breeding. The failures expose human *fallibility* quite directly and cause horses to suffer. We know that a diverse breeding pool (*pluralism*) helps preserve the long term health of any given breed or population of horses. We should use our accumulated knowledge of the *nature* and *development* of horses to breed for sound minds and bodies and so *ameliorate* (improve) the prospects of individual horses as well as the species. This will also make successful human-horse relationships more likely. Even if we change breeding practices, though, there would be more to be done. Not only do these human actions cause physical problems for horses, other human actions related to how we "keep" horses cause many physical and behavioral problems.

CONFINEMENT

"Vices" are usually responses to stress in artificial confinement. Very few domesticated horses have range to wander. Pastured horses are less confined than stabled or stalled horses, but most domesticated horses live lives that do not mirror natural conditions. Confined horses are often overfed, underexercised, undertrained, petted, and coddled—not things that make them happy (Budiansky, *Nature of Horses* 107, 264). Many horses develop stereotomies common to captive animals kept in zoos and labs—weaving, pacing, chewing, and cribbing. These not only are bad for their physical health but also indicate mental and emotional stress. Confinement and a limited feeding schedule result in digestive disorders and increased risk of parasite infections—this has the further consequence of humans pumping horses full of dewormers. Their hooves can suffer from the lack of natural wear, their teeth from the lack of grazing, their coats from our desire to keep them clean (clipping their hair and blanketing them). The fact that many horses live together and travel frequently (to competitions, clinics, new homes) means diseases spread and so more frequent vaccinations and testing are required.

How might horses benefit from any of this? With good care, they can lead longer, healthier, less stressful lives. With a proper feeding program, turnout, and waste management, most of the negative aspects of their confinement (disease, boredom, and colic) can be mitigated. With proper care by a veterinarian, farrier, and dentist, most of these side effects of confinement can be addressed as well. However, none of this adds up to a benefit, just to the mitigation of the potential harms. The benefit, on both sides actually, comes in the social relationships and accompanying mental stimulation.

In free-living horses there are long standing relationships in herds and the maintenance of these relationships and hierarchies, along with feeding and reproduction, take up most of their time. These needs and wants still exist for domesticated horses, but they are satisfied more quickly with regard to food, and often the primary social relationship is with a human rather than with other horses. Because of their sociality, it is not generally a good idea to keep horses alone, hence the common use of goats or other animals as companions. Most horses are kept with other horses, but increasingly in separate paddocks and stalls. They can see, smell, and call to each other, but actual contact is limited in order to decrease the risk of injury. This is, in large part, due to the fact that they move around so much. Horses do injure each other in establishing and/or challenging the hierarchy. This is not a constant battle in free living situations, or in stable domestic herds. However, in most domestic situations horses frequently come and go, increasing the risk of fights. Since many of these horses have metal shoes on their back feet, the risk of serious injury is real. There is much to consider here, including whether it is fair to keep horses alone, or move horses around based on our interests with little or no regard for their relationships with other horses. "Having a best friend to rely on always makes life easier, especially for a horse. As herd animals, horses have deep-seated needs for companionship, which adds to the stress if one is isolated for a period of time" (J. Williams 48).

With all that said, domestic horses have proven to be quite adaptable. They form relationships with humans and other animal beings and we need to pay attention to and respect these relationships as well. There are stories of horses with special friendships with goats, chickens, dogs, cats, and many cases of close human-horse relationships. "Goats, sheep and other grazing animals are also often kept as pasture buddies, and in some cases the horse gets very attached to his unusual little herd" (47). This raises questions about the frequent practice of selling horses when one "outgrows" them. They are attached to many of the beings in their environment—including the human beings. Abrupt moves are disorienting to the horses moved and to those left behind.

With their physical needs being met in a matter of hours, domesticated horses have even more time to invest in their social relationships. When this includes some "training" we find that many seem to enjoy the physical and mental challenges their work presents. Our activities with them may be a form of play for them and so provide pleasure. This may explain the enthusiasm some horses show for competitions and showing (Budiansky, *Nature of Horses* 101). They even seem to take pride in doing their work well. This will be discussed more in the sections on entertainment and competition, but for now it is important to say that humans owe domesticated horses mental and social stimulation.

PRAGMATISM'S RESPONSE TO ABUSE AND NEGLECT

Pragmatism, being *naturalistic* and *developmental*, would address issues of neglect and abuse by seeking to understand the basic needs of horse beings. For horses who are dependent on humans, these needs must be met by humans. Common sense and the law tell us that starvation and severe neglect are unacceptable. But what about the more ambiguous practices?

What about the basic approach to forming a relationship in the first place? Pragmatism, being *experimental*, requires us to explore a variety of approaches. Being *pluralistic* and *fallibilistic*, it does not expect any one method or approach to have all the answers. It does, however, require humans to be open, flexible, and always seeking to learn how they might improve (*ameliorate*) the well being of the horses with whom they are involved. The current focus on natural horsemanship techniques provides an interesting example.

Natural horsemanship is the philosophy of working with horses by appealing to their instincts and herd mentality. It involves communication techniques derived from wild horse observation in order to build a partnership that closely resembles the relationships that exist between horses. The use of various forms of natural horsemanship is probably a helpful move to counter the use of force or drugs found in some "training" techniques. However, it may suffer from issues as well. Many (but not all) of the practitioners of natural horsemanship are very skilled and have extensive experience. A Pragmatist, being interested in the natural and developmental history of horses, applauds the fact that this kind of approach (despite the variation among the practitioners) starts by asking what kind of creature a horse is: what are its needs, fears, methods of communication? For many in natural horsemanship this has come from observing wild horses. Many of the techniques they suggest can be very helpful. But, most humans who work with horses are working with domesticated horses. While they do retain many of the traits of wild horses, domesticated horses often exhibit differences as well—some of which are seen in breed characteristics.

For instance, we work with domesticated horses of widely different sizes. These horses also exhibit differences in flight response, ability to focus, and level of aggression. One also needs to consider how various horses were raised and handled. For instance, it can make a big difference if the horse was raised in a herd with other foals, and so learned about horse communication. This may not have occurred if the horse was an only baby. What rank did their dam have in the herd? What kind of rank do they hold themselves? Being pluralistic, Pragmatism recognizes that there is no one-size-fits-all solution or approach. Many people take the advice of the various natural horseman[6] in this way—as an absolute—and this can lead to problems and put both the human being and the

---

6. Some well-known examples include Monty Roberts, Buck Brannaman, Pat Parelli, Tom Dorance, Frederic Pignon and Magali Delgado of "Cavalia."

horse being in a dangerous situation. Taken as one set of tools, among many other sets of tools, they can be very helpful.[7] Taken as the *only* way, they can be unproductive or even dangerous.

In considering a horse-human relationship, we must understand the human side as well as the horse side. As with dogs and training approaches such as those offered by Cesar Millan (the "Dog Whisperer"), for the techniques being taught to work the human being must be able to assume a certain demeanor and role. It is helpful to coach people in how to do this, but not all will be capable of being the "pack leader" with dogs or the "alpha" with horses. Not all will be able to control their emotions, remain calm, or exude confidence. People need to make use of a variety of techniques so they can be effective while they learn these skills. They also need to find ways to be effective if they don't ever learn to embody these qualities. Human beings, like horse beings, have different individual temperaments and ranks. This is why matching human and horse beings well is so important. A very dominant horse being with a timid human being will not make a good match. Neither will most cases of pairing a very timid horse being and a very dominant human being, unless that human being has learned to soften his approach when necessary or appropriate.

We all respond differently to different leadership styles in our jobs and home lives. So too with horses. One may be a very successful parent with some children but not all. One may be a very good teacher or coach for some students or athletes but not all. One may be very good at working with some horses or horse breeds but not all. I, for instance, have found that many people who work with Quarter horses quite well have difficulty working with a Morgan or Arab, and vice versa. If the humans don't read horses well and modify their training techniques to fit various horse breeds, they can produce explosive or unresponsive behavior from the horses. This happens with individuals as well. None of my horses could be handled or worked in exactly the same way. The key, as one of my instructors (Charles DeKunfy) used to say, is to know and ride the species, not just an individual. This is, of course, hard for those of us who don't make our living working with horses. Most of us ride only a few horses (and often only a few individuals from a few breeds of horses) in our lifetimes.

---

7. While most of the practitioners do not sell themselves as the final answer on working with horses, some do. Further, many of the people learning from them misinterpret their message and universalize and absolutize their approach.

So, I do think learning from those with more experience is essential, and I am happy that training approaches that foster understanding over attempts to control are flourishing. As a Pragmatist, though, I have some worries. For instance, while I'm happy the Humane Society of the United States (HSUS) has partnered with Pat Parelli to promote his training methods, with a special focus on helping rescued horses, I do worry this kind of move might create more absolutist approaches to training among the less expert horse people. This is a problem with how people take in what Parelli does and says, not with what he actually does and says. Parelli recognizes the individuality of horses and the need to adjust one's training approach to meet the individual. He says, "Horses . . . are like snowflakes. They're individuals with unique personalities." He says he needs to know a horse, come to understand their "likes, dislikes, and fears" to better communicate with them (Allan, "Long Way Home" 15). The Humane Society judges his techniques to be more humane—"a kinder, gentler method of training, one that works with the animals and not against them." I agree that Parelli is a showman who can bring his techniques to large audiences, but even he agrees that what he does in training is nothing new or unique. "'It's the most natural way to relate to horses,'" he says. "People have been doing it for years, but no one's ever talked about it. No one ever gave someone a ribbon for doing it'" (18). I appreciate Parelli's ability (and that of others like him) to communicate the benefits of moving beyond "traditional, dominance-based models of horsemanship" (16), but I worry that his techniques can be problematic when the horse is in less experienced hands. He has spent a lifetime with horses; he has absorbed a great deal and that time and experience cannot be absorbed second hand. This kind of teaching is great for opening minds and starting a change, but most people will need consistent and continuous hands-on guidance to learn to work with horses in this way. The three-day clinic model most of these practitioners use does not provide that.

I think the rescue horses whom Parelli works with will have a much better chance at a successful and happy adoption than horses who do not get this kind of work. However, when people see him make it look easy they think they can do it too. Some of these people do have the experience, knowledge, and feel to make it work. Others, however, will find themselves in over their heads. The Humane Society wants to move people beyond the view that rescue horses "are somehow less behaviorally sound. Less healthy, or less worthy of saving" (Allan, "Long Way Home" 16). But, the truth is, as with rescue dogs, many of these horses *do* have special needs. It does not do them a service to hide this fact. It may help them avoid the immediate fate of slaughter, but it may set them up for lives that include frustrations with training or performance that land them back facing the same fate once again. This kind of approach is a start, but we need more sustained support for these horses and the people who adopt them, as well as for horses in general.

Horses can end up facing slaughter through a variety of avenues. Some are older or injured pets, show horses, or lesson horses. Some are wild horses and many more are race horses who are no longer making money for their owners. Since euthanizing a horse costs money—the Humane Society estimates it costs $450 for euthanasia and disposal—many try to gain a final few dollars and send their horse to an auction. Many of the buyers at these auctions are buying horses and ponies to sell them for their meat. The USDA reports that more than 100,000 horses were slaughtered each year for the purpose of human consumption (*All Animals*, Summer 2007, 12). Recent legislation closed down the slaughter of horses in the United States for human consumption, but that has now been reversed.

Those in support of a ban often say that we shouldn't be slaughtering horses because horses are noble. Even Nancy Perry, the vice president of government affairs for the Humane Society, said that the meat industry need not worry that the ban on slaughtering horses will lead to the end of slaughtering cows or chickens. "There is a slippery-slope argument suggesting that ending the slaughter of animals not bred for meat and not consumed in America will lead to a ban on slaughtering all animals for meat, ... Such fear mongering simply aids the interests of foreign corporations operating on US soil who buy our stolen and auctioned horses" (*All Animals*, Summer 2007, 20). This is a very problematic position. Why are some animals conceived as being for meat and not others. This varies by time and culture. One is hard pressed to point to something that differentiates horses from cows, pigs, or chickens that justifies slaughtering and eating one but not the others. This is simply a matter of prejudice. In this case the prejudice is protecting horses. However, the reports of starving and abandoned horses went up during the ban on slaughter. Some horses were forced to live with painful injuries and conditions because their owners wouldn't pay to put them down; they just waited for them to die. Many horses simply had to endure longer transport to slaughter facilities in Canada and Mexico. I agree with the Humane Society that someone who can afford the monthly care of a horse can afford the one-time cost of euthanasia. As the Humane Society says, the average monthly expenses of keeping a horse come to $300–$350. In many cases more is spent. If this is the case, most horse owners can pay the $450 to provide a humane end for their horse companions.

But many of these horses are not primarily companions. They are seen as money pits and the goal is to spend as little as possible, or they are seen as money earners and the key is to keep costs down to keep profits up. This applies to race horses, "worn out" lesson horses, and injured show horses. Even when these horses have been loved and cared for when performing for their people, that love doesn't always extend to the time when they can no longer do what the person wants. With the "need" to get a new horse to replace the old or injured horse, people look for ways to "unload" the less desirable horses. If they can't sell them, they might give them away, but there are no guarantees that these horses won't end up facing the same fate of starvation, abandonment, or slaughter at a later point. Ending slaughter may seem like an admirable goal to many, but it does not address the root of the problem. In fact, such a position reflects an approach to ethics that seeks a universal and absolute position and fails to recognize the tensions, contradictions, and problems caused by the proposed "solution."

Here is an example of why a Pragmatist approach might be helpful. Rather than being driven by a principle, regardless of consequences, the Pragmatist first asks some questions. Why do we slaughter horses currently? Given the array of reasons for current practice, what are the probable consequences of a ban likely to be? Are any of these probable consequences problematic? If so, can they be mitigated in some other way? If not, does that change our assessment of the proposed ban? The answers to such questions may differ in different times and places and so a response informed by context may result in multiple approaches to an issue rather than a universal or "all or nothing" approach.

Further, without real consideration of how and why horses end up facing slaughter in the first place little will really change for most horse's lives. If we don't change the attitude toward horses and horse care, these same horses will still face the ultimate in abuse and neglect—a prolonged and painful process of dying. Pragmatism calls on us to respect and honor the continuum of life, not just serve our own interests. This may be an instance of an action that made many humans feel better, but made many horses suffer.

Use in Research and Biomedical Contexts

Human beings use many other animal beings in research. Some of the research is aimed at improving the lives of the various species of other animal beings. However, much of it is aimed at improving the lives of human beings. Given that we share an evolutionary history with these other animal beings, this may make good sense—but not always. No two species are exactly alike, not even different sexes within a species are alike in all respects, and biomedical research shows this. For instance, the antibiotic chloramphenical works well for dogs, but it is very harmful to cats and horses. Another antibiotic, cleocin, is regularly used for cats, but it kills horses (Greek 62–64). Differences are important to keep in mind. For instance, horses cannot vomit, and that often has an effect on how diseases affect them. As a result, they do not always make good models for research to be applied to humans. Further, since the research often places the horse in circumstances that fail to meet their basic needs and desires, the results of the research must be examined carefully. The findings may or may not be accurate or helpful.

Horses are used in research on diseases and conditions that affect horses. Horses are often infected with a disease, such as West Nile virus and Equine Protozoal Myeloencephalitis (EPM) in order to test treatments and vaccines. In order to study serious conditions faced by domestic horses, some horses are intentionally made to founder, colic, or tie up. Then treatments and surgeries can be studied and improved. Veterinary schools and some equine hospitals keep horses as colostrum and blood donors. It is interesting to note that the American Veterinary Medical Association (AVMA) recently (2011) reaffirmed its commitment to fund an Institute for Companion Animal and Equine Research. They note that

> Funding for health-related research dedicated to companion animals (dogs and cats) and horses, is virtually nonexistent in comparison to research funding for human and livestock animal health. The national

annual $16 million investment in companion animal and equine
health research is estimated to be less than 0.12% of the annual
$13 billion biopharma and companion animal food industries sales in
2005. . . . (avma.org)

They note the need for such research to improve health care for these
animal beings. Less is said about how to care for and respect the animal
beings involved in such research.

It is important to note that the average horse person cannot afford, or
will not pay for, some of the advanced procedures available today. Such
research is primarily paid for by those who use horses in profit making
activities—high-end racing and showing. This raises questions about
how much of even horse-focused research is really for the benefit of
horses and how much is for the benefit of humans who use them.

While the above examples are uses of horses in research that appear to
have the primary focus of helping other horses, there are also uses of
horses in research and biomedical procedures that are aimed at improving human life. For example, horses were involved in early attempts to
prevent tetanus. "Equine tetanus antitoxin (horse derived) was the only
product available for the prevention of tetanus prior to the development
of tetanus toxoid in the 1940s. Equine antitoxin was also used for passive
postexposure prophylaxis of tetanus (e.g., after a tetanus-prone wound)
until the development of human tetanus immune globulin in the late
1950s" (immunize.org). Today, horses are used to produce Premarin
(PREgnantMARe urINe) for hormone replacement therapy in women.
Though their use is in decline, up to 60,000 mares have been used in a
year to produce this drug (E. Anderson 220). Not only are the mares bred
repeatedly, they are confined and hooked to machines that collect their
urine. Their foals are usually sold at auction. There are rescue operations
for these mares and their foals, but there are not enough homes. The
recent ban on slaughter resulted in even more horses in need of homes.
With high hay prices, fewer people are willing to take on the commitment
of buying or adopting a horse.

In addition to these cases where the use of horses produced something
useful to human beings, there are also cases where the use of horses in
research may have slowed advances in human medicine. Researchers
have used horses to understand and treat coronary artery disease. Much
of this research has focused on the connections between cholesterol and
heart disease. Since the other animal beings used in research did not

develop clogged arteries as the result of a high cholesterol diet, it took researchers a long time to see this link in humans (Greek 158).

PRAGMATISM'S RESPONSE TO RESEARCH AND BIOMEDICAL CONTEXTS

Being *fallibilistic* and *pluralistic*, Pragmatism would examine the use of horses in these various research and biomedical activities and not assume it is all good or all bad. Being *naturalistic* and *developmental*, Pragmatists would want to know if such research resulted in usable information. They would also want to know how the horses are affected, and whether they benefit (does it *ameliorate* their lives). Being *experimentalists*, they are open to research generally, but other concerns may impose limits on research. First, are horses good models for human diseases and reactions? (Greek 119, 64, 62, 158) When the research does have beneficial potential, what are the conditions for the horses during and after experimentation? Uses such as Premarin production are hard pressed to pass through a Pragmatist examination. Such use may benefit human beings, but has no benefit for horse beings. In fact, it requires frustrating many of the natural behaviors of horse beings. The mares are confined and hooked to a catheter. As already discussed, this kind of confinement poses both physical and psychological harm for horses. They also are subject to repeated pregnancies. Their foals are not just prematurely weaned, but transported to slaughter or adoption sites. These foals are at high risk for infection due to the stress of early weaning and they are likely to have long term behavioral issues. Foals learn a lot from their dams—acceptable herd behavior and body language (things humans use in forming their relationships with them). This kind of activity fails to respect what we know about the nature and social relations of horses.

Premarin production also finds itself in a contradictory position regarding the continuity of human beings and horse beings. Given that this hormone production works, we must acknowledge that we share enough biologically to be able to use each other's hormones. However, we simultaneously deny continuity as we deny the horses' need to move and form relationships with their offspring. The same can be said of the tetanus research and use in the past.

Research on horse beings that is for their own benefit, or the benefit of other horse beings, creates more complications for the Pragmatist, as does keeping horses as sources of blood or colostrum. A Pragmatist is hard pressed to say such research is wrong since Pragmatism is experimental in temperament and seeks to improve the conditions of life and promote growth. Research does allow for advances in care and quality of life for horses. Nevertheless questions arise about the numbers of horses used, the conditions in which they are kept, and how they are obtained. We should try to work with horses that present with a given disease or condition rather than induce the disease or condition in an otherwise healthy horse. We should work to reduce the numbers of horse beings used in research—and they should be used only for pressing and horse related issues. We could, for example, take the approach of the Great Ape's Bill of Rights in New Zealand. This allows only experiments that benefit the apes themselves. We could limit the use of horses to research from which horses benefit and keep the numbers to a minimum. We would also need to address how they are kept. We need to find ways to provide them with turnout when possible, interaction with other horse and human beings, and mental stimulation. This would not only be good for the horses but also would improve the research, as it would produce more reliable results by removing the complicating effects of bad care. Good experimentation requires understanding and respect for the nature and development of the beings involved. We also need to be pluralistic and fallibilistic—that is, open to new and different approaches and to learn from our mistakes.

Use in Entertainment

In the world of horses, entertainment and competition often overlap. Rodeos provide an obvious example. Horses and humans compete, but people also come to be entertained. Television contracts for professional rodeos just further blur this line. Keeping this overlapping in mind, I will make an arbitrary, threefold division into entertainment, competition, and work. This will allow me to highlight differences that emerge as the emphasis shifts from profit to pride on the part of the human beings who are involved in various practices with horses. For entertainment, I will focus on examples in which humans pay to watch horses perform; for competition, I will explore activities that have winners and losers; and for work, I will address practices that emphasize profit. Here, rather than try to be comprehensive, I will focus on several well-known examples of entertainment practices: circuses, movies and television shows, and riding exhibitions.

CIRCUSES

Horses have been used in circuses since early times. There were Roman and medieval shows. There have always been worries about abusive training techniques and the unnatural lives horses lead in such shows, as well as about the apparently demeaning nature of some of the acts (E. Williams 307, 310–311). Some horses are used for vaulting—people performing acrobatic acts atop a moving horse. These horses are selected for physical structure, physical ability, and steady temperament. Other horses may wear clothes and "dance" or do tricks. Some argue this is demeaning, but much of what the horses do is not that different physically from what is asked in various competitions. So, the question becomes more one of providing acceptable training techniques and respecting the physical abilities of the horse. Another kind of question arises concerning the dignity of the horses as they are presented. While wearing a tutu may not harm a horse directly, this kind of presentation can encourage humans to view other animal beings as dolls or toys. This is a dangerous perception and one Pragmatists would not want to perpetuate. Such presentation fails to respect the horse's natural and developmental history, and will probably result in a failure to meet their basic needs and desires. Most of the concerns about circuses have focused on the exotic animals involved—elephants, big cats, bears, and wolves. But horses and dogs are used as well and share in the problematic life of confinement, travel, aggressive training, and overwork with the repeated performances.

As mentioned, some of the activities and training for horses in circuses are not that different from the activities and training they encounter with any human-horse activity. However, compared to most other horses, circus horses tend to face more extreme conditions of confinement, more frequent travel, and a busier work schedule. They endure frequent changes in feed and water. The confinement and travel puts them at an increased risk for disease and colic. They face changes in the footing they work in and this, combined with the frequent performances, can stress their bodies. Traveling circus horses also often do not receive regular veterinary care. The conditions of circus horses change, however, when circuses become permanent fixtures in a single location. Animal shows—circuses included—sometimes settle down in one place; Las Vegas is a prime example. There are shows with knights on horseback, there are Lipizanner shows, and there are circus performances. These more settled circuses reduce stress in some ways, but not all. For all circuses, regulations are in place to address these issues. Exhibiting animals, or having them perform, requires a license that entails documenting veterinary care and providing rest periods between shows (E. Williams 286–287). Nevertheless, these regulations may not sufficiently respect the needs of horses and considerably more money and staffing would need to be provided in order to enforce these regulations effectively.

MOVIES AND TELEVISION

Horses have long been used in movies and television shows. Westerns are an obvious example, as are period war pieces. The Budweiser Clydesdales are among the most famous horses in the United States; their popular Super Bowl commercials are just one example of how they are used—I will discuss this further in the section on work. Here I want to discuss what we see in many television shows and movies. What is entailed in this kind of use?

There are of course questions about training techniques that attend any use of horse beings. There are also concerns about some of the specific things they are asked to do. Westerns and war movies frequently require horses to race fast and fall. Falling always risks injury. Further, in many movies people who can't ride are doing the riding. One frequently sees horses tossing their heads and gaping their mouths—usually signs of rough hands in the rider or some kind of physical pain due to poor fitting tack or to some kind of injury or mistreatment in training. Older and injured horses are sometimes used to accommodate the lack of skill on the part of the riders. This has obvious consequences in terms of pain and suffering. Many concerned with animal rights and welfare also question both the years and hours of use for individual horses. This is exacerbated when the actors don't know how to ride—they bounce on the horse's back and their unsteady hands cause the bit to hit the horse in the mouth.

Sometimes actors do learn to ride, though, and even take horses home with them when a show is done. Viggo Mortenson, for example, bought both the horse he used in *Lord of the Rings* and T.J. from *Hidalgo*. Clint Eastwood has also bought some of the horses he's worked with and given them to members of his family. Most recently, Steven Spielberg's *War Horse* is an example where an actor (Jeremy Irvine) learned to ride. More than that, he participated in the training of one of the young horses for the movie. He noted the difference between learning to ride on lesson horses which were like "a little beat up car" and working with the highly trained horses on the set which he compared to "a Formula One race car." (The plight of the lesson horses will be discussed in the section "Use in Work.") The trainer for this movie, Bobby Lovgren, used one of his own horses (a horse he'd purchased after working with him on the movie *Seabiscuit*) for many of the central scenes in the movie. He notes the importance of "[t]horoughly understanding each horse's individual behavior and temperament . . ." (insidemovies.ew.com). Such exceptions, though, may only highlight the general problem of those who do not take the well-being of the horses seriously.

EXHIBITIONS

The most famous of the travelling performance shows would be the Lippizans of the Spanish Riding School of Vienna and their many immitators. There are big differences in the quality of care and training between the famous, high-level shows and the more local, low-level shows. As we will see with horse shows, the more amateur level shows entail more problems for the horses and it is these kinds of shows that account for the majority of horses working in exhibitions. There is only one Spanish Riding School of Vienna and they rarely travel. While there are stresses, to be sure, the horses' needs are looked after at great expense. Knock-offs of this show continuously tour the United States, though, and perform in places like Las Vegas. There are also countless local drill teams, which vary a great deal in their skill and knowledge. Exhibitions such as jousting or other reenactments also raise issues of training, travel, and care.

PRAGMATISM'S RESPONSE TO ENTERTAINMENT

Pragmatists would want to examine the conditions of care and safety. In all of these a Pragmatist is most concerned with the conditions of training and use. What is too much use? What is problematic use? What conditions of confinement and travel are acceptable? What isn't acceptable? In many of the shows the people involved have varying levels of expertise and knowledge. The horses are often seen primarily as a way to make money by the proprietors and as a source entertainment by the audience. There is also the added concern of promoting the view that other animal beings are objects whose purpose is to entertain us. This can promote an attitude that makes it harder to call on human beings to respect those other animal beings and their own natural and developmental histories. Being fallibilists and pluralists, Pragmatists do not offer absolute guidelines. From the Pragmatist perspective a ban is not called for, but there are limits on the use, and there are requirements for the care of the horses. We have regulations, but these may not be sufficient. Further, they may not be guided by the needs and desires of horses themselves. I will develop this further after looking at issues related to competition.

Use in Competition

Exhibiting animals requires USDA licenses except for private collections, horse shows, animal racing, and most rodeos (E. Williams 286–287). They police themselves. Racing is covered only by state laws and these are enforced by a state's gaming and racing commission. The Professional Rodeo Cowboy's Association monitors rodeos. Horse shows have the United States Equestrian Federation (USEF—formerly the American Horse Show Association [AHSA]). Self-policing is not always the most effective or responsive. This is especially true when there is money and prestige on the line. There are many forms of competition. Here I address just a few: racing, rodeos, shows, and pulling competitions.

HORSE RACING

I will begin with racing since it is the kind of competition most seen by the general public—whether in person or on television. Racing has been around at least since Greek and Roman times. Chariot races were very popular (E. Williams 319). Today, most people think of running horses under saddle when they think of racing—the Kentucky Derby for example. There are many racing circuits for this kind of thoroughbred racing. Such racing began in the United States at Newmarket in 1605 in New York.

Other tracks emerged and the major track at Belmont opened in 1905. In the United States there are also quarter horse races, harness races, and steeplechase races. The majority of these horses are not on the "A circuit" of these various racing enterprises, though. The top end of racing rests on several levels of lower circuits that get much less attention and scrutiny.

Most race horses today are thoroughbreds. Training can run $22,000 a year, stud fees range from $2,500 to $150,000. But the potential winnings and selling of foals still makes this a potentially profitable activity. There is also the prestige of producing a winner—prestige that increases profit and reputation.

Even with good training, though, racing comes with a high risk of injury. "More than 1,200 horses suffer catastrophic injuries on the track every year in the US" ("Race to Save Thoroughbreds" Fall 2009, 13). One reason for the injuries is the young age of most of the horses. Most horses shouldn't even be ridden until they are three years old. Here they are racing at two. Famous examples of racehorse breakdowns have been in the news recently. One of the most well known cases of breakdown occurred in 1975 when the filly Ruffian broke down in front of the cameras as the race was broadcast. She had to be euthanized and the tragedy left a mark on the racing world. More recently many are familiar with the case of Barbaro, who shattered his leg while running the Preakness Stakes in 2006. His owners made extensive efforts to save his life (how much of this concern was for the horse and how much for future stud fees can be debated), but in the end he too was euthanized. Eight Belles' collapse in the 2008 Kentucky Derby also caught the attention of media—she had fractured both of her front ankles. These just add to the list of Charismatic's broken leg in the 1999 Belmont Stakes (he was later sent to Japan to stand at stud), and the break down of two fillies—Go For Wand (shattered ankle) and Pine Island (dislocated ankle) in the 1990 and 2006 Breeders Cup Distaff. We see and hear about some of the more public injuries and breakdowns, but they represent just a small portion of the overall number of injuries.

The majority of injuries and deaths occur in the lower levels of racing. Seventy percent of races in the United States are claiming races in which less talented horses are bought and sold. As recently reported in *The New York Times*, casinos have entered the business and raised the purses of these races so that they often exceed the value of the horses in the race.

They also often pay through last place to encourage owners to enter their horses. This provides an incentive to race injured horses and get a little more money out of them. Many are raced while drugged and medicated and pose a risk to all the riders and horses in the race. In 2010 *The New York Times* had reported on a jockey boycott at Penn National Race Course. One owner had nine horses die in races in ten months. When a horse breaks down in a race there is a risk of serious injury too all horses and riders who might get caught up in a fall. In this case concerns for the well-being of the human riders motivated the actions. But there is also concern for the horses. While some owners see racing as a "business" or a "game," others worry that the increased money in racing has turned horses into "trading cards for people's greed." The 2012 *New York Times* article reported that, on average, twenty-four horses die a week at US racing tracks (nytimes.com).

In addition to the obvious problems of injuries and death, there is another more widespread and hidden risk—"retirement." When horses do not succeed in racing, or come to the end of their winning days, they are seen as a financial liability. Only recently has the industry put pressure on breeders to buy back a certain percentage of the horses they produce. Over 50,000 thoroughbreds are bred each year in the United States, but only a small number successfully compete ("Race to Save Thoroughbreds" Fall 2009, 13). We need to control breeding more closely if we do not want excess and unwanted horses. Many race horses end up at the slaughter house. During the recent ban on slaughter most just faced the extra trauma of being shipped to Canada or Mexico and then slaughtered. "Of the 100,000 American horses transported in cramped trucks from the US to slaughterhouses in Canada and Mexico every year, more than 12,000 are thoroughbred racehorses. Others are shipped to Japan for racing and breeding, and they, too will eventually become dog food" (12). This even happens to horses who have prestigious racing careers, including Kentucky Derby winners. Charismatic (mentioned above) won the Kentucky Derby and then broke his leg in the Preakness. He went to Japan to breed, but he has not been successful. Similarly War Emblem won both the Kentucky Derby and the Preakness Stakes. He too went to Japan to breed, and he too has been unsuccessful (13). If they can't breed, they are considered worthless.

There are attempts to stop the slaughter of racehorses. For example the New York State Racing Association has a zero tolerance policy for breeders, owners, and trainers who directly or indirectly send horses to slaughter. Some tracks have joined this prohibition—Portland Meadows, Santa Anita, and Pimlico. Emerald Downs (in my neighborhood) has a fund to help place ex-race horses in new homes and careers. Some ex-racehorses are bought and retrained for other activities—trail riding, jumping, and dressage. There are rescue groups who facilitate this transition. This is helpful, but not as easy as it sounds. Ex-racehorses have physical and mental issues, and often require careful and expert handling. Yet many end up in the hands of inexperienced amateurs who do not have the necessary knowledge and skills. This can lead to a chain of selling the horse over and over again. So, while many are successfully and happily moved into new lives, we can't keep up with the numbers being bred and we must be careful about overselling the success of this "solution." All of these efforts only begin to make a small difference and may not change the attitude of many involved in the industry. Here is an example of the attitude that needs to be addressed: "'Some go to slaughter, some go to new homes,' Mariotti says about the horses he auctions off on the first Sunday of each month. 'A horse is a product, just like a cow or a steer. The bleeding hearts who've got it in mind that they're going to save every one, they're idiots.'" (Thompson). To be clear, the end of slaughter is not a pretty one for horses (or other animal beings). They are held in crowded pens and their movement and vocalization are evidence that they are unsettled. A report by an HSUS investigator gives the following account. "A worker grabbed the back of her neck, feeling for the spinal cord. Seconds later he stabbed her and she fell hard to the ground, then stood upright. Again the hand struck her. This time she did not get up; her body quivered while workers cheered" (Malkin 20).

RODEOS

The shift to agriculture has led to human dependence on domestication and often to the subjugation of nature and living creatures. For many, this subjugation can be found in rodeos (Serpell, *Company of Animals* 175, 179). The events in rodeos have their roots in the work horses did (and in some cases still do) on ranches. The work itself raises one set of issues; the transformation of these tasks into competitive events that occur on a circuit raises still other issues. Breeding and training horses to buck as hard as they can is different from riding a young horse who bucks when first feeling the weight of a rider.

Some horses bred and trained for some of these specific activities seem to really enjoy the chance to perform and compete, but not all. Further, when in the hands of less skilled humans, these horses almost inevitably experience overwork, injury, and breakdown. Further, male horse owners are found to be more aggressive and dominant, while female horse owners are more easy going and less aggressive (Serpell, *Company of Animals*, 33). While women dominate barrel racing, men are more prevalent in bronc riding, steer wrestling, cutting, and reining. When not properly performed, or not properly understood, rodeo activities can promote the idea of dominating other animal beings. The allure of the cowboy image includes, for instance, long roweled spurs—something few have the skill to use carefully and humanely.

Almost all animal welfare and animal rights groups oppose rodeos. They point to the dangers and stress involved with the frequent transportation of the animals. They also point to the injuries sustained: broken necks from roping, burns from bucking, sores from the overuse of spurs (E. Williams 318–319). There are also tendon and ligament injuries from reining, cutting, and barrel racing.

Another problem is that rodeos regulate themselves. The Professional Rodeo Association is responsible for developing and enforcing regulations. The Horse Protection Act does not apply to rodeos (E. Williams 287). As with other competitions, the most significant problems develop in the "low end" of these competition circuits. This is where less skilled riders, with less money to invest in care, encounter less oversight—a bad combination for the horse.

HORSE SHOWS

The first horse show in the United States is thought to have taken place in 1853. The main idea of such shows seems to have been to establish which horses were "best" and so should be used for breeding. A related purpose was to "prove" the success of a farm's breeding program. Today there are many breed shows and discipline shows. Some showing focuses on conformation only, some looks at conformation and performance, and other showing looks at performance only.[8] As with rodeos, there is a concern

---

8. I am including three-day events and combined driving events here.

about horse shows developing and enforcing regulations. The show people police themselves. The United States Equestrian Federation is the main governing body in the United States, and it works alongside breed and discipline organizations such as the American Morgan Horse Association, the American Quarter Horse Association, and the United States Dressage Federation. Different breeds and disciplines have different standards. As noted earlier (in the "Abuse and Neglect" section) over two hundred drugs are banned by the United States Equestrian Federation (USEF) and there are a variety of banned training practices. The fact that all these things need to be banned tells us something about the mindset of some of the humans involved in showing horses. According to the Horse Protection Act, these bans are self-enforced when it comes to horse shows. None of the bans and restrictions can realistically be applied to the training that *precedes* the shows. Interestingly the ASPCA does note this concern, though they offer no way to address it. They say that

> The ASPCA is not opposed to animal shows, fairs, and exhibitions of breeding and/or performing stock . . . if held under the auspices of established, well-regulated sponsoring organizations that have clearly stated and vigorously enforced rules against harsh or abusive treatment of both competing and "target" animals. . . . The ASPCA's concern extends beyond the show venue to ensuring humane methods of breeding, raising, training, preparing for exhibition, transporting and housing show stock and in providing humane care for animals who are no longer to be used for this purpose. (aspca.org)

Since no organization can monitor every horse, the only way to effectively change the treatment of horses as they are prepared for competition is to get humans to rethink this relationship.

To make horse shows, especially at the lower levels, less problematic, we need to make sure they become more than popularity or beauty contests. As we will see with dogs, shows and classes that focus on conformation (halter classes) do have some detrimental side effects. First, horses who win these titles tend to dominate the breeding population and so shrink the gene pool and increase the risk of congenital defects. This is especially true when judges become political (choosing horses presented by trainers employed by the rich and powerful, for example) and do not remain focused on how the horse is put together. Second, many of the halter horses no longer compete in performance classes. This can result in breeding individuals who cannot hold up to the basic physical activities most horses enjoy. Third, most halter horses (and many other kinds of show horses) are kept in stalls most of the time. This is to make sure they don't get any scrapes or scars, or pull shoes, and to increase the likelihood that they will "show themselves" well in the class. Here, too, is one of the greatest risks for abuse. Some horses (and dogs) are trained to "model" by using tools such as cattle prods to get them to pay attention and look alert. They learn to hold a pose, but at what cost? Further, many competition horses are being used at too young an age. Horses take time to grow and mature; different breeds and different individuals develop at different rates. Nevertheless, riding a horse before three is too young for almost all horses. Yet the classes with the most money tied to winning are futurity classes. These are classes for two- and three-year-old horses. This means they have been in training even earlier.

People who show need to focus on learning to have respectful relationships with horses. This is not promoted when high profile trainers get caught in bad practices. Quarter horse trainer Cleeve Wells was recently fined $10,000 and suspended by the Professional Horseman Association. This ruling was upheld by the American Quarter Horses Association after hearing testimony regarding his abuse of horses in his training program. A horse was found tied in his stall, unable to reach food or water. His mouth was swollen (two pieces of his mandible had to be removed), there was a tongue laceration, and infected spur injuries that ran the length of his sides. Pus was oozing from the wounds and there was no evidence of medical care. At the end of the one-year suspension, Wells must show cause for reinstatement. If cause is shown and he is reinstated, Wells will be placed on indefinite probation. While one might applaud the fact that action was taken, many clients said they knew about his abusive practices but also knew he could win competitions. This attitude raises concerns about the ethics of showing and competing with other animal beings.

Similarly, evidence of policing exists in the world of Tennessee Walkers, but that same evidence raises serious concerns about how humans treat horses and our ability to protect these horses. Tennessee Walkers are known and judged on the high stepping action that is part of their unique gait. Soring is a banned practice that is used to exaggerate this action and gait. Methods include: using caustic chemicals to produce painful blisters on the legs, burning or cutting on the legs, inserting nails or screws into legs, cutting the foot to the sensitive quick before adding the pressure of shoes (and sometimes marbles). These practices are illegal under the Horse Protection Act and condemned by the AVMA. Nonetheless, according to the Humane Society, "Just last year inspectors observed more than 400 violations of the law at the 71st Tennessee Walking Horse National Celebration in Shelbyville, Tenn. Another 243 were recorded at this year's event, representing 9 percent of the inspections conducted" (Sharp 8). They further note that "(t)he practice continues in part because funding shortfalls prevent the USDA from sending inspectors to more than 5 percent of shows. Advocates have serious concerns about what happens at the other 95 percent, where industry insiders conduct the inspections" (8). Progress is being made as more money is being provided to increase the inspections called for by the Horse Protection Act. But clearly there is a long way to go. Inspections, suspensions, and fines don't seem to help many of the humans involved develop a new attitude of respect.

HORSE PULLS

Horse pulls are found mostly at fairs these days. Draft horses (and some others) were bred to pull heavy loads. In the past, farmers gathered in friendly competitions to see whose horses could pull the heaviest loads over prescribed distances. Today we have tractor and truck pulls that have picked up from these competitions. Though fewer horses are used in pulling work than in the past, the competitions continue. Asking horses to pull more than they are physically able and prepared to do comes with obvious risks. When pride is on the line, some human beings will risk the well-being of the horse beings.

PRAGMATISM'S RESPONSE TO COMPETITION

As with entertainment, the issues of competition are both obvious and hidden. In all cases, problems attend the transport of horses. However, most high-level performance and competition horses travel in style. While there are always the risks of accidents and the increased chance of colic, dehydration, or contracting respiratory diseases, most horses at high levels of performance and competition travel safely. While the most publicized breakdowns and abuse cases come from these high-level performances and competitions—the Kentucky Derby, Grand Prix jumping, Pro-rodeo—this is just a small part of the picture. There is no doubt that there are abuses when there is serious money and reputation on the line. This is true of high-level human athletes as well. However, the bulk of horse beings are performing in lower-end shows and competing on lower-level circuits. Here, the number of horses involved, the increased amount of money involved, the lack of oversight, and the prevalence of less skilled and knowledgeable trainers continue to create a great deal of suffering.

Using the Pragmatist perspective one realizes that, given the *natural* and *developmental* history of domesticated horses, there are horse beings who want to perform, who want to run, who want to pull, who want to jump, who want to cut cattle, who want to run barrels, who want to model, who want to demonstrate the power and precision of dressage. *Experiments,* and the willingness to learn (*fallibilism*), have taught humans a great deal over the five thousand to six thousand year relationship with horses. As long as one has appropriately matched the activity with the physical and psychological abilities of the horse and is able to work with the particular personality and interests of the individual horse (respect the *plurality* of horses), there is nothing *inherently* wrong with these activities from the Pragmatist point of view.

For example, Donald is the horse with whom I had the longest relationship. We met when he was one and he has recently died at age thirty-two. Needless to say, we knew each other pretty well. When Donald was young we showed in the Morgan shows in English pleasure and pleasure driving. He always made it clear he preferred driving to riding. He pranced around once he saw the harness and he couldn't wait to get going once he was hooked to the cart—even in his thirties. At the age of twenty-seven, he went to a local Morgan show as company for Hank, the younger horse in my life. I put him in a driving class just for the fun of it. I wasn't sure he could sustain the trot as long as the judges might ask. By then the ligaments in his hind legs were stretched out due to age and he didn't have much strength in his hindquarters. So, I figured we'd just do what he wanted—this was just for fun. True to form he barely stood to be hooked. He was quiet in the warm up ring, but was willing to go. But then we entered the show arena. He started to really come alive and move out. When people started clapping he moved out more. Then a horse passed him. He hit a trot I hadn't seen since his early teens! The crowd went crazy and Donald just turned it on. He got second place and left the arena in full stride. Then he started to walk. The walk back to the barn was a slow one, but he was alert and very animated. Once there, he started to whinny—not something he regularly does. It seemed he was telling Hank what he had done. He did the same when we returned to our home barn the next day.

Donald always did better when he had an audience. In his teens we made the conversion from saddle seat to dressage. We would work on movements at home and he would do them, but without much power or presence. When we would get to a show or a clinic, however, he was a completely different horse. He had more energy and presence. Hank is different. Naturally a forward and energetic horse, he can be difficult

Figure 3. Competing with Donald who preferred to drive. Often working well but unimpressively at home, he would really come alive when he had an audience at a clinic or a show. Even at the age of twenty-eight he enjoyed the chance to perform at a show, getting inspired when the audience began to clap and cheer for him. (Photo by Bob Moseder.)

Figure 4. Competing with Hank is one way to respect his individual nature and desires. While not all horses enjoy such activities, some do. Also pictured (standing) are Dan and Julie Williams—trainers who excel at matching horses with activities that suit their conformation and personalities. They often take horses who are deemed uncooperative or dangerous and find what they love to do. (Photo by Howard Schatzberg.)

when it comes to paying attention and staying calm at home. When we get to a show, though, he is all business. Despite the chaos of the show grounds he doesn't spook or get wound up. He clearly has the energy as he won't stand still while I get him ready, but once I'm on he goes to work and once we enter the dressage arena and salute the judge he's a different horse. He is happy when he does something well and hard on himself when something goes wrong.[9]

9. In 2008 circumstances made it possible to take Hank (Nonesuch Second Smoke is his registered name) to the Morgan World Championship and Grand National show in Oklahoma City. He was fifth in the world in training level and he won amateur first level division. Being a World Champion seems to suit him fine.

These are examples of horses who love to go to work. But loving work is not the whole story. Making sure the horse is doing work for which they are well suited is also important. As happy as Donald was working and showing, things got better for him when we switched from saddleseat to dressage. It clearly suited his conformation and his temperament better. That is one reason it is important to match all horses with the activities that suit them best. They also need the right person. Donald wouldn't work for everyone and certain kinds of people (aggressive riders and farriers for instance) make Hank very nervous and he shuts down. In my years working in training barns I have seen horses who were pushed into activities that did not suit their personalities and they usually broke down in some way. In addition to physical break down, their minds were often affected negatively. Such horses would blow up unexpectedly and were labeled uncooperative and dangerous. I have also had the good fortune of working with trainers who inadvertently specialize in helping such horses make a comeback.[10] Over the years I have watched them take these horses no one else would touch and through time and patience discover what work these horses want to do and help them learn to do it. There is usually that awful moment, though, when someone wants to buy the horse. They usually just see the winning horse and don't see what has gone into helping the horse thrive. When the buyers don't keep these horses with these trainers, the horses often relapse into old ways of behaving as they get pushed too far or in directions that don't suit them. Soon, they "disappear" from the show world and one wonders about their fate.

Honoring the horses is important. When one invests in feed and training that allows a horse to develop safely, and when a person has the ability to help the horse succeed, rather than get in their way or make the task harder, there is the opportunity for the kind of rich connection I described at the start of the chapter. Most horses, however, do not find themselves in this situation. The bulk of horses are in the care of inexperienced amateurs who have very limited knowledge. Humans who are matched with the wrong horse often develop bad habits and attitudes. Riding a horse who can't or doesn't want to jump, for instance, can cause a rider who wants to do nothing else to learn abusive ways of coercing horses.

---

10. These trainers are Dan and Julie Williams of Williams Training Stable in Adamsville, PA.

They also learn to see a horse as a kind of thing that is just there to do something for them and hopefully win while doing it. The horse is always seen to be at fault when things don't go as planned or as desired. After pushing the horse as far as they can, such people usually just sell them and buy another one hoping the next one will do more for them. Some people succeed with this approach, but most are simply repeatedly frustrated, trading horses on a regular basis. They never stop to consider that a different attitude and approach might be in order. If they do rethink this approach, though, humans can potentially gain a great deal from their relationship with a horse and the horse can thrive.

In addition to the pleasure (physical, mental, emotional) one may gain from working with horses, there is also an altered sense of community that is important to consider. This does not generally happen when the horse is seen as a commodity or object, but it is increasingly the experience of many horse owners and riders. Some gain a sense of kinship and some gain a feeling of connection to life in general. To get this kind of relationship one needs to go with the nature and ability of the individual horse, not just the human's interests—jumping, dressage, roping, endurance trials, driving, or whatever. One needs to honor the interests of the individual horses as well as horses in general. One needs to get to know them, understand their personality, and respect them as the individuals they are. This may include competing with them. *Some animal advocates consider all competition coercive and wrong. But to take showing away from some horses would actually show a lack of respect for them. Pragmatically speaking, such action fails to respect their natural and developmental histories. That is not say that this is so for all horses, and there are plenty involved in activities that do not suit them. But a sweeping claim that all competition is abusive also fails to respect many horses and the history of horse and human relations.*

Horses demonstrate desires, needs, and purposes. In fact, if they didn't have these characteristics it would have been hard if not impossible to domesticate them in the first place. Domestication is not something done by force and coercion—especially with such a large and strong animal. "A skilled horseman needs to respond to his horse as an individual, to follow the workings of its feelings, to use his imagination to understand how things are likely to affect it, what frightens it and what attracts it . . . ." The treatment of domestic animals has never been impersonal. It has depended on the human capacity to attend to, and to some extent understand, the moods and reactions of other species (Midgley, "Mixed Community" 213). We must continue to pay attention. It is naïve to say it is unethical to ask horses to do anything not of its own inclination, but it is equally foolish not to consider the horse's nature and preferences at all (Budiansky, *Nature of Horses* 2). When we fail to respect the nature and preferences of horses, respectful relationships are not possible. Experts and amateurs alike fall prey to this problem.

Even when inexperienced amateurs seek "expert" help they often find people who sell themselves as trainers and instructors when they too have very limited experience, making it hard for anyone to learn what they need know in order to have a successful and ethical relationship with the horse being in their lives. In these circumstances it is highly probable that a horse and rider may be mismatched, that the horse and the competition activities in which it is engaged are not a good fit. Examples include pairing a timid rider with a "hot" horse or a laid back horse with a human who wants to gallop and jump. The equipment used may be inappropriate and/or not fit properly. This is likely to cause injury and soreness. This may lead to performance "issues" that are then approached with "training." In inexperienced hands it is not uncommon for the "training" to default to attempts to force the horse to do something. This is likely to start a cycle that requires increasing levels of force and fight. The horse soon is seen as a problem horse—uncooperative or even dangerous. The person may quit riding (letting the horse just sit), may sell the horse (maybe for better or for worse for the horse), may send the horse to someone to be "fixed." Depending on the expertise and ability of the trainer the horse may get help. The rider may not change, though, and once the horse returns home the difficulties start all over again.

Under these circumstances, the competitive activities can be quite dangerous for the horses (and riders). If the horse has not learned to bend, use his/her hind end, and be in balance for instance, barrel racing, cutting, dressage, and jumping will put a great deal of stress on the horse's body. Training techniques may be misused or not adjusted to the particular needs of an individual horse. At the lower levels of competition, there is often over-use—over-competition—and horses' bodies break down. There may not be the money or knowledge to provide the proper trimming of feet or shoeing that is appropriate to the activity. There may not be the knowledge of the body that enables one to spot injuries or disease early on or get veterinary care. Preventive care is highly unlikely.

Often, well-meaning attempts to help a horse will actually cause problems. Inexperienced hands wrapping a horse's leg can increase the likelihood of injury, overfeeding can create weight problems that result in back and leg problems, medicines and drugs may be administered improperly. Horses at this level may be transported often—shows every weekend. The trailer may not be hooked up properly (adding stress to the horse's legs), the trailer may not be the right size for the horse (it may have been bought when they had a different horse), and the horse may not load and unload safely (an easy way for the horse to get hurt).

Similarly, race horses (and jockeys) who do not make it to the A circuit find themselves racing more often than they probably should, find themselves under the care of less knowledgeable and attentive trainers and grooms, and find themselves worth less to their owners and consequently do not receive the best care. Horses may be put in a claiming races and spiral down to worse and worse racing circuits—not to mention the horses who begin and end on the bottom end. Then their careers are over. If they are lucky, they may be retired as someone's pet or retrained to perform in some other way—jumping, dressage, trail riding. This takes patience and knowledge. However, we know the racing industry breeds more horses than the industry can use. They bear little responsibility for the "excess" horses. Some barns do buy back a percentage of their foals. But all of this is just a drop in the bucket.

Similarly, competitive horses come to the end of their competitive careers (as do all athletes—human or horse). This may be due to age or injury. Some horses are raced or shown through this for awhile with the use of drugs—despite their illegality. When the end comes, some are retired and stay with their people. For many people, though, keeping a "useless" horse is too expensive and so the horse is sold or given away to make room for the next competition horse. Some of these horses land in good homes and live out their lives in great circumstances. Many, however, may get "used" all over again. The new people may try to race, show, or use the horses beyond what their health allows. Many become lesson horses (see the next section on work).

Pragmatism approaches these complex issues, not by trying to find a sweeping solution or proposing a ban, but by exploring particular circumstances and issues. The answer is not to ban racing, but to get the industry to be more responsible about breeding, retiring, training, and running horses. The answer is not to end all competition with horses, but to get better and real regulation all the way down to local schooling shows. It is to invest in training and education for all who are involved with horses. Done well, these activities actually fit the nature and developmental histories of specific horses and provide an important outlet for expressing their physical abilities and mental capacities.

A specific challenge of this view is that it asks people to understand the horse being before them in some complex ways—the history of domestication and how it impacts their needs, the different breeds, conformation and temperament, the unique personality and interests of individual horse beings. Unless, as mentioned before, working with horses is the way one makes a living, one will probably have close relationships with only a few horses in a lifetime. Under these circumstances, how can one learn enough or have enough experience to prepare one to do the best one can? This takes real commitment. Entering into a relationship with a horse should not be done lightly or casually.

Further, there is a challenge in asking people to be open to a variety of approaches to training and competition. Pragmatism's commitment to pluralism does not mean that all training approaches are equally acceptable or equally successful. For Pragmatism, such pluralism does not include harmful techniques and practices. However, what is harmful in some circumstances may not be harmful in all. But how can amateurs know if a trainer is qualified or if they themselves are ready to try particular things with a horse? The horse is the one most likely to suffer for our errors (though humans get hurt and scared as well). *Surprisingly, many riders think they are beyond the need for lessons and the help of trainers. Pragmatism requires people involved with horses to always be learning. They should always seek to improve their skills and work to improve the lives of horses.*

Some would say the risks are too great for the horses. Since people have to learn, and will make mistakes, it would be better if people just left them alone. They certainly shouldn't be pushing the limits of their physical and mental health by competing with them. While one can understand the sentiment that motivates such a position, from a Pragmatist's point of view it does not make sense. There is a lot lost and risked with the absolutist approach. Humans have a long history of mutually transformative relationships with horses. Bad relationships need to be fixed, but leaving relationships altogether cuts off too many possibilities for both human and horse. Human children are over-trained, given steroids, or are cosmetically altered as parents push them in athletic and beauty competitions. We could ban the competitive activities, though most call for reform and regulation instead. But I do not know of many who suggest we stop having relationships with children altogether in order to make sure there is no abuse or misuse in such relationships. While this may seem like a far-fetched comparison, my point is that the Pragmatist position seeks to avoid over-correction in response to problematic situations. All-or-nothing positions do not make sense and usually create new problems that must be addressed. For those who compare the position of domesticated animals to slavery, even the end of slavery did not call for the end of all forms of labor exchange.

Use in Work

Keeping horses is expensive—even when done at the most basic level. To help pay for the horses' food and care, many people involve the horses in some kind of work. Other people work with horses as a job themselves—this can be for additional or primary income. Here I examine just a few of the more obvious kinds of work in which horses are engaged: lesson programs, therapeutic riding programs, rental operations, police and ranger work, carriage rides, ranch work, and commercials.

LESSON HORSES

A common way for horses to "earn their keep" and to make money for the people who care for them is to be a lesson horse. Some horses are trained from the start to be lesson horses. That is all they know. Many lesson horses, however, are retired competition horses. Once such horses get too old for the level of competition their people desire, they are often sold or retired into a lesson program. Or, if injured to a degree that they cannot come back to the desired level of competition, they often end up as a lesson horse. Having people learn to ride horses is always potentially harmful to the horses. Even when horses were the main form of transportation many humans were not good riders or handlers of horses. The hope is that the humans will learn to ride and to develop a willing partnership with a horse, but the learning curve is steep.

As my own horse Donald got older, it made sense for me to get another horse if I was going to make much progress in my own learning of dressage. We had not competed in years, but we would go to clinics. His back legs were eventually no longer up to the work. I couldn't afford to keep two horses, though. Many people suggested that I either lease Donald to a beginning rider or let a barn use him for lessons in exchange for his board. In this case, I couldn't see how this was fair.

As I mentioned, we'd been together since he was a yearling. My father's rule was that I had to sell my horse when I went to college. He didn't say for how much, though. So, I "sold" Donald for a dollar to friends of mine who raise and train Morgans. While I went to work for them during the summer to help pay for his care, I also said it would be okay to use him in some lessons. They were doing me a huge favor and it didn't seem right to put them out any more than I had to. So I decided Donald would have to help pay for himself for a few years. After just a few lessons, someone fell off. This is not uncommon when one is learning to ride. To my knowledge, however, no one had ever come off of Donald before. He had only been ridden by a handful of people, all of them experienced riders. Once someone came off, though, Donald quickly learned he could remove unwanted riders. He started to "lose" riders regularly. He wasn't mean, he'd just stop or turn quickly and then look around at the rider on the ground. But when the trainers would ride him he wouldn't try anything. So we decided he didn't want to give riding lessons. Since he loved driving, we tried using him for driving lessons and he was fine. In fact, he seemed to really enjoy it.

Given this past, I was reluctant to consider using Donald for riding lessons, and there isn't much call for driving lessons where I live. For any horse, riding lessons are a dicey affair. Beginner riders are often out of balance, pull on the reins, give incorrect aids but blame the horses if they don't do what the human wants. The rider is rarely able to get the horse working in the correct frame and this takes a toll on the horses' bodies. They are often used in many lessons every week, even in a given day. Some barns take very good care of their lesson horses. Many, however, think of them as "just" lesson horses and they receive inferior farrier and vet care, use tack that isn't fitted to them, and get used more often than they should be. This can cause them to break down at an early age. Camp horses are a subset of lesson horses who are particularly at risk for over use and substandard care. These horses are often in the care of young, inexperienced camp counselors in addition to having young children bouncing on their backs and pulling on their mouths. These children often have no particular interest in "learning" to ride, they just want to be on the horse. Their goals and commitment rarely go beyond the end of summer.

For people to ride, though, there have to be horses who have beginner riders on them. Is it unethical for people to learn to ride given the discomfort and possible damage for the horses? I don't think so, *if* we pay attention to how this is done. There are some horses who seem to genuinely like helping inexperienced riders. They are very careful with them and demonstrate amazing patience. But we should not exploit that nature. From the Pragmatist point of view, special care and consideration must be given to horses involved in teaching people to ride. We should probably increase the use of simulators as well. Good simulators exist, but currently they are very expensive. They also fail to provide the connection and experience with the living being and so are not a complete substitute. Some other options include not letting riders use a bit in the horse's mouth until they are balanced in the saddle and not letting riders jump until they have a secure seat.

There also needs to be a focus on understanding the natural and developmental history of domesticated horses and a willingness to adjust the human expectations to fit with the needs and desires of specific breeds and particular individuals. Riding is a privilege—not an economic one but an existential one. We must start to instill respect for the skills of one experienced with horses and teach people to be open and flexible in their approach to riding and handling horses. They should focus on their own fallibility and inability, not the horse's. The better instructors do make the basic point that if things don't go as planned it is usually due to "rider error." While, of course, the horse may need training or conditioning most of the time, once you fix the rider's position the horse quickly follows. Humans must strive to improve in order to earn the right to enter the relationship with the horse. This requires an ongoing commitment to learn and improve.

THERAPEUTIC RIDING PROGRAMS

In addition to retiring competition horses to lesson programs, some choose to donate older or injured horses to therapeutic riding programs.

These programs use horses to help with the mental and physical therapy of humans. I have volunteered at several of these programs and in many ways they are amazing. I watched a woman, who had ridden and jumped horses most of her life, relearning to control her body after a car accident. When trying to walk her balance was not steady. When on a horse, however, she was more balanced, and she used and strengthened muscles she needed in order to walk. I have also worked with a young woman who could not remember things she learned for very long, making progress on tasks very slow. She was impatient with trying to learn new things. However, when it was time to ride she focused and always made an effort. Her mother said she learned more about riding and the games we played on the horses than anything else she did. She clearly had an emotional connection with the horses that motivated her work. The programs often also include an opportunity for the humans to compete on the horses—either in races and games or in more standard horse show classes. This provides social opportunities for the humans and often helps build their confidence generally.

However, many of the adult riders with physical challenges pose difficulties for the horses. They are sometimes heavy and do not have the control of their bodies needed to maintain balance and control when on the horses. This means the horses must compensate with their own bodies. Most young, healthy horses can do this. But, as I said, many of the horses donated to these programs are older horses or horses who have sustained some kind of injury. This means they may not be up to this kind of use. Further, horses in such programs often do not get exercised in other ways. These horses need to be as strong and fit as possible, yet they often do little but be turned out in pasture (if they are lucky), be longed to get any excess energy out, and then walked and trotted in the program with riders who cannot properly balance on their backs.

So, is it wrong to use horses in this way? Again, Pragmatists would acknowledge it can be a problem, but if done with care it can work out well for all involved. There are guidelines for such programs. The North American Riding for the Handicapped Association (NARHA) states that one of its core values is "providing a culture of safety, understanding and ethical treatment of humans and horses engaged in equine-assisted activities and therapies." Beyond this, a Pragmatist would want us to consider the individual horses involved. We have to consider the benefits and drawbacks for both humans and horses and not just assume that all programs engage in the "ethical treatment of humans and horses." There is little, if any, oversight of these programs. I have volunteered at one program that was very aware of safety for the horses and humans and took great care of the horses in the program. I have volunteered at another program, though, that paid little attention to safety issues, used older and injured horses, and offered substandard care for the horses. Such programs should not be a dumping ground for older or unwanted horses, but a place where horses with certain temperaments can thrive. It is also possible that some humans simply cannot sufficiently control their bodies or emotions and so should not be involved in this type of therapy.

RENTAL HORSES

Another career for horses is the life of a rental horse. As with lesson horses, some of these horses are trained from the beginning with this work in mind. Others end up in this line of work when their competition days are over, or when people "outgrow" them. The life of the rental horse is generally harder than the lot of lesson horses as it is almost guaranteed that the people who ride them have either never ridden or have not ridden regularly enough to be very skilled. Nor are they there with the purpose of learning or improving in mind. The horses are there to provide a service to the humans. They also do the same thing over and over— that is ride the same route on the trails or the beach. They often know exactly where they are to walk versus where they might be asked to trot (if they ever do more than walk). Horses used to pack people into the mountains, either for a trail ride or to leave them at a camp site, have the added challenge of needing to cover rough and dangerous terrain with unschooled and unbalanced riders on their backs.

I have, myself, rented horses on several occasions. When traveling in Colorado for instance, I have gone on trail rides with non-rider friends. Such rides tend to line the horses up in single file and walk a trail route well-known to the horses. On one of these occasions, I was asked to ride a horse who had been a guide's horse, but who had recently been "misbehaving" on the trails unless she was in the lead. Since guides need to be able to take up any position in the line, she was in danger of being out of a job. They wanted me to ride her just one or two horses behind the lead horse and get her to relax. I agreed. It was not a relaxing or enjoyable ride for either of us as the mare reared and spun on the narrow trail. There are ways to retrain horses who either want to be in front or only want to follow, but this takes time, patience, and consistency. While we made some progress that day, it could easily be undone with the next ride. It is unlikely I did much to help her situation. The bigger question is why she developed this behavior in the first place. I will never know about her case in particular, but it is not uncommon for horses who are bored with what they are doing to act out or develop resistant behaviors.

In addition to the repetitive nature of such work, most operations like this one get the horses groomed and tacked up in the morning and they remain saddled and tied between rides. In the United States, with our litigious society, many horse rental operations have closed down. Those that do remain in operation make sure the horses they use are tired and docile in order to lessen the chance of anyone getting hurt. My experience in Great Britain has been different, though similar issues remain for the horses. In England I have ridden horses at riding academies that both gave lessons and took people out on trail rides. These horses had attitude and fought any deviation from their routine. On these rides there were places to trot and canter and any attempt to not do those things made the horses unhappy.

In Scotland I had different experiences. A horse friend and I went to one school that offered rides on the beach. When we got there, there were no papers to sign, no riding helmets available. Since we rode, she asked if we'd be willing to ride two of her young horses. She wanted to save her more experienced horses for other people coming that day. She also needed to get the young horses ready for the summer season. The horses jigged all the way to the beach. Once at the beach they trotted out. The beach was strewn with logs and rocks, but our guide asked if we wanted to canter. I would not have done more than walk one of my own horses given all the opportunities for serious injury. But these horses took off in a full gallop. Trying to stop or slow any one of the horses would have been more dangerous than to keep going. We slowed and stopped when the beach ended and they jigged all the way home. The horses had had a great time, but this is not necessarily what their future life will be like.

Later that week we went to a different barn and my friend's mother joined us on the ride. Since she is not a regular rider I was worried. This school had helmets for all of us, though. They also had a list of rules and watched everyone ride in the arena before we set out. They changed horses for a few riders based on this evaluation. Then we were off.

They walked to the beach. This beach was clear and open. One guide took my friend's mother and another rider one way down the beach at a walk. The rest of us went the other way at a fast trot. As our guide said that we could canter when we reached a certain point, all the horses quickened their pace and without any cue from us they took off in a gallop. This was all more controlled, though, and on a safer beach than the ride earlier in the week. It was, however, clearly routine for the horses. Nonetheless, they seemed to be enjoying themselves. Everyone walked home calmly but with purpose. These different experiences show that such work does not have to be complete drudgery for the horses, but making it less boring entails that riders take on more responsibility and risk.

A subset of rental horses are the ponies used for "pony rides." Many adults have memories of going on a pony ride. This might have happened at a fair, at a circus, in a parking lot of some store, or at a birthday party. All the risks and concerns about frequent travel apply to these ponies. Such operations maintain a string of ponies who are usually tied into an automatic walker and they walk in circles all day. While this is boring and repetitive work, there are usually height and weight limits for the riders and they do not have reins to pull on the ponies' mouths. They do not go faster than a walk and so the riders don't get too out of balance. But, they often walk on hard surfaces, in the heat, and may get kicked and hit by rough children. The focus is clearly on the desires of the humans, as is the case with most rental situations.

What would Pragmatism tell us about these experiences? What would it tell us about the practice of hiring out horses at all? Again, one has to consider the specific horse and the specific activities. In Scotland, I had the experience of those barns matching riders with horses—this made good sense for the well-being of horse and human. In the United States I have seen more of the attitude that the horse should accommodate any rider and any work. The litigious nature of US society adds to the idea that there should be no risk involved in riding. Despite waivers that require the rider to acknowledge that riding is a risky activity and to accept that risk, if something goes wrong people look for someone to blame and often sue. This has only encouraged the idea that horses should be docile and obedient—maybe even rendered unable to cause harm. This attitude does not seem to fit with the idea of respecting the needs of the horse beings called for by Pragmatism. So, it's not a yes or no answer. Rather, some instances are unacceptable and others are acceptable. The question is how can we work to make the respectful options the norm? This will not occur if animal advocates simply call for a ban. Rather, such advocates need to learn about horses themselves and then work with those engaged in real relationships with horses to provide situations that respect the nature and abilities of the horses involved. It may also require rethinking how the United States approaches risk and liability generally, not just with regard to horse-related activities.

POLICE HORSES, PARK SERVICE, AND BORDER PATROL

In another field of work, horses are used for crowd control by mounted police and as a way to improve relationships with communities. People will approach a police officer to ask to pet the horse. Similarly, they are used by park service rangers. Horses allow the rangers to work in the back country and also make them approachable by the hikers and campers. For similar reasons they are also used to patrol the US border. They are able to work off road more quietly than motorized vehicles.

Some cities are cutting or shutting down mounted police forces due to cost. Some of these include Boston, Massachusetts; Roanoke, Virginia; San Jose, California; Toledo, Ohio; Columbia, South Carolina; and others (Krikstan 69). New York City, however, continues to see their mounted patrol as essential to the safety of the city. They choose large, calm horses who can handle the hours on the pavement and the potentially spooky environment of the city. Not all horses prove suited to this kind of work and those that don't adapt well are returned to the farms from which they were purchased.

> Currently, 62 horses serve on the force, with about half based in Manhattan. In general, the horses do not go out when the temperature is 18 degrees or colder or 90 degrees or above. . . . "Our horses are kept warm in the cold and refreshed with baths during extreme heat, but if the Department needs horses in emergencies, we are deployed. Everyone earns their keep." Most horses would envy such keep. The stalls here measure 10 by 10 feet and are kept immaculately clean. All five city stables are certified by the New York State Horses Health Assurance Program. . . . Horses are fed six times a day. . . . The horses are shod every six to eight week with steel shoes that have borium cleats." (Price 46–47)

Both the riders and the horses are given intensive training and being in the mounted unit is a coveted spot. They are seen as important for counterterrorism efforts, as the mounted officers can see above the crowds; they are also important for crowd control. This work is not without risk, however, and horses do get spooked. Horses have been known to bolt in fear—posing a danger to themselves and the humans around them (Price 48).

Horses fulfill similar duties for the Park Service. One of my sister's horses was donated for this kind of work. One of my first horses, Abraham, was donated for border patrol work. He had been trained using some rough techniques and had at one point been badly cut up when he ran through several fences trying to get away from abusive use of a whip. I liked him and my parents bought him to be my first show horse. He was, however, always unpredictable. Every time I got on, Abe would spin and rear. If I just rode through this, he would settle down. I loved him, though he proved not to be a good show horse. This was partly due to his conformation. He also had a tendency to spin off the rail if anything spooked him and I was still too young and inexperienced to correct this behavior. I told my parents I didn't really want to show and was happy to just ride at home. My parents wanted me to have a more "successful" experience of showing, though, and they (probably rightly) didn't trust him. It is hard to completely restore trust after a horse has been abused.

One cool fall day I decided to ride Abe down the road. He was always spooky and so it was a bad decision to go on this day, and worse yet to go bareback. All was going well, when some steers in our neighbor's pasture charged at the fence. Abe spun and took off. I stayed on for a ways, but when he turned sharply to go back up our driveway I came off. It turned out I had a gash on my head (no helmet in those days) and a punctured lung. While I explained to my parents that it was *my* bad decisions that had resulted in my injuries, they decided Abe should go somewhere else. Ultimately he was donated to the Southern California border patrol.

For police, ranger, or border patrol horses, daily life is full of hard work. All of this kind of work entails long hours under saddle, sometimes standing on concrete, sometimes covering many miles. For some horse this may be ideal work, but not for all. We were told Abe was adjusting well to his new job. A few years later he was featured in an article on the use of horses in border control work. By all accounts Abe had a close

Figure 5. Abe. He had been abused with a whip when he was young and as a result was always a bit unpredictable. He did not like showing and was not well-suited to a young rider. He was donated to the Border Patrol and was said to be happy in his new work. Work can be an important outlet for some animal beings, though there are issues to consider.

relationship with a particular officer and enjoyed his job. The long hours suited him. I have always wondered if I should I trust this account. Was this view of things just a way to make me feel better about how his life turned out? Pragmatists favor the idea of finding the place and activities that suit the horse. If Abe was happier out on patrol, then it was more than worth my feelings of loss. Humans need to learn to put the interests of other animal beings before their own.

OTHER WORK

Driving horses may work to provide romantic carriage rides in a city park, or at a wedding. They may carry people in a parade or be used as a taxi to traverse city streets. There is a campaign to end the use of carriage horse on the streets of New York City—stress is usually cited as the primary concern, as well as the risk of physical injuries from cars. Inhaling car exhaust is another problem, as is the often inadequate stabling available in the city. The Humane Society reports that

> The horses often labor in extreme heat or bitter cold, despite a law against forcing them to work in adverse weather conditions. They breathe exhaust fumes and must contend with motorized forms of transport, which can spook them and result in accidents that are sometimes fatal. . . . They stand for hours with no shelter from the elements and walk on pavement that takes a toll on their legs. . . . [M]any of them are warehoused on the west side of Manhattan in stalls . . . that barely allow them to lie down. Carriage horse companies, rather than taking care of retired horses for life, frequently sell them for slaughter. (Hettinger 12)

There is now a proposal to replace horse-drawn carriages with classic cars.

Other horses are still used to work livestock, especially on cattle ranches. If not abused with overwork or abusive training, this can be a very good life. Often pastured for the winter, the horses also get to use the skills they were bred and trained to have. They round up and cut out livestock. They are used to rope calves and to check the fence line. Interestingly the ASPCA states that they are not opposed to horses being used in ranch work "provided that all the animals' physiological and behavioral needs are fully met and that no cruel practices are used in raising, training and maintaining the animals, including when their period of useful service is over" (aspca.org). They do not mention any other "approved" work for horses, though.

Horses used for hauling, pulling, and plowing are another kind of ranch horse. Some people who are trying to farm in less invasive ways use horses to work their fields. Others who try to harvest trees in more sustainable ways use horses to pull out individual trees from forested areas rather than engage in the practice of clear cutting,

Horses are also used to advertise products. Sometimes the pictures or videos used are taken in the course of other activities in which the horses are engaged. Rolex has ads that connect to jumping events, as does Budweiser. (The Budweiser Invitational is a premier jumping event.)

Other commercials involve separate training and use of the horses. The commercials for Budweiser that involve the Budweiser Clydesdales, or the Wells Fargo commercials that have the team of draft horses pulling the stage coach, are examples of how horses help sell an image. They also make live appearances at various events. These are usually horses already involved in performance shows or competition. The issues involved in various forms of work are many of the same issues raised by entertainment and competition.

PRAGMATISM'S RESPONSE TO WORK

The varied ways in which horses are used in work means there is no simple stance on the ethics of using horses in work. The main response from the Pragmatist perspective is—"it depends." It depends on the conditions in which the horses work; it depends on the care they are provided; and it depends on the concern for, and attention to, their well-being. Some lesson horses seem to enjoy the work and are well cared for. Others are clearly seen as a means of making money and are simply maintained so they can work. The same can be said for all the forms of work. The Pragmatist's aim is not to ban such work, but to try to match horses with appropriate work and then ensure good care and attention to their safety and well-being. If their health and safety cannot be guaranteed within reasonable limits—perhaps carriage horses in New York City are an example—then it may be time to modify or eliminate these work activities. But even if that is the case, does that mean all carriage horses everywhere should be removed from such work? These are the kinds of discussions the various concerned groups need to be having. Extreme or absolute positions do not help foster such conversation.

Death

Horses (especially ponies) can live a long time. This provides an opportunity for long-term relationships. Despite this, most people see their time with a particular horse as short term. First, horses and ponies can literally be outgrown. Others may be outgrown as the person's skills and ambitions send them on to another horse. And then, when horses get injured or old, they are often replaced. Some people keep an old or hurt horse while they begin to work with a new horse. Given the expense of keeping horses, though, many lease, sell, or donate older horses so they can afford the new horse. This means that many people who are involved with horses for a long time never actually experience the death of a horse. Nevertheless, almost everyone with horses has dealt with the threat of death. Colic can come on at any time and affects horses of all ages. Life-threatening injuries can also occur at any time. To live with horses is to live with the very real presence of the possibility of unanticipated death.

Pragmatism is well positioned to help us understand and deal with the deaths of other animal beings (as well as human beings). Because Pragmatism understands all live creatures as beings who are born, grow, and develop, and then deteriorate and die, it is not prone to denying or trying to avoid the processes of life and death. Death is part of the natural development of any organism and must be addressed thoughtfully if a life is to be respected. This does not mean people do not experience a sense of loss or tragedy when injury, illness, or death occur. Rather, Pragmatism offers a way to understand and approach it. This includes taking responsibility for the life and death of another animal being.

With horses, one can face these decisions at any time. There is concern that some use euthanasia as a way to avoid dealing with an injured horse. Given the time and money involved, some seem to see death as a more expedient option. Others may see it as more humane than selling a rehabilitated horse who might be used beyond what their body can bear. If one chooses to live with older horses, it is almost inevitable that one will face the choice of death. An older horse may colic, and this can be very painful. If it is not resolvable, one would have to decide about ending the horse's life. Laminitis is another condition older horses are prone to, and it is also painful and debilitating. It makes it difficult for a horse to stand. There are treatments, but no guarantees as to the results. When is such a life intolerable? There are other conditions older horses are likely to face: severe arthritis can make it hard for horses to get up and down, worn teeth can make it hard for them to hold weight, their digestive systems can fail to absorb and utilize nutrients. Organs can begin to fail. At some point one may need to decide if the horse can be a horse. Is the horse enjoying life? This varies for different individuals, but it is important to respect those things that make life worth living to a horse and make decisions from their perspective.

Further, if the decision is made to end the horse's life, should they be sent to slaughter or gently euthanized? One practice makes money; one costs money. As mentioned before, the absence of the option of slaughter may actually increase the suffering of horses as they are either left to die or they are shipped long distances to foreign slaughter facilities after having gone through the process of sale at auction. At an auction, horses are often housed poorly and handled roughly by strangers. For a horse who has been in a loving home, this can be an especially traumatic experience. Then there are concerns about how the slaughter facilities handle their death. Because the horses are frightened it can be difficult to achieve a quick and painless "kill." A benefit of slaughter, however, is that a horse's carcass is put to use. They may be used for food or other raw materials. This is also the case when euthanized horses are picked up by a renderer who processes the carcass. Increasingly, though, people bury or cremate horses. This may ultimately return them to the earth, but it does require the energy inputs to dig the hole and move the body, or to burn the body. If not buried deep enough, euthanized horses pose a risk to the various animals (wild and domesticated) who may dig them up and ingest fatal amounts of the drugs themselves.

While there is no *one* way to handle the event of death, Pragmatists would be concerned about letting beings suffer and increasing their suffering with travel and unfamiliar handling and experiences (auctions and slaughterhouses). This does not necessarily mean a ban on slaughter, but perhaps a different approach. Though many of the conditions of slaughter are currently unacceptable, as noted before, as long as we presently find it acceptable to slaughter cattle, pigs, and chickens, there really is no ground for objecting to the slaughter of horses as a whole.

We have USDA mobile slaughter trucks for livestock. Could they also process horses? This would remove the hardship of travel and unfamiliar circumstances. Would veterinarians be willing to lose fees to encourage low-income families to opt for euthanasia? Could horse protection groups raise money to help cover the costs associated with the death and handling of the body? These possibilities deserve our careful consideration, but the main point here is that facing and handling the death of a horse is part of a respectful relationship with horses.

For a Pragmatist, living with horses entails taking them on their own terms. They are not simply objects of use or instruments of glory. We have developed partnerships with each other (transactive relationships) that can entail both the worst abuses and the best possibilities of ourselves. Horses deserve our respect and demand our willingness to help them live and die well. This is what all friends deserve.

THREE

AMERICAN PRAGMATISM

The Continuity of Critters

Now that we have seen the kind of discussion that might occur if we used American Pragmatism to guide the discussion of the relations among humans and other animal beings I turn to a longer discussion of the philosophical perspective itself. Many readers may never have heard of the philosophical tradition of American Pragmatism. For those who know something about American Pragmatism (or neo-pragmatism), it may seem an odd philosophy to choose in order to develop a discussion of respectful relationships between human beings and other animal beings.[1] There are some reasons for this possible confusion.

First, a superficial understanding of Pragmatism may lead one to believe it would support a kind of "application of intelligence" to control and manage other animal beings for human beings' use. I believe it is a more complex and nuanced outlook. Nevertheless, Pragmatism does not

---

1. I will use Pragmatism as shorthand for some of the general views attributed to classical American Pragmatism. I am capitalizing "Pragmatism" to distinguish the philosophical ideas from the ordinary use of the term "pragmatism."

ignore issues of human use and in some instances does tend to put human use more front and center than some other philosophies (animal rights and deep ecology) appear to do. Further, while Pragmatists are pluralists and remain open to exploring various practices, Pragmatism does not suggest being short-sighted or greedy when settling on our desired ends, nor does it justify denying our connectedness with the rest of nature. It is not about expediency.

Second, the more "public" perception of Pragmatism is often one of a mechanistic, problem-solving approach that uncritically endorses science and technology as a "solution." This is a very unfair and misleading account of Pragmatism. I encourage readers to read on in this chapter to see some of the ways Pragmatism understands human embeddedness in a variety of transformative relationships with the rest of nature. It pays attention to the way humans can move beyond interaction with the rest of nature to transactional (mutually transformative) relations. It also acknowledges the complex ways these transactional relations can be understood and improved.

Third, if all one knows of Pragmatism is the work of Richard Rorty and other neo-pragmatists, the discussion here may come as a surprise. Pragmatism is not all about language and communities of interpretation. The other animal beings in our lives are flesh and blood beings with whom we interact; they affect our lives. They have changed us as much (or more) than we have changed them—not just conceptually but literally, that is, physically, socially, and mentally.

And finally, some of the leading figures of Pragmatism (William James and John Dewey) said some things about other animal beings that demonstrate a lack of understanding and respect for these beings. In this they join many thinkers in many philosophical traditions. However, they each also said things that argue for greater respect and understanding and their overall views demand an approach of respect and understanding.

As I mentioned in Chapter 1, I think it is important to add American Pragmatism to the philosophical and public discourse concerning the relationships among human and other animal beings. The conversation has been dominated by the views of utilitarians such as Peter Singer and rights-based theorists such as Tom Regan. Continentalists such as Kelly Oliver and Donna Haraway are making inroads and there are more feminist voices now, voices such as those of Carol Adams, Jospehine Donovan, and Val Plumwood. In addition to care ethics, virtue ethics

(Martha Nussbaum) has also begun to make an impact. Despite the wide variety both among and within these views, most fall prey to the assumption that humans are something both physically separate from other animal beings, and ontologically distinct and exceptional. This supports the idea that humans are in control of other animal beings. On this view those animal beings whom we do not control should just be left alone. These free-living or "wild" animal beings are seen as somehow uninfluenced by humans much as "wilderness" is often conceived of as free from human influence and impact. From a Pragmatist perspective this makes no sense. As soon as human beings began to emerge we began to influence our environment and all the creatures in it, just as the environment and the creatures in it influenced us. There is no radical separation or distinction. Rather there is inter-relatedness and transaction from the start.

However, when one hears William James say, "The world stands really malleable, waiting to receive its final touches at our hands. . . . [I]t suffers human violence willingly" (*Pragmatism* 115), one begins to think of Pragmatism as supporting a notion of human privilege and human dominion. This kind of statement implies a human-centered approach to understanding the rest of nature and suggests we see nature as a resource for our use. It doesn't do much to change one's impression of Pragmatism when we hear from John Dewey, "To prefer the claims of the physical suffering of animals to the prevention of death and the cure of disease . . . does not rise even to the level of sentimentalism. . . . It is accordingly the duty of scientific men to use animal experimentation as an instrument in the promotion of social well-being . . ." ("Ethics of Animal Experimentation" 100).

Given Pragmatism's own claims, however, these statements are not representative. Pragmatism, in general, does not see the rest of nature as simply a resource for satisfying our human needs and desires. Instead, Pragmatism highlights our connectedness with the rest of nature. Pragmatists point out that after Darwin the idea of a radical separation of human beings and other animal beings, which supports the idea of mastery and promotes the exclusive focus on use value, makes no sense. Instead, along with C. S. Peirce, we need to remember that all life exists in a continuum. His notion of synechism is the idea that all things are connected. "In a synechistic world . . . all borders are continuous and consequently are inherently vague" (D. Anderson 87). From this beginning Pragmatism calls us to respect the continuity and complexity of our relationships with the rest of nature. This continuity is not just about shared genetics, evolutionary history, and physical structures. It is also that we share a desire for affiliation, a propensity to rivalry, a capacity for affection, and often can be motivated by fear and greed (Sabloff 49).

Remembering what was said at the end of Chapter 2, I will offer a general Pragmatist view that I find useful for examining human relationships with horses, dogs, and cats. This Pragmatic view borrows from some of the most relevant aspects of the work of Charles S. Peirce, William James, John Dewey, Charlotte Perkins Gilman, and Alain Locke. I will also use some of the work of Jane Addams, but not here in the general account of Pragmatism. I will turn to her work in the final chapter as I suggest some ways to make things better for the relations between human and other animal beings.

What I provide here is a very general and superficial version of the story of Pragmatism. I do not pretend to do justice to the full history of Pragmatism or to any of these individual thinkers. The purpose is to provide a framework for using Pragmatism to discuss the issue of human relations with horses, dogs, and cats. I do include critiques of the views presented at the same time that I point to the parts of the Pragmatist perspective that I find important and helpful for these discussions. I do this to be honest about the history of these views and to point out one of the strengths of Pragmatism—the capacity to change and correct one's view. Both William James and John Dewey, for instance, change their perspective on animal beings over time. This demonstrates the importance of reflective thinking that responds to experience and experimentation. Rather than take dogmatic or absolutistic positions they engage in ongoing inquiry.

General Ideas of Pragmatism

Very generally, classical American Pragmatism emerged in the second half of the 1800s with the work of Charles Sanders Peirce, William James, and John Dewey. It was developed and put to work in the world in interesting ways by people like Jane Addams (dealing with issues of immigration, poverty, and gender), Charlotte Perkins Gilman (dealing with issues of gender and economics), and Alain Locke (dealing with issues of race and violence). These six thinkers also had something to say about how humans treat and interact with other animal beings, though this was never their central concern.

From Peirce we gain the idea of human ontological continuity with the rest of nature. This entails the possibility of understanding and communicating with the rest of nature. We also get the idea that life is always in process. I will present his views as grounding the *naturalism* of Pragmatism.

From James we get the call to respect others who are different. Continuity does not mean sameness and much can be learned from stretching oneself and encountering others from a variety of perspectives. While James himself sometimes failed to remain open to the differences of other animal (and human) beings, this was not always the case. His views definitely call on us to include such perspectives in our understanding in order to engage the world around us in satisfactory ways. I will present this as Pragmatism's embracing of *pluralism*.

With Dewey I will emphasize the Pragmatist insight that life is *developmental*. Life is always changing and generally seeks growth and "improvement." Such growth, if it is to be successful, engages any particular aspect of life or situation as being in a web of relationships with other life. No one and no thing stands alone. Individual and species development depends on transactive (mutually transformative) relationships with the rest of the environment (living and nonliving). As with James, Dewey also sometimes fails to follow his own views consistently. Until late in his life, he tended to set humans apart from the rest of nature more than did Peirce. This caused problems for him as he tried to deal with emerging scientific information about intelligence, emotions, and consciousness. His own theory should have committed him to a continuum of such traits, not some kind of human exceptionalism. Later in his life he moved in this direction and his work in general provides many resources for understanding current work in biology, anthropology, ethology, and cognitive ethology—all fields that contribute to our understanding of our relations with other animal beings.

While Dewey is usually the primary example of one who fully embraces the *experimental* approach Pragmatism calls for, I will use Gilman to exemplify that here. I do this because she engaged in actual experiments with changes in living conditions in order to improve the position of women in society and so to allow for the continued growth of the human species. She connected some of this work to the position of those animal beings commonly seen as pets. While the position she arrives at in regard to such animal beings may not ultimately fit with the Pragmatist view I present here, her method and approach to experimentation does, and we can learn a great deal from looking at her work in this light.

And finally, to exemplify the *fallibilism* that Pragmatism calls us to recognize (first called for by Peirce), I turn to the work of Alain Locke. He understands the idea that every being is the result of the mixing of genes and cultures and that this kind of mixing has been going on all along. This, as with James's pluralism, cautions us against promoting any kind of superiority for any particular individual or group. Our current possibilities depend on this past mixing and this undermines the idea that one group or individual has all the answers. We are always mistaken in some respect when it comes to understanding ourselves or others. Moreover, when we offer experimental solutions to problems we encounter we should acknowledge our uncertainty. Locke's own experience with intolerance (he was one the first African-Americans to receive a PhD in philosophy in the U.S. and the first African-American Rhodes Scholar) highlighted for him the importance of being open to revising one's views as one encounters ways of being that challenge basic assumptions.

These thinkers, then, yield the five basic dimensions of Pragmatism that will be examined here: *naturalism, pluralism, developmentalism, experimentalism*, and *fallibilism*. (Again, in the final chapter I will turn to Jane Addams to discuss Pragmatism's focus on *amelioration*.) For examining our relationship with pets, this means we need to understand the evolutionary (naturalism) history of the various animal beings and we need to examine the ways we have influenced and transformed each other. We need to be open to seeing the world from the perspectives of all the animal beings (pluralism) with whom we live if we want to develop mutually satisfactory relationships. We need to recognize that these relationships are always in process (developmentalism) as is the nature of both the human and other animal beings. We need to experiment (experimentalism) with new and different ways to sustain and to improve the relationships, and we need to be willing to admit when we make mistakes (fallibilism) in understanding ourselves, other animal beings, and our relationships with each other. Chapter 2 began such an examination with regard to horses. The following chapters will proceed with this kind of examination with regard to human relations with dogs and cats.

The reader may wish to stop at this point and proceed to the chapters on dogs and cats. That can be done. However, I think Pragmatism provides an important alternative to the most well known philosophical approaches to animal issues—Singer, Regan, and Nussbaum—and so deserves further consideration. The rest of this chapter will provide additional detail on the views of Peirce, James, Dewey, Gilman, Locke, and Pragmatism in general. This will be used to examine human-pet relations.

While each of the five figures I discuss here is a Pragmatist, and so takes a naturalistic, pluralistic, developmental, experimental, and fallibilistic approach, I emphasize just one of these traits in connection with each thinker to help further develop these ideas at the same time. This is an artificial emphasis, but it does help to highlight some distinctions among various Pragmatists. Pragmatism is not itself a singular view but a pluralistic philosophy that is still developing as it works in the world. It might best be described, not as set of doctrines, but as a style or attitude that entails the critical engagement of philosophy with problems of the world. To do this entails having an openness of mind, an experimental spirit. It calls on us to deal with the reality of change, development, and the temporal dimension of existence; we must give up certainty but not knowledge, and we must deal with birth and death.[2]

PEIRCE—NATURALISM

While it is unusual to think of Peirce as taking an interest in animals, among the early Pragmatists he is one of the most interested. Peirce set out to rethink the "order of nature" and emphasize the continuity within nature. He rejected the notion of a stable universe that is bound by order and necessity. Instead, he suggested that there is real chance and diversity

---

2. Some may note the absence of George Herbert Mead. He, among the Pragmatists, probably says the most directly about other animal beings. I have chosen not to address his work here because so much of what he says about other animals beings has been countered by more contemporary research and his focus is more specifically on psychology. His overall view does have implications for this project, but there is too much to overcome in regard to specific claims. I leave that work to others. Another notable absence might be Jane Addams. She is not directly addressed in this chapter but I will address her work in the concluding chapter when I move to suggesting how we might make changes to some of our current relationships with other animal beings. Addams's work on how to mediate understanding and agreement among people with very different experiences and perspectives will be helpful as I try to bring together very different views on what is appropriate in the relationships between human beings and other animal beings.

in a universe that is constantly evolving. Moreover, this universe reveals real continuity among beings and uncertainty about the future. We face the uncertainty together and, because of our continuity, Peirce argued that our interests are connected to the interests of others. This means our interests should not be limited to just our own concerns. Instead, our interests

> must not stop at our own fate, but must embrace the whole community. This community, again, must not be limited, but must extend to all races of beings with whom we can come into immediate or mediate intellectual relation. It must reach, however vaguely, beyond this geological epoch, beyond all bounds. He who would not sacrifice his own soul to save the whole world, is, as it seems to me, illogical in all his inferences, collectively. (*Essential Peirce I* 149)

Logic is important for Peirce and he sees it as clearly one important part of the full range of human reasoning. Logic, as a theory of inquiry, seeks to describe and prescribe, in a general way, scientific practice. What impressed Peirce most was that many scientists of the modern period were coming to understand nature, to find out truths about it through the experimental method. And the history of science confirmed, from a Pragmatic point of view, that the ideas of the sciences reveal their truth in history through their effectiveness in dealing with the world. True ideas bear an experimental track record. "We call them in science established truths, that is, they are propositions into which the economy of endeavor prescribes that, for the time being, further inquiry shall cease" (*Collected Papers* 5:589). This does not mean they are settled for all time, as Peirce's fallibilism reminds us. We can see this in the study of other animal beings and ourselves. We continually learn new things and regularly revise theories.

If scientists are to be successful in such inquiry, though, the human inquirers must be able to know nature, at least in part. This means nature must be intelligible to human inquirers. "The only end of science, as such, is to learn the lesson that the universe has to teach it" (*Collected Papers* 5:589). This means the human inquirer must be *able* to know nature; and nature must be *able* to be known. On various occasions Peirce stated that persons have an instinct for "guessing right"—not all of the time, but more often than not. Creating and selecting fitting or plausible hypotheses from an infinite realm of logically possible hypotheses requires this instinct for guessing or imagining. "It is somehow more than a mere figure of speech," he argued, "to say that nature fecundates the mind of man with ideas which, when those ideas grow up, will resemble their father, Nature" (*Collected Papers* 5:589). On the side of Nature, he maintained, "Nature only appears intelligible so far as it appears rational, that is, so far as its processes are seen to be like processes of thought" (*Collected Papers* 3:422). Nature must have an element that is idea-like, that is akin to the working of the human mind. This clearly applies to other animal beings. This should not be surprising if the human mind is itself a feature of nature and figures in a continuous line with other minds that have naturally evolved. Thus the process of inquiry must be based on a working, living analogy between inquirers and nature. By virtue of evolution on earth, we share a lot in common with other animal beings and this is part of what makes the scientific study of their behavior, communication, and consciousness possible in the first place.

Trading on evolutionary theory, Peirce recognized human beings to be a natural result of evolution—humans are a feature of nature. However, the human ability to inquire and to know seems to establish a duality in the midst of nature. As inquirers, we become nature knowing itself: "we are all of us natural products, naturally partaking of the characteristics that are found everywhere throughout nature" (*Collected Papers* 5:613). This accounts for the affinity between our ideas and Nature's laws, but it also insists on a fundamental otherness. There is an inner and an outer, a subject and an object, and so forth—all *within* nature. The key is to see these as functional features *of* nature—they are not extra- or super-natural. For Peirce, our experience is itself the key indicator to us of the otherness—what he called the "outward clash" in nature. "Experience," he believed, "means nothing but just that of a cognitive nature which the history of our lives has forced upon us" (*Collected Papers* 5:539); it refers "to that which is forced upon man's recognition, will-he, nill-he" (*Collected Papers* 5:613). Individually and communally, our beliefs are resisted by nature's otherness—this is the truth of any empiricism. And when as inquirers we experiment, we aim to make sense of this external constraint on our thought. Peirce thus described "experiment" as "a question put to nature" (*Collected Papers* 5:168 [5:57]).

Understanding nature requires more than a bare acquaintance with individuals; we seek the intelligibility of the relations of things and the regularities of their behavior. The habits of animal beings are like natural laws, and this is what we study in animal sciences. Peirce's rejection of nature's uniformity was not a rejection of its regularity (Pearson, 99). And it is precisely this regularity about which the scientist hopes to learn. Even a statistical rather than a deterministic regularity shows that individuals in nature have habits and ways of behaving that are general. This is evidenced by the past regularity of the actions of things as well as by the predictability of the future.

We cannot think and act just as we please. We encounter a natural world. In describing gravity in a lecture, Peirce maintained that we come to believe by way of experience that any stone dropped on earth will behave in a reasonably similar way. Similarly we understand species by general traits. We find a natural law that enables us to tell what would be the case in the future under certain circumstances. A law's reality, its independence from what you or I think about it, is what enables us to make predictions according to it: "it is a prognostic generalization of observations" (Pearson 68). It's our very scientific and experimental use of nature's laws that reveals and confirms their pragmatic meaning— gravity, for example, is found in its would-be consequences. "The scientific man," Peirce said, "looks upon a law . . . as a matter of fact as objective as fact can be" (Pearson 74). Only it cannot be an individual fact; in order for prediction to be possible through its use, a law must be general and apply to an indefinite range of possible events.

Finally, Peirce claims that generality, or laws, are real; this means that nature itself reveals generality and continuity to us as inquirers. It does this through lawfulness, but it also does so through some features of our experience. For example, we on occasion experience sympathy with other living beings and we quite routinely experience communication with other animal beings. In order for me to sympathize with other human or animal beings, there must be continuity between their experiences and mine. Since species are continuous with one another, (what Peirce calls synechism),

> there is no ontological obstacle to the possibility of communication across species. . . . At the very least, there would be borderline beings whose species home it is difficult to discern; and it would be reasonable to suppose that such borderland creatures could communicate with each other and with those on either side of the border. . . . He [Peirce] claims that animals have an instinct for communication: "for some kind of language there is among nearly all animals. Not only do

animals of the same species convey their assertions, but different classes of animals do so, as when a snake hypnotizes a bird. Two particular important varieties of this Species of study will relate to Cries and Songs (among mammals and birds chiefly) and to facial expression among mammals" (CP 7:379). In short, Peirce's synechism makes possible the experiences we have of animals from different species acting in communication, and making sense of Peirce's suggestion that we can study the semeiotic, or sign-using, habits of all animals." (D. Anderson 87)

Most humans who live with other animal beings participate in such cross-species communication every day and "Peirce's synechistic ontology and theory of perception make sense of this instinctive confidence in ways that many nominalistic, scientistic ontologies and rationalistic epistemologies cannot" (D. Anderson 88). We read each other's body language and facial expressions; we interpret each other's states of mind. Peirce says, "I can tell by the expression of face the state of mind of my horse just as unmistakably as I can that of my dog or my wife" (*Collected Papers* 7:379). He thinks other animal beings can share in humor and in the appreciation of music. They also enter into a kind of dialogue with us when we engage in joint activities. "In riding a horse, I understand him and he understands me; but how we understand one another I know hardly better than he" (*Collected Papers* 7:456).

Thus, simple everyday experiences bring home to us the real generality of nature. In scientific work we also find such continuity suggested. Evolutionary theories tend to argue for a process that moves forward by "insensible degrees." Thus, in identifying species, Peirce argued, the naturalist notes that the qualities of his specimens "are not precisely alike." Therefore, "the differences are such as to lead him to believe that forms could be found intermediate between any two of those he possesses" (*Collected Papers* 2: 646). The upshot is that natural kinds are real, but the borders between them are continuous. New species may appear, and some individual specimens may partake in both species. So there is no radical separation of humans from the rest of nature. If there were, it would not be possible for humans to inquire about nature, which we do; nor would it be possible for humans to successfully communicate with the rest of nature, which we do as well.

Some further evidence of this can be found in the ways humans and other animal beings can modify their instincts. Peirce discusses several examples of free living animal beings who must modify their instincts in order to survive: a toad who has lost an eye must revise habits of hunting, honey bees carried to new parts of the world will abandon instinctual activities that are of no use in their new environment. He suggests humans also regularly modify their instincts. This means that in both human and other animal beings instincts are important, but so too is the ability to adapt and change. This ability to modify and change habits is part of what makes it possible for species to live together. He says,

> Some people are so inobservant as to suppose that the training of dogs and horses is simply forced upon them from without, and consequently that very rude conduct on the part of the trainer must be persisted in. But it is quite the other way. When they once under-stand what is wanted they try to learn until fatigued. My wife has a black poodle . . . who has learned a great many "tricks" under affec-tionate treatment exclusively; but those of them that do not seem to him to have any practical or moral purpose he is not very fond of doing, unless indeed, a stranger is present, before whom he can show off . . . . ("An Essay" 467)

Here we see both successful (two-way) communication and modification of habits.

Peirce also ascribes personality to other animal beings. "Peirce main-tains that 'personality is some kind of coordination or connection of ideas.' A personality is not a concrete thing but a general idea, a living feeling, that reveals itself through a kind of immediate self-consciousness (*Collected Papers* 6:155). Moreover, a personality involves directionality and growth. By these criteria, Peirce's horse and dog certainly seem to *be* personalities" (D. Anderson 89–90). This has implications for how we form relationships with other animal beings. We need to approach these relationships with "attentive perception and a sympathetic apprehension of animal life" (D. Anderson 91). The continuity between human and other animal beings allows for just this possibility.

> Our relations with animals constitute an ongoing experiment that needs to be informed by a full understanding of animal life. Peirce is not blind to the viciousness of animals or humans; on the contrary, he is well aware of animal fallibility. Furthermore, he understands that community requires reciprocal relations. It's not just that we must be nice to animals: animals too must come to join in the community's

well-being to the extent they can. If this at first seems a stiff requirement, we need only think of the roles pets play in family life to see the
possibilities for reciprocity. (D. Anderson 93)

With James we ultimately learn that since we are continuous with the rest
of nature and nature is changing, continuous, uncertain, and developmental, we need to stay open to many possibilities. William James exem-
plifies the call for pluralism. But he doesn't start there. His view gets
corrected and changed over time. In his 1890 *Principles of Psychology* he
says of other animal beings—specifically dogs—

> They are enslaved to routine, to cut-and-dried thinking; and if the
> most prosaic of human beings could be transported into his dog's
> mind, he would be appalled at the utter absence of fancy which reigns
> there. . . . To wonder why the universe should be as it is presupposes
> the notion of its being different, and a brute, which never reduces the
> actual to fluidity by breaking up its literal sequences in his imagina-
> tion, can never form such a notion. He takes the world simply for
> granted, and never wonders at it at all. (353)

Why assume the absence of fancy rather than a different focus of fancy?
How does James purport to know that these "brutes" are "enslaved to
routine?" There are numerous examples of inventive play by a variety of
species. We tend to think animals who play are "smart"—mammals and
birds. Birds tease dogs. Cats and dogs play with each other and engage
in play behavior with the human beings in their lives. Who can share
a home with other animal beings and not have many examples of play
and pretending. While they may not wonder at the nature of the universe
(we don't know if they do), these are not beings without fancy and
imagination.

James (like Dewey) further denigrates the reasoning abilities of other
animal beings when he says, "The results of reasoning may be hit upon
by accident. . . . Cats have been known to open doors by pulling latches,
etc. But no cat, if the latch got out of order, could open the door again,
unless some new accident of random fumbling taught her to associate
some new total movement with the total phenomenon of the closed door.
A reasoning man, however, would open the door by first analyzing the

hindrance" (339). There arc many examples of "accidental" success and imitation in the world of other animal beings—as there are in the human world. Most of us learn by imitation, trial and error, and happy "accident." However, there is plenty of evidence that this is not the only way human beings or other animal beings interact with their environments. There are plenty of examples of complex problem solving by a variety of species. Some of the clearest examples of the ingenuity of other animal beings come from their attempts to foil the wishes of their "keepers." Examples abound of escapes that require observation, planning, and real insight. Further, they accomplish these feats without being taught or encouraged to do so. While many of the most cited examples of this kind of intelligence come from the realm of apes, dolphins, and elephants, they are not absent from the animal beings with whom most of us live. There are plenty of examples of horses, dogs, and cats escaping human attempts to confine them. Horses break into feed rooms, dogs into refrigerators, and cats into (and out of) all sorts of places. They also prove capable of re-thinking their practices when they foil the human beings' attempts to prevent future break-ins or escapes. We even see cooperation among individual animal beings to get what they want. A friend of mine had a horse, Charlie, who could open a wide variety of latches and often freed his neighbors to join him on excursions.[3]

In another shortsighted moment, James remarks, "The dog singles out of any situation its smells, and the horse its sounds, because they may reveal facts of practical moment, and are instinctively exciting to these several creatures. . . ." Further, "Man by his immensely varied instincts, practical wants, and aesthetic feelings, to which every sense contributes, would, by dint of these alone, be sure to dissociate vastly more characters than any other animal; and accordingly we find that the lowest savages reason incomparably better than the highest brutes" (344–45). But human's limited sensory capacities mean we miss a great deal as well. The inherent racism and speciesism here and elsewhere in James's writings, contradicts the openness and tolerance he comes to call for in his 1896 essay "On a Certain Blindness in Human Beings."

Specifically, James shows some insight into our common prejudice against other animal beings and cautions against it in "On a Certain

---

3. Charlie belonged to Michelle Hoedeman. He apparently continues his escapes with his new owner as well.

Blindness in Human Beings." The blindness to which he is referring is "[T]he blindness with which we all are afflicted in regard to the feelings of creatures and people different from ourselves. . . . Hence the stupidity and injustice of our opinions, so far as they deal with the significance of alien lives. . . . ." Though James deals with several themes in this text, he notes his blindness to his dog, an example upon which I will focus.

> Take our dogs and ourselves, connected as we are by a tie more intimate than most ties in this world; and yet, outside of that tie of friendly fondness, how insensible, each of us, to all that makes life significant for the other!—we to the rapture of bones under hedges, or smells of trees and lamp-posts, they to the delights of literature and art. As you sit reading the most moving romance you ever fell upon, what sort of a judge is your fox-terrier of your behavior? With all his good will toward you, the nature of your conduct is absolutely excluded from his comprehension. To sit there like a senseless statue when you might be taking him to walk and throwing sticks for him to catch! What queer disease is this that comes over you every day, of holding things and staring at them like that for hours together, paralyzed of motion and vacant of all conscious life? (629–30)

James recognizes that human beings and other animal beings often have different interests and so engage in different behavior. This can result in some misunderstandings and miscommunications. James goes on to say of this blindness that "It absolutely forbids us to be forward in pronouncing on the meaninglessness of forms of existence other than our own; and it commands us to tolerate, respect, and indulge those whom we see harmlessly interested and happy in their own ways, however unintelligible these may be to us" (645).

Here James acknowledges the intimacy of the tie between a human being and a dog being. He also shows a deep understanding of, and sympathy for, a being of a different kind and recognizes the need to respect this difference. He does not assume that the dog has no interests, plans, or purposes, but just that the dog's interests, plans, and purposes often differ from our own. The dog's existence is not meaningless because of this difference and James exhorts us to respect the meaning of its existence on its own terms and not unduly interfere with this existence. Stephen Budiansky, in *If a Lion Could Talk*, makes a similar point when he critiques most current research into the "intelligence" of other animal beings. This research tends to adopt a "self-centered definition of intelligence" (xiii). He suggests, as does James, that we should respect the "intelligence" of each species. He says, "Modern cognitive science and evolutionary ecology are beginning to show that thinking in animals can be complex and wonderful in its variety, even as it differs profoundly from that of man" (xxvii).

I won't recount the vast amount of evidence suggesting or proving (depending on one's perspective) the complex reasoning capacities of many animal beings.[4] Many animal beings need complex reasoning and inferencing capacities to survive in free living situations. These don't necessarily disappear with domestication. "Consciousness quite possibly arose when social animals (a category that could include certain insects, don't forget) reached the point at which they were required to understand the intentions of the other animals. In Darwinian terms, consciousness would thus be one final, vitally important, and beneficial adaptation" (218). And successful domestication requires such awareness.

James's denigration of the abilities of other animal beings is not beyond question given the observational and experimental evidence available to us today, nor is it consistent with his call for tolerance and respect. It also fails to pay attention to his own call for understanding and respecting pluralism. A consistent Jamesian perspective suggests, instead, that human beings should seek to understand the motivations and actions of other animal beings. There is no reason to try to reduce their being to the most simplistic explanation. Such reductionism may, in fact, get in the way of productive understanding and successful relationships. Successful and respectful relationships require that we are open to a plurality of being.

DEWEY—DEVELOPMENTALISM

John Dewey agrees with James's recognition of pluralism and with Peirce's concept of nature and embraces the continuity and uncertainty of the universe. One of the many questions he takes up is how to approach ethics in such a world. Given the world in which we live, we cannot have an ethics based on a fixed reality, fixed boundaries, or a certain end. As a

---

4. Here is just a small list of some useful sources on this: Marc Bekoff's *Minding Animals*; Donald Griffen's *Animal Minds*; Alan and Bekoff's *Species of Mind*; the Premacks' *The Mind of an Ape*; the Goulds' *The Animal Mind*; Marion Stamp Dawkin's *Through Our Eyes Only?*

result Dewey focuses on possibility and growth as ways to judge our practices and actions. Nonetheless, Dewey is (as is James) often not good at staying open to the intelligence of other animal beings. As someone who takes Darwin and Peirce so seriously, it is surprising to find Dewey so blind to some of the most obvious consequences of our relatedness to other animal beings and to the developmental histories of these animal beings. For example, while Dewey agrees that unnecessary suffering is not warranted, he does not see any need to protest the use of other animal beings in experimentation. This is because he denies the psychological and social suffering of other animal beings—something not warranted by Peirce's continuity thesis, nor by experience, nor by his own view later in life. Dewey foreshadows some of the approaches of animal rights, animal welfare, and virtue ethics but, as do thinkers in those areas, also falls prey to an unwarranted human exceptionalism. In his article "The Ethics of Animal Experimentation," Dewey says,

> Different moralists give different reasons as to why cruelty to animals is wrong. But about the fact of its immorality there is no question, and hence no need for argument. Whether the reason is some inherent right of the animal, or a reflex bad effect upon the character of the human being, or whatever it be, cruelty, the wanton and needless infliction of suffering upon any sentient creature, is unquestionably wrong. There is, however, no ethical justification for the assumption that experimentation upon animals, even when it involves some pain or entails, as more common, death without pain—since animals are still under the influence of anaesthetics,—is a species of cruelty. (98)

Defending the freedom of scientific inquiry, he argues against any restrictions being placed upon such experiments and says that there is no reason to believe the scientists would harm their subjects anyway. He bases this human "right" to experiment on other animal beings on his belief that such beings are capable of physical suffering only, and this suffering can be addressed with drugs. Social welfare and psychological suffering are reserved for human beings alone.

Dewey's disregard for the complex social and psychological lives of other animal beings is only possible if he denies the developmental history of these beings. This denial is also evidenced in some things he says in *Democracy and Education*. He says, "The relative ability of the young of brute animals to adapt themselves fairly well to physical conditions from an early period suggests the fact that their life is not intimately bound up with the life of those about them. They are compelled, so to speak, to have physical gifts because they are lacking in social gifts. Human infants, on the other hand, can get along with physical incapacity just because of their social capacity" (48). However, many other animal beings have relations of dependence. All the animal beings commonly domesticated and kept as pets are social beings—even cats—and require relatively long periods of learning in order to survive and thrive. They were domesticated by humans who played a role that fit with various social relationships—relationships that were already a part of how the other animal beings negotiated their world.

Dewey also, at times, assumes that other animal beings lack the reasoning ability needed to achieve desired ends through intelligent selection and performance of various means to those ends.

> As a matter of fact, imitation of ends, as distinct from imitation of means which help to reach ends, is a superficial and transitory affair which leaves little effect upon disposition. Idiots are especially apt at this kind of imitation; it affects outward acts but not the meaning of their performance. When we find children engaging in this sort of mimicry, instead of encouraging them . . . we are more likely to rebuke them as apes, monkeys, parrots, or copy cats. Imitation of means of accomplishment is, on the other hand, an intelligent act. It involves close observation, and judicious selection of what will enable one to do better something which he already is trying to do. (41)

Again, experiments that show creative problem solving and learning among other animal beings contradict Dewey's conclusions, as do the many examples of ingenious escapes. Further, even "simple" imitation of ends may demonstrate intelligence. Recent experiments show that horses are more likely to learn from watching and imitating high-ranking horses. They do not imitate low-ranking horses. This entails selection about whom to copy and may not be so "simple."

Another example of his mistaken stance on how other animal beings develop and negotiate the world can be seen when he discusses what he takes to be an absence of memory and anticipation in other animal beings. In *Reconstruction in Philosophy*, he says,

> Man differs from the lower animals because he preserves his past experiences. What happened in the past is lived again in memory. About what goes on today hangs a cloud of thoughts concerning

similar things undergone in bygone days. With the animals, an experience perishes as it happens, and each new doing or suffering stands alone. But man lives in a world where each occurrence is charged with echoes and reminiscences of what has gone before, where each event is a reminder of other things. Hence he lives not, like the beasts of the field, in a world of merely physical things but in a world of signs and symbols. . . . And all this which marks the difference between bestiality and humanity, between culture and merely physical nature is because man remembers, preserving and recording his experiences. (80)

Again, there are plenty of reasons to question Dewey's conclusions based on current research in animal communication and cognition—even on his own terms. Peirce acknowledged that other animal beings used signs to communicate. Further, while they may not write about their past experiences there is no reason to assume "experience perishes as it happens." Pets frequently anticipate activities based on past experience. They remember people and places.

Importantly, in all of this, Dewey shifts his position with time. Some thirty years later, in *Human Nature and Conduct*, he admits that, "The intelligent acknowledgment of the continuity of nature, man and society will alone secure a growth of morals which will be serious without being fanatical, aspiring without sentimentality, adapted to reality without conventionality, sensible without taking the form of calculation of profits, idealistic without being romantic" (11). Pragmatism is based on the idea of human beings as live creatures in a transactional relationship with their physical and social environments. Dewey is adamant that we should not make the mistake of buying into dichotomies such as mind/body, reason/emotion, or culture/nature. These are continuous transactive relationships, and human beings and other animal beings are (and have been since humanity emerged) engaged in transactive relationships that build on the continuity and are mutually transformative. Our developmental histories are intertwined. For instance, it is because dogs and humans have a long, complex, and intertwined history that dogs, but not wolves, follow the looks and pointing cues of humans.

Dewey also attributes the development of intelligence in human beings to their social complexity. Our physical dependence and increased complexity of social arrangements evolved together. Our increased brain capacity comes at the cost of increased developmental time. We are vulnerable for a long period of time and must be cared for, protected by, and learn from a social group of our kind. For Dewey it is an important fact that as human beings we are born to and dependent on other human beings. We are, from the beginning, associated. This applies to most mammals, though, to one degree or another.

> There is no sense in asking how individuals come to be associated. They exist and operate in association. . . .
>
> There is, however, an intelligible question about human association:—Not the question how individuals or singular beings come to be connected, but how they come to be connected in just those ways which give human communities traits so different from those which mark assemblies of electrons, unions of trees in forest, swarms of insects. . . . When we consider the difference we at once come upon the fact that the consequences of conjoint action take on a new value when they are observed. . . . Individuals still do the thinking, desiring and purposing, but what they think of is the consequences of their behavior upon that of others and that of others upon themselves. (*Public and Its Problems* 250)

No human being in nature can claim to be an isolated individual. Even the choice to "leave society" is influenced by one's social experience and nurturing. Similarly, though, reproduction, for the social mammals (many of whom have relatively long periods of nurturing) requires association and survival requires ongoing nurturing relations. Extended nurturing and caring for other beings, however, is what Dewey uses to distinguish human associations from the association of electrons and other animal beings. It was once thought that cats hunted simply by instinct. In fact, they learn from their mothers. Horses learn from their mothers as well and their status in the herd is often dependent on her status. Puppies weaned too early will be harder to socialize and prone to anxiety. In fact, human beings took advantage of the social and developmental natures of these animal beings in order to tame and domesticate them in the first place. Again, it seems Dewey would need to reform many of his views of other animal beings based on current evidence. Further, human beings are not just associated with other human beings, but with many other animal beings—and they with us.

With the recognition of our interdependence, human beings begin to take others (other human beings and other animal beings) into account when making decisions about what to do, how to act, and what to believe. Our behavior is affected by anticipation of the responses of others. It is our awareness of our connectedness that allows us to direct our behavior to certain goals and it is this ability to give intentional direction to our actions that, Dewey believes, makes human beings different from many other beings in our environment. But we know other animal beings effectively anticipate our reactions and purposes—if not, domestication would not have worked. Further, social complexity is thought to be the foundation for intelligence and the ability to communicate and plan. Since many of the domesticated animal beings commonly kept as pets live and grow in complex social worlds and require nurturing and learning to survive and thrive, how different are we? Social dependence requires that these animal beings be aware of "the consequences of their behavior upon that of others and that of others upon themselves," at least to some degree. It seems that, regarding the social, psychological, and intellectual lives of animal beings, Dewey is simply wrong and as a Pragmatist would need to modify his position accordingly. And he did.

If social complexity is seen as the root of intelligence and language, and pets display social complexity, why should we deny that they are likely to have similar capacities of intelligence, self-consciousness, and language—though different from our own? If the simplest explanation is the best, why do so many people go to such great lengths to deny even the great apes such capacities, much less the animal beings with whom they live? Dewey eventually came to see this himself. Interestingly, it was a relationship with a milk goat that seemed to change Dewey's mind. In his letters we catch glimpses of a Dewey who respects the individual personalities of dogs and horses, and who ascribes intelligence, planning, and meaningful communication to such animal beings. Then we see the defense of his goat. He describes her rich emotional life and her surprising attachment to Mrs. Dewey.

This shows up in published work most obviously in *Knowing and the Known*, co-authored with Arthur Bentley. In this work animal behavior is taken as evidence that other animal beings are capable of inquiry, planning, and adjustment. In a note related to producing this book, Dewey acknowledges that other animal beings are in transactive relations with each other and their environments and that these transactions include the use of signs ("Note on 'What is it to be a Linguistic Sign or Name?'"). In another essay written around the same time he acknowledges what a mistake it is to see humans as isolated from the rest of the physical world, or on different level than other animal beings ("Modern Philosophy").

The critical, fallibilistic approach of Pragmatism enabled Dewey to revise his views in the face of experiential and experimental evidence. Here, experimental evidence finally helps Dewey see that other animal beings have rich and complex developmental histories that need to be understood and respected.

GILMAN—EXPERIMENTALISM

Gilman also believed in evolution and the constant development and change present in the universe. By experimenting with the social arrangements she thought we could help shape such change. Gilman believed that reshaping the material conditions of human existence can reshape human beings. Gilman did not think that there was anything inherently wrong with human nature, but she believed it had been kept back by the wrong conditions and ideas. She believed that one of these wrong ideas, which must go before the rest can change, is the subordination of women. She often compared the position of women with the position of animal beings kept as pets. On her account, both needed to change.

Gilman believed that the root problem for women was that the natural division of female as mother and male as father has led to confining women to the role of mother and had given to the male all the activities in which both men and women could and should strive. "To the man, the whole world was his world; his because he was male; and the whole world of woman was the home; because she was female. She had her prescribed sphere, strictly limited to her feminine occupations and interest; he had all the rest of life; and not only so, but having it, insisted on calling it male" (*Man-made World* 23). With the androcentric culture firmly rooted in our minds and habits, the division has been further exacerbated— made to seem natural and inevitable—by placing women in a state of complete economic dependence. Such dependence has made women into the creature the androcentric picture had painted of her. She is seen to have no purpose outside of the domestic sphere, so no education is provided to fit her for anything but her domestic role. Then it appears that she is not fit by nature to do anything outside her domestic role and so the cycle has been perpetuated—a self-fulfilling prophecy.

But as it is not a natural condition of women (as is made evident by the many exceptions to the rule), but a social arrangement, it can be changed and on Gilman's view must change if the human race is to continue evolving. "The whole position is simple and clear; and easily traceable to its root. Given a proprietary family, where the man holds the woman primarily for his satisfaction and service—then necessarily he shuts her up and keeps her for these purposes" (*Man-made World* 39–40). The same can be said for other animal beings human beings keep in their homes. They are shut up and kept for our purposes. She was especially critical of the breeding of lap dogs as they represented the extreme of an artificial, created being who is totally dependent on another for its survival. They mirror the condition of women with which she was so concerned.

Evidence of this concern can be found in some of her fiction writing. In her novel *Herland*, there are no domesticated animals (including live-stock) except for cats. But the cats are not "kept." Interestingly, though, these cats do not make any sounds and they do not hunt birds—with experimentation they have been "improved." In *Moving the Mountain*, she again directly addresses several animal issues. These include the breeding of animal beings for food, hunting and fishing, bull and cock fighting, and the illness and defects that result from inbreeding. She points out how other animal mothers teach their offspring in much the same way human mothers do. She acknowledges that our brains differ, but only by degree. That is, until we domesticate them. When we "tame" an animal being, she thinks we give them a large part of their nature. "Look at the instinct of the wild dog and the instinct of the tame dog. Who gave the dog what we now call his '*nature*'—faithful, obedient, self-sacrificing. We have developed those instincts by making the crea-ture perform the action whose repetition formed the instinct" ("Our Brains" 46). This is her position on the "nature" of women as well.

Perhaps the best illustration comes in Gilman's short story "When I Was a Witch." Although this was written in 1910, not that much has changed for cats, dogs, or parrots, though there are fewer horses employed in the city streets today. In this story, the woman hears the calls of the cats in the city. "'Poor Kitty! It is a shame!' And I thought tenderly of all the thousands of hungry, hunted cats who slink and suffer in a great city" (23). She then wishes that all the cats were "comfortably dead." The city goes silent. She had also wished "that every person who strikes or otherwise hurts a horse unnecessarily shall feel the pain intended—and the horse not feel it!" (22). The next morning she witnessed just this as a man jerked the bit of the horse pulling the garbage cart, teamsters used the whip on their teams, and a boy hit the horse pulling the market wagon. As she realizes her wishes are coming true, she boards a streetcar. Across from her she finds a woman and a dog.

> A poor, wretched, little, artificial dog—alive, but only so by virtue of man's insolence—not a real creature that God made. And the dog had clothes on—and a bracelet! His fitted jacket had a pocket—and a pocket-handkerchief! He looked sick and unhappy.
>
> I meditated on his pitiful position, and that of all the other poor chained prisoners, leading unnatural lives of enforced celibacy, cut off from the sunlight, fresh air, the use of their limbs; led forth at stated intervals by unwilling servants, to defile our streets; over-fed, under-exercised, nervous, and unhealthy. (25)

Contemplating the unhappiness of such creatures, she wishes that all the unhappy dogs in the cities would die—and they did. The woman with the dog doesn't even notice her dog is dead until she gets off the streetcar.

As the narrator realizes her power, she further considers the horses. "As I watched the horses at work that afternoon, and thought of all their unknown sufferings from crowded city stables, bad air, and insufficient food, and from the wearing strain of asphalt pavements in wet and icy weather, I decided to have another try on horses" (26). She also takes on the parrots. The parrots began to demand to be let out, and they began to speak their minds. This is exactly what Gilman wants for human women as well—to be let out and to be able to speak their minds.

Gilman argued that, to liberate human women, the androcentric home must change if we hope to produce people capable of becoming democratic citizens. Not only are women and girls hindered in their development, but fathers and sons are perverted by their power. "For each man to have one whole woman to cook for and wait upon him is poor education for democracy. The boy with a servile mother, the man with a servile wife, cannot reach the sense of equal rights we need to-day. Too constant consideration of the master's tastes make the master selfish . . ." (*Man-made World* 42–43). If we want to produce people capable of looking to the needs of others as well as their own, the model of men in competition for personal ownership must give way to the model of women in cooperation for the individual development of all. We need to experiment with a different social arrangement.

In order to develop her gynocentric model, Gilman started with the fact that humans are born of a woman and into relationships of dependence. Gilman sees the mother/child relationship as our most basic relationship and the ground for developing the possibilities of humanity. She argued that with primitive man involved in hunting, death and power became his central concerns. With primitive woman involved in birth and cultivation of children, planting and cultivation of food, growth, and the improvement of others became her central concerns. Gilman believed that as humanity evolved and men became more settled, they saw the care and service women gave to the children, animals, and crops as desirable for themselves (*His Religion* 207). Not only did they want to have control of her eventual products, they wanted her to serve and care for them. So, the custom of a man possessing a woman began. Equal partnership was replaced by a relationship of domination and subordination. So too with other animal beings.

On Gilman's view subordination to and dependence on another is a perverse relationship that adversely affects both the one in power and the one who is disempowered (*His Religion* 213). This applies to women and other animal beings. Gilman extended this argument to critique slavery and capitalism. "In the family, with its subordinate and dependent woman, its children long held to be the property of the father, even man's sense of justice was aborted. The conditions of slavery, of ownership, of authority, with the dependence and submission of the owned, check the growth of ethics completely. This dominance underlies the despotism of officer, priest, and king, and still finds expression in the attitude of our 'captains of industry'" (*His Religion* 150–151). The familial and social arrangement that results from the patriarchal structure promotes obedience and submission rather than self-governing thought and activity. Patriarchy, then, produces individuals incapable, on Gilman's view, of being ethical. We extend this way of thinking to our relationships with other animal beings and seek their obedience and submission. If Gilman were alive today I think she would be disappointed at how little we've progressed in liberating other animal beings from our dominance. We need to promote a more ethical relationship with other animal beings.

Ethics, for Gilman, is not a matter of obeying certain rules or customs. She believed that what particular action is right or wrong will change as conditions change. Human life is a changing life, not a static one, and so particular mores will change too. What does remain stable, however, is the drive to modify and direct behavior to promote the improvement and happiness of the human situation. This includes our relationships with other animal beings—especially the ones closest to us. Ethics is an experimental science.

> Ethics is a social science,—the social science, in fact,—being a consciously apprehended system of modifying our behavior in the interests of our common happiness and progress. Ethics covers all our inter-relationships, in economics, in politics, in ordinary intercourse. Its basis is an understanding of the nature of society, its structure and functions. That conduct is right which tends to the best development of humanity; that is wrong which injures it. The relative importance, the degree of rightness or wrongness in a given act, is according to the amount of good or evil in its effect upon society. (*His Religion* 149)

While this is vague, it is clear that some notion of development (like Dewey's notion of growth), is what should guide our decisions and is the signpost by which we can judge any action or social arrangement. We must ask whether the ways in which human beings treat other animal beings contributes to the development of humanity or injures it. She clearly thinks that most of human behavior in relation to other animal beings injures our development and theirs. So, we must experiment with change.

LOCKE—FALLIBILISM

To experiment in the ways Gilman suggests, we have to be willing to admit something is not working or that we might have been mistaken in some aspect of our past arrangements. This is the meaning of fallibilism. To change relationships that are or have been oppressive requires a belief in such fallibilism. While I am using Alain Locke to exemplify the notion of fallibilism, it is important to remember that this piece of Pragmatism began with the work of Peirce and is central to any Pragmatist analysis. To help make my point here, I will link this discussion of fallibilism and Locke to issues that arise in ecofeminism.

Many feminists talk about what they call the "interlocking systems of oppression." These are usually listed as race, class, and gender. Some ecofeminists add species to the list, and we can see the start of such a position in Gilman above. Ecofeminists contend that oppression of all kinds, including the oppression of nature and other animal beings, shares a common origin in dichotomous and hierarchical thinking—something the Pragmatists also critique. Karen Warren, for instance, identifies three characteristics of what she calls an oppressive conceptual framework. Value dualistic thinking is the kind of thinking that has characterized much of analytic philosophy—separating beings and values into exclusionary opposites. This kind of thinking fails to see interconnections and has no sense of the world as a continuum. Often added to this way of thinking is what Warren calls value hierarchical thinking. This means that not only are things divided into oppositional pairs, but that we then assign more value to one part of the dyad. This has again been common in the history of philosophy, and feminists have addressed the problems that emerge for women since women find themselves on the down side of the male/female and up/down dyad.

Nonetheless, Warren acknowledges that these ways of understanding the world could be accurate descriptions of the world we encounter. However, she finds that they occur under a more systemic logic of domination. This logic of domination is what makes these ways of thinking oppressive and dangerous. The logic of domination is a way of thinking that legitimizes the notion of seeing difference or inequality as a justification for subordination. So while a parent/child relationship might be a neutral example of a value hierarchy with an unequal distribution of power, if such a relationship is understood through the logic of domination it becomes abusive and oppressive. Ecofeminists contend that women, nature, and other animal beings share the fate of having been set in opposition to men, culture, and reason and that philosophy (and our society in general) has put more value on the male side of the dichotomy. Since the logic of domination is well entrenched, this has resulted in an oppressive way of conceiving of, and treating, women, nature, and other animal beings.

Ecofeminists offer a variety of alternatives to these ways of thinking and acting. Some logically dismantle the dualisms, some argue with the value assignments that have been made, and some use empirical evidence to show the damage of operating with oppressive frameworks as our guide. Others seek a more spiritual approach, asking people to see their interconnections with nature and other animal beings to develop a sense of oneness. These approaches to ecofeminism have sometimes been at odds—falling into their own dualism of philosophical versus spiritual approaches to the issues. Philosophers tend to take the more "hard headed" approach to the arguments and evidence, while the spiritual ecofeminists take a more "fuzzy" or "soft" approach that entails rituals and meditation. This divide among ecofeminists mirrors the very kind of thinking that they think got us into the trouble in the first place. With a now strong history of feminist philosophy to draw on, why can't ecofeminism avoid this trap? I contend it is because most feminist philosophies (and most animal related philosophies) draw on the history of analytic philosophy that has the dichotomous, hierarchical way of thinking at its core. Here is one place Pragmatism can be of some help.

Pragmatism, in all its variety, rejects the oppositional, dichotomous, hierarchical way of thinking. It sees complex relationships and continuums instead. We have seen this with Peirce, James, and Dewey. Gilman began to dismantle oppressions and make connections between human beings and other animal beings. Alain Locke, as a gay black philosopher, was also well positioned to understand the logic of oppression. He is motivated to find alternatives to oppositional, dichotomous, hierarchical ways of thinking. His philosophy clearly works to do just that as he blurs borders and calls for tolerance. However, his philosophy is also joined by his interest in the Baha'i faith. I will argue that these two ultimately prove to be incompatible when viewed through their approach to nature and other animal beings, but his work reveals a tension that is informative as we seek more respectful relationships with other animal beings.

Alain Locke embraced the tenets of the Baha'i faith. Many of these tenets are quite compatible with the critical form of Pragmatism represented by Locke, but some are not. The Baha'i faith takes an evolutionary perspective, embraces science, sees that all human knowledge is fallible, and embraces pluralism. The Baha'i seek a unity built out of real diversity, not out of sameness or indifference. For example, "[I]ts principal tenets are intellectual integrity, the complimentary roles of science and religion, the essential unity of all religions, and the brotherhood of all mankind. It provides for a new highly democratic system of participatory government crowned by a world assembly, and for the application of spiritual principles to social as well as individual conduct" (Huddleston 27). Like Locke, the Baha'i faith sees and seeks real brotherhood (and sisterhood), not the tolerance of indifference (Huddleston 39). One way of making this possible is to embrace a very Pragmatist fallibilist approach and give up prejudice. "If our chalice is full of self, there is no room in it for the water of life. The fact that we imagine ourselves to be right and everybody else wrong is the greatest of all obstacles in the path toward unity, and unity is necessary if we would reach truth. . . ." (Adbu'l-Baha in Huddleston 45). There is a continual emphasis on being open to new information and on embracing both science and religion as part of the path to learning.

The Baha'i faith also embraces the equality of the sexes.

> Women, in some respects, have different areas of capacity than men and a distinctive viewpoint; partly, of course, as a result of upbringing, but partly also from the very difference in physical make-up and their unique function in society. The capacity and the contribution they can make to the general good of society are just as important as the capacity and contribution men make. Consequently, when women are prevented from reaching their full potential, society is thrown off balance and suffers accordingly. (Huddleston 73)

However, some of the Baha'i views have a tendency to essentialize and even romanticize the feminine. For example, some claim that war will end if women become equal and we focus on the feminine attributes of love and service. Similarly, while the Baha'i quite progressively deplore the persecution of homosexuals, they nonetheless see homosexuality as a sickness (Huddleston 85). Homosexuality, according to the writings of Baha'u'llah, is spiritually condemned. But this does not mean that one cannot help advise, or sympathize with, people so afflicted. It does mean, however, that it is not a permissible way of life.

> No matter how devoted and fine the love may be between people of the same sex, to let it find expression in sexual acts is wrong. Immorality of every sort is really forbidden by Bah'u'llah, and homo-sexual relationships He looks upon as such, besides being against nature. . . . But through the advice and help of doctors, through a strong and determined effort, and through prayer, a soul can over-come this handicap. (Shoghi Effendi in Huddleston 86)

So, here we begin to see some of the contradictions emerge. Despite a fallibilistic approach that embraces science as a path to learning, the Baha'i faith still ends up with essentializing and dogmatic positions with regard to women and homosexuals. Locke, himself a homosexual, must have felt some discomfort with such positions. Given his version of critical Pragmatism, he must have seen the contradictions between the Baha'i emphasis on teaching children to think for themselves, the Baha'i desire to overcome prejudice, the Baha'i commitment to fallibilism, and the Baha'i proclamations on the nature of world. Locke himself says,

> In a pluralistic frame of reference value dogmatism is outlawed. A consistent application of this invalidation would sever the trunk nerves of bigotry or arbitrary orthodoxy all along the line, applying to religious, ideological and cultural as well as to political and social values. Value profession or adherence on that basis would need to be critical and selective and tentative (in the sense that science is tentative) and revisionist in procedure rather than dogmatic, final and *en bloc.* ("Pluralism and Intellectual Democracy" 57)

This tentative holding of value is what is meant by Locke's critical Pragmatism. There is pluralism and revision, but also a set of limits: tolerance, reciprocity, parity. "Value assertion would thus be a tolerant assertion of preference, not an intolerant insistence on agreement or finality. Value disciplines would take on the tentative and revisionist procedure of natural science" (57). There would be acknowledgement of, and respect for, other value assertions as long as they too are open and respectful. This is different than ethical theories that assert a universal principle or ethicists who demand agreement (in thought and action) with their conclusions. For instance, Regan says,

> I regard myself as an advocate of animal rights—as part of the animal rights movement. That movement, as I conceive it, is committed to a number of goals, including: the total abolition of the use of animals in science; the total dissolution of commercial animal agriculture; the total elimination of commercial and sport hunting and trapping.
>
> There are, I know[,] people who profess to believe in animal rights but do not avow these goals. Factory farming, they say, is wrong—it violates animal's rights—but traditional animal agriculture is all right. Toxicity tests of cosmetics on animals violate their rights, but important medical research—cancer research, for example—does not. The clubbing of baby seals is abhorrent, but not the harvesting of adult seals. I used to think I understood this reasoning. Not any more. ("The Struggle for Animal Rights" 176)

This absolutist stance does not allow for new information to come and views to be revised. It requires complete agreement by others and so eliminates the possibility of dialogue. Locke replaces this kind of approach with critical Pragmatism.

Another example of a contradiction Locke faced has to do with the Baha'i view of the "natural order." As do the Pragmatists, the Baha'i embrace an evolutionary approach. However, the evolutionary perspective of the Baha'i is one that embraces a strict hierarchy with human life at the top. This hierarchy does not seem to be seen as a hypotheses, as a truly fallabilistic approach would dictate, but as the established order of things. "Just as the animal is more noble than the vegetable and mineral, so man is superior to the animal. The animal is bereft of ideality; that is to say, it is a captive of the world of nature and not in touch with that which lies within and beyond nature; it is without spiritual susceptibilities, deprived of the attractions of consciousness, unconscious of the world of God and incapable of deviating from the law of nature. It is different with man" (Abdu'l Baha in Huddleston 29).

Interestingly, however, the Baha'i want to improve the human treatment of other animal beings. With regard to diet, they envision a vegetarian future: "The food of the future will be fruit and grains. The time will come when meat will no longer be eaten" (Adu'l Baha in Huddleston 59). A contemporary Baha'i author notes that "[w]hen this happens there will be no necessity for the mass killing of animals which now blunts the spiritual qualities of the whole race of man so much" (Huddelston 53). He continues, "It should be added that our concern should not stop at our fellow human beings. As the most intelligent and powerful creatures on earth we have grave responsibilities to protect all other living things. Animals may only be killed in self-protection or to meet our genuine needs for food and clothing, and even then there must be no cruelty" (68). Abdu'l-Baha argues that other animal beings share with human beings the ability to feel. Since they share physical sensations, we must work to reduce their suffering.

> If it is harmed a thousand times by man it is not able to defend itself in words nor can it seek justice or retaliate. Therefore one must be very considerate toward animals and show greater kindness to them than to man. Educate the children in their infancy in such a way that they may become exceedingly kind and merciful to the animals. If an animal is sick they should endeavour to cure it; if it is hungry, they should feed it; if it is thirsty, they should satisfy its thirst; if it is tired, they should give it rest. (Abdu'l-Baha in Huddleston 69)

All of this care and concern for other animal beings, however, is basically human centered. Treating other animal beings well will make us better people—a kind of virtue ethic. Even contemporary Baha'i concerns for the environment are basically human centered. This strict divide of the human from the rest of nature is problematic for the more naturalist bent of Pragmatism which recognizes a continuum. It also seems to violate the notion of unity embraced by the Baha'i and by Locke himself. He sought a pluralism that would "provide a flexible, more democratic nexus, a unity in diversity rather than another counter-uniformitarianism" ("Pluralism and Intellectual Democracy" 53). As mentioned, Locke focused on tolerance, reciprocity, and parity as the groundwork for a workable plurality. This approach can be applied to human beings' relations with other animal beings. We need to be open to the similarities and differences among human and other animal beings; we need to acknowledge the reciprocal exchanges and make modifications in the relations among species.

Further, Locke has three corollaries of cultural relativity: cultural equivalence, cultural reciprocity, and limited cultural convertability. Cultural equivalence looks for functional similarities among different cultures. Cultural reciprocity recognizes the many reciprocal contacts between cultures. And limited cultural convertability sees the organic selectivity and assimilative capacities of cultural exchange ("Cultural Relativism" 72). We can see these operate in terms of human relationships with pets. Functional similarities can be seen in attempts to communicate. There are functional equivalents in body language and facial expressions that convey fear, aggression, happiness, or submission. There are postures that convey a willingness to play or the commitment to fight. We can see how such functional equivalents are important to successful cross-species relationships. Just as one example, "natural horsemanship" relies on understanding the body language of horses and finding ways for humans to enter into dialogue with them based on these functionally equivalent forms of communication.

With regard to cultural reciprocity we have already seen, in looking at the history of domestication, that both human and domesticated animal beings live in highly composite cultures. We have been changing each other for thousands of years. Just as one example, cats, while helping humans with rodents, were selectively bred and changed themselves at the same time that they altered religious and social practices in specific human cultures.

And, related to this long history, we see evidence of both cultural exchange and assimilation—limited cultural convertability. Dogs, for instance, have been changed and assimilated into human culture in ways that wolves have not. Yet they remain canine beings. In *Natural Relations*, Ted Benton notes a similar human/animal continuism and points to five comparisons that make Locke's concepts of cultural equivalence, cultural reciprocity, and limited cultural convertability applicable. These are (1) an organically limited life-span; (2) temporal phasing of organic growth, development and decline in individual life-spans; (3) sexuality; (4) social co-operation in the meeting of organic needs; and (5) stability of social order and the integration of social groups (53–54). We can see these operate with other animal beings we consider to be pets and this makes the mixing of cultures all the more possible.

In addition to these ideas about cultural mixing, though, Locke's call for cultural relativism, a form of fallibilism, would apply here as well. With this in mind,

> we reach a position where we can recognize relativism as a safer and saner approach to the objectives of practical unity. What is achieved through relativistic rapprochement is, of course, somewhat different from the goal of the absolutists. It is a fluid and functional unity rather than a fixed and irrevocable one, and its vital norms are equivalence and reciprocity rather than identity or complete agreement. But when we consider the odds against a complete community of culture of mankind, and the unlikelihood of any all-inclusive orthodoxy of human values, one is prepared to accept or even to prefer an attainable concord of understanding and cooperation as over against an unattainable unanimity of institutional beliefs. ("Cultural Relativism" 71)

With this approach, other animal beings do not have to be just like us in order to be worthy of our consideration. They would, however, need to be part of what we consider when we take on the "task of reconstructing our basic social and cultural loyalties or of lifting them, through some basically new perspective, to a plane of enlarged mutual understanding" ("Cultural Relativism" 72). Under Locke's philosophy we need to respect other animal beings for who they are and not seek to dominate them.

At the same time we can continue to build understanding and engage in mutually transformative relationships. He says we need to

> recognize the legitimate jurisdictions of other cultures as well as to respect the organic integrity of the weaker cultures. . . . Through functional comparison a much more constructive phase of cultural relativism seems to be developing, promising the discovery of some less arbitrary and more objective norms. Upon them, perhaps we can build sounder intercultural understanding and promote a more equitable collaboration between cultures. ("Cultural Relativism," 74)

And we can now add—between species.

As Leonard Harris says, "Locke faced his cultural groundings, engaged in their critique, and offered a way of valuing that requires us to continually engage in emancipatory revaluation and transvaluation" (17). Why limit this to the community of human beings? If, as Warren argues, the basic oppressive conceptual framework is shared by all forms of oppression, then we should address such oppression in all its manifestations. Recognizing our interdependence with other human beings is a first step toward recognizing our interdependence with other animal beings and the rest of nature. It is a first step toward seeing the common sources of oppression. I believe that a consistent, critical Pragmatist perspective requires that we reevaluate our view of, and relations with, other animal beings. It also requires us to engage in value formation and evaluation in an open, tolerant, and fallibilistic manner. On this view ethics is not about offering universal or absolute principles. It is not about working out final answers to emerging ethical and social problems. It is about providing a framework for understanding and guiding ongoing discussions of complex emerging issues. To repeat Locke,

> But when we consider the odds against a complete community of culture of mankind, and the unlikelihood of any all-inclusive orthodoxy of human values, one is prepared to accept or even to prefer an attainable concord of understanding and cooperation as over against an unattainable unanimity of institutional beliefs. ("Cultural Relativism" 71)

This is the kind of approach that can open up the possibility of currently opposed animal-related groups working together. This will be developed further in the last chapter with the help of Jane Addams.

So let's examine two more fairly common kinds of other animal beings who qualify primarily as pets in the United States— dogs and cats. As with horses, I choose to focus on these animal beings because they are the beings with whom I have had the most personal experience (the place all Pragmatists should start) and they represent the most commonly "kept" animal beings outside of livestock.

FOUR

DOGS

Respecting Perception and Personality

Dogs are "contaminated" by humans; by this I mean that they take on emotional coloration from contact with humans. It is therefore impossible to know what dogs would be like if they did not live in human communities.

—Jeffrey Moussaieff Masson

In order to really enjoy a dog, one doesn't merely try to train him to be semi-human. The point of it is to open oneself to the possibility of becoming partly a dog.

—Edward Hoagland

Now I turn to animal beings with whom many people have relationships. One estimate says that there are almost as many cats and dogs in households as televisions (Serpell, *Company of Animals* 19). In 1986 there were an estimated 48 million dogs in the United States, and today that number is roughly 74.8 million (xxi 9). As they do with horses, some animal advocates see human relationships with dogs as a kind of slavery. But, this interpretation seems flawed. Of all the animal species on the planet, only about a dozen have been domesticated. And dogs and humans may have been in relationship longer than any of the rest. This relationship may have started from fourteen thousand to fifteen thousand years ago—long before humans could have completely controlled the relationship (Budiansky, *Truth About Dogs* 17). As has the human relationship with horses, the human relationship with dogs has transformed human beings as much or more than it has transformed dog beings. Dogs have been used for food, transportation, protection, hunting, and herding. Such uses opened up new and different possibilities for human life. Today, relationships with dogs continue to be profound and personally and socially transformative.

I have always lived and worked with dogs, just as I have always lived and worked with horses. My immediate family always had dogs, as did the families of my aunts and cousins. Every barn I worked at had dogs as well. The rule in my family was that you could get your own dog when you turned nine. The idea was that you were then old enough to be responsible for the dog's care and training. Being the youngest in the family, I was frustrated to be the only one without a dog of her own, but it also meant I had relationships with many dogs. I clearly remember Rocky, a collie belonging to my oldest sister Candace. There were Circus and Casey, two poodles belonging to my other sister, Megan. Then there was Po (Apollo), a smooth haired fox terrier belonging to my brother, Carl. Since my brother is five years older than I am, Po and I grew up together. I was four when he joined the household and there were clearly questions about the proper order of the pack. He ate many of my stuffed animals and tore up my favorite blanket. He would push me out of my bed and when I tried to get back in he would growl at me. We worked it out. Terriers are tough little dogs and he taught me how to assert myself.

When I turned nine we moved from a ranch with plenty of room for all these dogs (along with twenty-plus cats, several horses, chickens, ducks, rabbits, and sheep) to the city. My sisters had moved out of the house by then and their dogs had died. So it was Po who would accompany us to the city. We had also inherited a very special cat from friends of the family—Sieglinda. She had always been an indoor cat and had not adjusted well to the ranch. She was to come with us too. It was decided that one cat and one dog were enough for the city so I would have to postpone getting my own dog. When I was thirteen we moved again, to a farm in Pennsylvania. Sieglinda had had to be put down by then, but Po came with us and I got a dog—thanks to my sister Megan. Tuffy was an Australian Shepherd. Since then there have been many dogs in my life: Pandora and Nemesis, both Australian Shepherds; Freckles and Tao, Australian Shepherd/Border Collie crosses; and now Maeve and Kira, both Australian Shepherds.

As with the horses, in my family the care of the dogs came first and they were the responsibility of the person who had chosen the dog. The choosing of the dog was an important education. We had to study breed characteristics and make an informed decision. Then, caring for the dog was another kind of learning experience. You could not expect others to do the chores associated with the animal beings—cleaning, feeding, medicating, exercising, and training. This responsibility did result in a real sense of what is involved in the life (and death) of another being and helped to develop respectful relations between human and dog beings. This included taking the dogs on their own terms.

For instance, Po, as a terrier, was bred to kill small creatures. Despite our best efforts to keep him away when kittens were born, on several occasions he killed kittens. One time he got to the box in the laundry room and broke the neck of every kitten in the litter and left them there. This same creature then wanted to sleep on my bed that night and offer me his protection. I also had to deal with whether it was fair to ask Tuffy, raised on a farm, to adjust to living in an apartment while I was in graduate school. When she developed a cancerous tumor, I altered my summer plans from staying at school and studying for my comprehensive exams to going to work for friends who train horses in order to get her back to a farm before she died. Pandora was a bit older when we found each other and I was told she had separation anxiety due to being passed around at a young age. She ate a couch, some shoes, and parts of my car. Then I figured out she had very sensitive skin and most of this behavior was due to skin problems. I learned Tellington TTouch and what was seen as her "problem" was cured.[1] Nemesis was always a handful—right up until her body gave out at sixteen. When she was a puppy, a veterinarian suggested that she be put on Prozac. I chose to work with her nature instead and took her to a herding class. I had no intention of learning to herd sheep, but rather to turn her over to the instructor. It turned out she wouldn't work for anyone else, so I began learning to walk backward over uneven pasture, wet with rain and sheep droppings—a wonderful way to spend Saturday mornings! Now, with Maeve and Tao, I have also done

1. "Using a combination of specific touches, lifts, and movement exercises, TTouch helps to release tension and increase body awareness. This allows the animal to be handled without provoking typical fear responses. The animal can then more easily learn new and more appropriate behaviors. By using the TTouch and a variety of other tools, like the Confidence Course, you can assist the animal in experiencing self-confidence in previously frightening situations. Even the most difficult problems are often eliminated. You can also learn how to apply the Tellington TTouch to assist with recovery from illness or injury, or just enhance the quality of your animal's life" (ttouch.com). Pandora did also seem to have mild separation anxiety, but looking into the range of issues she faced made a big difference.

some sheep herding. It seems to be good work for Maeve, but Tao tends to get too excited—not so good for the sheep. Each dog being is different and a responsible relationship with them requires the human beings to adjust as well. As species, we have been adjusting to each other for a long time now and need to continue to be attentive and responsive. There is no one fixed way of interacting—we need to remain open to a variety of possibilities.

The domestication of dogs probably began fifteen thousand years ago, in some places before the domestication of plants and other animals. This is a *long* relationship. There is evidence of burial with dogs twelve thousand years ago (Clutton-Brock, *Natural History* 58–59). Other fossils date back fourteen thousand years. The dog is believed to be the first domesticated animal, entering human communities thousands of years before any other animal (Coren 18). While there are many animals, only a few have ever entered human communities in this way and become domesticated. Even fewer have become pets, and only dogs and cats have regularly reached the level of companion. Dogs and cats usually do not need

Figure 6. Po the terrier presented the challenge of reconciling different aspects of his nature. He would offer protection to his humans, but he would also kill kittens if he got the chance. It is important to understand the nature of specific breeds and work with the individual dog.

Figure 7. Pandora was adopted at a slightly older age and was said to suffer from separation anxiety. She would chew on herself, as well as shoes, couches, and cars. Paying attention to her behavior it became clear she suffered from allergies that made her skin itch. Adjusting her diet and using Tellington TTouch addressed her anxiety and destructive behavior.

to be forced to stay with humans. Dogs have done so well (and been so vulnerable) with humans because they form such strong social bonds (Serpell, *Company of Animals* 100–101).

The wolf is considered the ancestor of the dog (56), but some have thought the domesticated dog might be the result of breeding that includes the wolf, coyote, and jackal (Coren 35). Mitochondrial DNA now shows the wolf and dog split 135,000 years ago, while the wolf and coyote split one million years ago. So it appears the wolf is the only ancestor of the dog despite earlier conjectures. By ten thousnad years ago there were distinct breeds and they were being used in a variety of ways. By 4000–3000 BC we start to see something like the greyhound or saluki. By Roman times there were six groups—guard dogs, shepherds, sporting dogs, war dogs, scent dogs, and sight dogs. Artificial selection and cross breeding helped to produce a variety of dogs. By the first century AD we had the extremes of lap dogs and guard dogs. Most of the breeds we know, though, are only one hundred to two hundred years old, and there were no registries until the 1870s (Budiansky, *Truth About Dogs* 29–30). There are now more than four hundred breeds registered with clubs and

Figure 8. Dog history.

there may be as many as eight hundred (Serpell, *Domestic Dog* 180; Coren 22). The "success" of this relationship is usually attributed to the fact that dogs and humans share a hierarchical social structure with a reliance on kinship and communication. Evidence of this success can be seen in the fact that in 1994 there were fifty-two million dogs in the United States (Coren 5). Today, there are an estimated 77.5 million (humanesociety.org).

A common story is that at the end of the ice age humans and wolves competed for food and so lived in proximity to one another. Young wolves were taken in by humans and alliances formed. Wolves are a highly social carnivore who mirror human social structure. Over time some wolves lost the tendency to react defensively to the unfamiliar and became submissive but not fearful (Coren 49–51). The dominant/submissive structure allows canine beings and primate beings to live in groups without continually killing each other. Another possibility includes the idea that the more submissive canides chose to associate with humans in a mutually beneficial relationship. The success of this particular relationship may have been augmented by the characteristics we share. Over time, humans have intensified the differences found in the canide species and developed specialized breeds.

Whatever the story of the initial process of domestication might be, some of the general effects of domestication include smaller size, shortened muzzle, floppy ears, changes in coat and color, increased licking, greater love of play, more docility, and reduced fear of new things. Much of this amounts to neoteny—the retention of infantile characteristics in adults (Coren 37–39).

It is important to remember that specific behaviors are not inherited, though heredity affects behavior (Serpell, *Domestic Dog* 5). Genetic differences have been developed under the influence of environmental factors. It is not that genetic factors appeared all at once to be modified by later experience. Behavior has been organized and reorganized over time. These are developmental changes (Scott 16–17). Even with similar genetics, early experiences can create a large difference between individuals. Pre-natal experience such as the mother being stressed affects development, as do neonatal handling and experience. Aggression, fears, phobias, separation-related problems all can be attributed to early experiences (Serpell, *Domestic Dog* 80–89). Behavior is never wholly inherited nor wholly acquired, but developed. As a result, breed stereotypes have some basis and need to be taken into account; there is a great deal of individual variation within any breed or dog population (Scott 384, 204). From a Pragmatist perspective, recognition of such development should impact approaches to training and working with dogs.

All of the incredibly diverse breeds are amazingly similar—digestion, gestation, and sensory ability are basically unchanged from the wolf.

Breeds are, however, also amazingly different in personality and intelligences. As with horses, it is important to consider what you want to do with a dog and what kind of personality will fit well with your own in order to form a successful relationship. The Humane Society of the United States (HSUS) and other shelters and rescues now administers a Caninality test to dogs and their potential human adopters. Dogs are rated on their temperament and activity level. Green dogs include the high energy, high intelligence herding dogs. These dogs can only be adopted by "green" humans—that is humans who are physically very active, can take their dogs with them a lot, like to engage in various kinds of training/learning activities such as herding, agility, or obedience work. Orange is for dogs with moderate energy and purple is for calm dogs. This kind of matching has helped to reduce the number of dogs who are returned to the shelters. Since generally a dog can only be returned a limited number of times before it is considered unadoptable and put down, this is not an idle concern. This kind of matching demonstrates a working assumption that dogs do differ by breed and by individual, and that like fits with like. It also acknowledges important differences among human beings as their personalities and lifestyles affect such relationships. All animal beings are shaped, limited, and enabled by their biological makeup, by the history of their evolution, and by their experience (Coren vii). We need to take this into account in order to be more adept in forming successful relationships.

For example, some dogs are predisposed to be effective watchdogs, others to be good hunting dogs, and others to be good herding dogs. Within each group (sporting, working, herding, non-sporting, terrier, hound), though, different breeds have different particular talents and personalities. So even if one knows one wants a herding dog, one must choose among border collies, corgis, shelties, Bouviers, or Australian shepherds (to name a few). Making this choice requires that you consider a variety of factors. Each herding breed has its own physical, mental, and emotional characteristics. There can be strains within a breed as well. My Aussies Pandora and Nemesis couldn't have been more different—one was the "quiet kind," the other the "bouncing barking kind." Yet, compare either of them to my mother's Jack Russell terrier or Dandie Dinmont and one cannot mistake that they were both Aussies and that Digby and Bentley were something very different.

Among dogs there is much individual variation. The last terrier my mother had (Digby) was difficult, even for a terrier! Tuffy and Pandora, my first and second Aussies, required very soft handling and lots of encouragement. Nemesis, however, required a firmer hand and clear limits. Tao (who is probably more border collie than Aussie) requires more in the way of calming down and learning to pay attention. And Maeve is like a combination of Pandora and Nemesis. As I mentioned in Chapter 2, one of my riding instructors says one needs to learn to ride the species, not a particular horse. Similarly, the more one learns about dogs *in general,* the better equipped one will be to handle the infinite variation one will encounter. However, to be successful with an individual horse or dog, one also needs to take the time to learn about breed differences and how best to work with different breeds and mixes. A human companion needs to love and know a kind of dog *and* the individual dog (Haraway, *Companion Species* 36). We need to get to know the individual differences just as we do with people (Rollins 30). We need to acquire the flexibility of learning to read and understand the individuals with whom we are working. If we don't do this, dogs will continue to be taken into shelters and killed because *they* are "out of control" or "stupid."

Our ability to live and work successfully with other beings (human and other animal beings) depends, in part, on our tendency to attribute mental states to them. We do this with other animal beings even if some scientists tell us not to. Such attribution goes too far when we claim dogs know it is their birthday, but in general it helps to assign mental states in order to negotiate our interactions successfully. Dogs stand out in this regard since we understand each other well—attributions of consciousness seem to go both ways (Masson 10).[2] We have evolved together with dogs and such attribution works to predict and explain their behavior. It is also how they communicate and work with us. This helps us build respectful relationships.

Some trainers fail to attribute real consciousness or reason to dogs, and this limits how they work with them. Training based on this assumption can create a relationship of complete dependency. This, then, feeds

2. It is important to note that many people have a similar ability to "read" or understand other animal beings with whom they work—cattle, horses, sheep, cats. Dogs have been living with us the longest, though, so there may be greater general understanding.

into the perception of dogs being "good slaves." For these people, dogs who do not accept human control are seen as "problem dogs" (Masson 14). This is one reason some animal rights people view training as a distortion of the nature of the dog and so as something to be avoided. But dogs are not wild; they are domesticated. If dogs run loose, they often get killed by cars or disease. Some training is necessary for successful mixed-species communities. But the insight that they do need to express their nature, and that training needs to respect this nature, is an important one. Working with dogs often makes the dogs happy, especially when the work fits their nature (Masson 123–24). Again, this requires getting to know breeds and individual dogs. Much training does not "take into account difference in the nature of intelligence among the various breeds of dogs or breed differences in temperament and willingness to work. . . ." Breed books usually focus on positive traits, not disease issues or "bad" traits, and this limited perception can make it difficult to create positive lives with these beings (Coren 11–13). Our understanding of dogs is better, and so our attempts to communicate and train them go better, if we assume dogs have feelings, fears, desires, beliefs, plans, and goals (Coren 68). For some this adds up to assuming they are conscious. In *The Intelligence of Dogs*, Stanley Coren notes that, "since we attribute consciousness and intelligence to other human beings, we have no right, in the absence of other data, to deny the same to other animals, certainly higher ones such as dogs." This is especially true since they have similar psychology and chemistry (73). Attempts to deny consciousness to other animal beings also fall prey to a limited understanding of consciousness as something one has or does not have. Peirce and James argue that consciousness is much more fluid and continuous than this suggests. Further, it doesn't make good sense to deny these traits. Their domestication depended on these very traits—why ignore them now? Such denial is not useful or respectful. The need to respect the consciousness of dogs, though, is why training and work can be very important aspects of a dog being's life.

Attending to their intelligence and consciousness, and using them in training, are ways dogs can benefit from domestication. As with horses, domesticated dogs are not spending their days looking for food. With their breeding generally under human control, most are not frequently engaged in raising puppies and teaching them to hunt and survive. Most are not kept in packs, so negotiating social relations with other dogs does not fill the day.[3] Training and work can become the replacement for pack socialization. Dogs are hierarchical animals and relationships need to be kept clear. Obedience work can be very important for establishing this sense of place. Other kinds of work can be important ways to get physical exercise and mental stimulation. The canine brain did not evolve to lie around all day—dogs travel, hunt, play, and form life-long bonds. They need work to do. Rather than dominate dogs, we need to use their capacity to learn and release the potential of each dog (Serpell, *Domestic Dog* 26). All mammals learn. Most dogs learn best when motivated by social companionship, not punishment and reward. If we use our knowledge of dogs, our relationships with them can be happier. We need to realize they are not just like us at the same time that we recognize our contintuity with them. Further, there is variation among dog intelligences (Budiansky, *Truth About Dogs* 128, 145, 237).

Just as there are various intelligences among humans (spacial, numerical, artistic, poetic, philosophical), there is variation among dogs. Some dogs are generally bright while others are more specialized. Some are better at solving problems, others at understanding spatial relations, and still others at social interactions (Coren 80–82). Providing training and the opportunity to learn can often diminish the differences among dogs. They have a general adaptive capacity that makes them fairly malleable (Scott 427). So all dogs can generally learn basic obedience and family routines.

Those who want to deny dog intelligence fall back on language as the marker of intelligence. This is a flawed approach. While humans have long relied on the marker of language as a sign of human specialness—specifically, as a marker of intelligence and consciousness—we see markers of consciousness and intelligence in other social animal beings. Speaking of dogs, Coren says,

> In essence, consciousness of its own states has given it the ability virtually to read the minds of others. At the positive end, this could open the door to empathic responses, such as sympathy, compassion, and trust, but it also makes possible treachery, double-crossing, and deceit. In other words, it allows the rich diversity of adaptive and

---

3. This is one thing that a Pragmatist would probably argue for—most dogs probably should not be only dogs (i.e., the only dog in the family).

> meaningful behaviors that we expect of humans, dogs, and other social animals. According to this theory, then, to be an effective social animal requires both intelligence and consciousness. If the theory is true, we can further assert the corollary that the very existence of complex social interactions should serve as evidence that an animal has both consciousness and intelligence. (84)

So while consciousness requires communication, it does not require language in the more narrow sense.

While consciousness, intelligence, and communication do not require language, it is interesting to note that the earliest stage of language development is language comprehension, not production. There are also gestures, signals, and body language. Dogs read body language very well and are very receptive to vocal communication. They are also very adept at learning. They learn based on observation, their environment, social interactions, and language communication (Coren 159). Humans communicate in a number of ways, but we rely heavily on body language and unconscious cues. Since this may account for as much as 93 percent of human communication with others, dogs are well positioned to understand us very clearly (E. Anderson 25).

Further, as mentioned before, there are different kinds of dog intelligence. There is adaptive intelligence, which includes learning and problems solving. This intelligence applies to planning, selecting, learning, retrieving information, and applying information. There is also working or obedience intelligence. This includes the desire to please, the ability to pay attention and not be distracted, and the capacity for flexibility. There is also instinctive intelligence. Some think that those with less instinctive intelligence seem to have more adaptive intelligence, and the reverse (Coren, 118–122, 127). Whether this is true or not, brains are the result of particular evolutionary histories, as are bodies (Coren 17). We should try to understand these evolutionary histories to understand and communicate with the individuals with whom we live. Trying to understand the mental and physical capabilities of various dog beings will help us negotiate respectful relationships.

Knowing the breed of a dog tends to be a good indication of instinctive intelligence, but adaptive intelligence is much more individualized. Individual personality is a big factor (Coren 160, 190–191). While it is difficult to influence instinct—one is unlikely to get a blood hound to herd sheep—one can orient a dog to accept human leadership.

Highly adaptive intelligence makes a dog more malleable, but it can also become a problem because such dogs are easily bored and act in ways many humans find less than desirable (Coren 209, 217, 232). We need to find appropriate outlets for the various intelligences. Work is one possibility.

Humans clearly benefit from some working dogs: bomb and drug sniffing dogs, police dogs, seeing eye dogs, aid dogs, therapy dogs, and seizure dogs. Now we have the possibility of training dogs to sniff out disease in human bodies. Specific dogs are selected for different work based on specific traits. So, if one is looking for a watch dog, one will probably do better to select a German shepherd or a Scottish terrier than to choose a bloodhound or Saint Bernard. Even with these breeds, though, a great deal of training is involved. Dogs often need to be capable of intelligent disobedience as well—that is they need to exercise canine judgment. For example, a guide dog needs to ignore commands if following them will put the person in danger.

In addition to benefiting from the work dogs do, we also enjoy their companionship. There is some evidence that people who live with dogs (and cats) may be healthier than people who do not—perhaps in part because if they exercise the dogs they get some exercise themselves. Further, it seems just the presence of the animals can help with blood pressure and provide motivation to stay mentally alert and responsible. One explanation for this is that "just as caring for a baby releases the oxytocin that helps mothers relax . . . so the nurturing aspects of domestication appear to have released a similar oxytocin effect on most of humanity" (Olmert 154). Oxytocin can strengthen immune response and protect us from infection as well as just make us feel good. Dogs are good for us.

Both dogs and humans can be altered for the better if we take the time to get to know the individual personalities of dogs and learn to respect the individual dog beings with whom we live. Again, purposive self-activity, intelligence, and valuing are all part of what allows domestication and furthers specialization. If we learn to honor these, both human and dog beings stand to gain, even if some aspects of the relationship must change. Teaching people that it is okay to dominate and dictate to other animal beings creates a harmful habit. We need to teach respect and so improve relationships. For example, a "faithful, well-treated sheepdog" acquires a "sense of identity from their quasi-membership in a family" (Franklin 124). And we can gain a different sense of our relationships with the rest of nature from these relations as well. "A fundamental change in our moral estimation of animals would require a corresponding change in our conception of our relations to nature as a whole" (Steiner 124).

For this kind of change to be a real possibility we need to honestly assess current relationships between human and dog beings. A Pragmatist approach entails getting acquainted with the people and activities we want to evaluate and possibly change. Without such an assessment of current conditions we are likely to overlook and/or misunderstand many problematic situations. This ignorance can lead to misapplied remedies and counterproductive "solutions." So, I turn now to assess some of the areas many animal advocates highlight as problematic for dogs who live within human society.

Abuse and Neglect

We love our dogs. Sixty percent of pet owners have a least one dog. These owners say they are more attached to dogs than to cats or other animal beings. They see dogs as more playful, affectionate, and emotionally supportive than other animal beings. As a consequence, people in relationships with dogs tend to spend more time interacting with their dogs than those humans in relationships with cats. They also spend more on them at the veterinarian. Despite our love for dogs, the Humane Society of the United States estimates that six to eight million dogs and cats end up in shelters in the United States each year. Sixty-four percent of puppies are discarded (Serpell, *Domestic Dog* 162–164). One estimate says that of dogs that end up at shelters, about 16.1% are reclaimed, 25.6% are re-homed, 55% are killed. The Humane Society estimates that 30% of dogs are reclaimed, and three to four *million* cats and dogs are killed each year in shelters. The numbers one can find clearly vary. But even the most conservative numbers show that loss, abandonment, and death of unwanted dogs are very large problems.[4]

Dogs can become "unwanted" in a number of ways. One study found that 21 percent of people surrendering dogs to shelters did so because

---

4. Some of the bodies of the dogs and cats who are killed in shelters are sent to renderers and turned into detergent and hog and chicken food. Beck and Katcher call this pet cannibalism (23).

they took too much time, work, or money. Nineteen percent said it was due to moving, 9 percent due to allergies, 4 percent because the dog was ill (E. Anderson 189). People are not always completely honest about why they are surrendering pets, and this is just one study, but it does reveal that human expectations about the dog and human preferences for how to spend their time and money are large factors in determining the fate of dogs.

Dogs aren't just abandoned; many are abused. Dogs are tied and left to live in their own feces and urine, they are left with little or no access to food and water, they are kicked, hit, burned, shocked, and shot. The Humane Society points out the connections between the abuse of pets in a home and the likelihood that children and/or women in the home are also abused. When such abuse is present, the pet is often used as part of the blackmail that keeps the abused in the home. The pets (and other humans in the home) may also be sexually abused. Pets risk being abandoned if the love of the humans goes away, if they behave "incorrectly," or if they do not provide the unconditional love that is expected (Haraway, *Companion Species* 38–39). Even well-loved pets risk lack of care when economic times are tough. During an economic downturn there is an increase in the number of animal beings surrendered to shelters. The rising cost of medical technology, ironically, makes many face difficult decisions about the health care humans can and should provide for the animal beings in their lives.

STARVATION, UNDERNOURISHMENT, AND OBESITY

Dogs need access to fresh food and water. While some suffer from the lack of adequate food, others suffer from too much or inappropriate food. Dogs who are tied are often left outdoors without adequate water, or the water becomes frozen or contaminated. Others are fed inappropriate human food on top of their regular food and become obese. This comes with limited mobility and a whole host of diseases—just as with human beings.

Hoarders may provide the best known cases of neglect and undernourishment. These are the extreme situations that capture the public's attention.

Patronek (1999) surveyed animal shelter operators about their experiences with people who hoard animals. Detailed information was obtained on 54 cases. An animal hoarder was defined as "someone who accumulates a large number of animals; fails to provide minimal standards of nutrition, sanitation and veterinary care; and fails to act on the deteriorating condition of the animals (including disease, starvation and even death) or the environment (severely overcrowded and unsanitary conditions), or the negative impact of the collection on their own health and well-being." These findings support some of Worth and Beck's conclusions. Most cases were female (76%), a large proportion (46%) were 60 years of age or older; most were single, divorced or widowed; and almost half lived alone. The most common animals involved were cats (65%) and dogs (60%). Based on the data collected, Patronek estimated that there are 700 to 2,000 new cases of animal hoarding every year in the United States. (psychiatrictimes.com)

News reports about such cases inform us of the conditions dogs frequently face in these situations—confinement, exposure to the elements, insufficient food and water, filth, and disease. "Household interiors were coated, often several inches high, with human and animal urine and feces, sometimes to an extent that the floor buckled" (E. Anderson 186). If that is not enough, these dogs often receive little social interaction or love. Sometimes motivated out of a desire to "save" unwanted animals, these hoarding cases are clearly examples of neglect.

As with horse abuse, extreme cases make us angry and make us wonder how someone could treat a dog this way. However, other more common forms of misdirected love also cause a great deal of harm. Humans often equate love and food. They can't stand to deny a dog more food or more treats. They share a little of everything they eat as well—it's only fair to share after all. This does not result in a happy, healthy dog, however, but a dog with great health risks. Obesity affects 9 percent of dogs and 14 percent of cats (E. Anderson 76). A Pragmatist perspective points to the need to know the needs of the particular animal being and to respect their developmental history—not to turn them into us or treat them as a thing. The most loving dog people are often the culprits in cases of obesity.

PHYSICAL ABUSE

While over-feeding may seem to many to be a relatively minor problem (a disease of the affluent), physical abuse of domestic animals is an ever-present problem. This can range from chaining a dog outside, to beating and kicking dogs, to inflicting burns and other wounds. Dogs are thrown out of moving cars, dragged behind moving vehicles, and dropped from buildings. Citing specific examples found in newspapers, Elizabeth Anderson tells us of a case in 2007 in which two teenagers put duct tape on a puppy's mouth and paws and cooked the dog in the oven—alive. In 2006, a woman in Utah wired a puppy's mouth shut so he would stop barking; robbers took a Yorkie at gunpoint and strangled the dog as the people fled (E. Anderson 194).

A less obvious problem is chaining dogs outside. Some dogs are chained up to serve as watch dogs. Others may be chained outside because they have soiled the house or destroyed things in the house. While chained, they may hurt themselves by straining and jumping against the chain (the injuries can result in death), they may be subject to attack by other animals, and they are often exposed to the weather. Being social animals, they can become anxious and aggressive from being chained. This can cause them to act out and harm other dog and human beings ("Breaking the Chain" 9).

Probably the bulk of abuse comes in the misapplication of training techniques and from human beings acting out of frustration or anger with dogs who have not been trained and so are exhibiting "undesirable" behavior. Some of the obvious abuse includes when dogs are beaten, kicked, or burned with cigarettes. But how does one judge more ambiguous cases of a firm reprimand or correction?

There are honest disputes about what counts as abusive training, just as there are disagreements about disciplining human children. Similarly, with signs of abuse, one has to be careful. Different breeds and individuals exhibit different levels of submissiveness and act in some of the ways one might expect from a dog who has been regularly hit or kicked. So, just as with children, there are signs of abuse one should attend to, but one must also be careful about misjudging a situation.

So why might people abuse dogs? Sometimes it's out of ignorance. Many do not know the damage that can be done by chaining a dog out in the yard; they may think strong physical corrections are part of effective training (and there may be times such corrections are appropriate). This can be addressed with education. Others, however, do it with cruel intent. They see animals as appropriate victims of their anger or as beings who don't deserve love or attention. For this group of people there is often a connection to how they treat other human beings in their homes. The Humane Society of the United States actually has an education campaign that points to the links between those who abuse human beings in their homes and the fact that they have often previously abused other animal beings. They point to other animal abuse as a warning sign of human abuse to come (if not going on simultaneously). This is an important insight, but it can promote the view that the abuse of the dog or cat being is not as wrong in itself. Some allude to it primarily as a precursor to escalating violence. Others, such as ecofeminist Carol Adams, have been very effective at pointing out how these kinds of abuse and violence are integrally linked.

She points out that most abuse cases involve male humans abusing female humans, young humans, and other animal beings. One of the techniques of abuse is to hurt or kill the animal being in front of the other members of the family. This is a kind of psychological violence in itself as well as a possible prediction that the violence will soon be turned on the human beings. It is also used as a way to control the human victims of abuse. "If you tell anyone what I've done to you, I'll kill the dog." For this reason, it is unfortunate that most women's shelters will not take in other animal beings. Some have programs for fostering the animals while the women are at the shelter, but since these animal beings are often a main source of comfort and psychological support, many women (and children) are unwilling to be separated from their pets. Further, if the women (and possibly their children) are trying to move out on their own, they are likely to be moving into an apartment. Many landlords won't allow pets. The lack of acceptable living options further traps these women.

There is also the very unfortunate connection of women and other animal beings in terms of sexual abuse by men. Given the secrecy of these issues, we don't know the actual rates of bestiality. Different estimates range from two to eight percent of people having engaged in sexual activity with other animal beings. We also know that sex with animals is used in cases of marital rape. Partners are forced to have sex with animals—often based on something seen in pornography (Adams, *Neither Beast Nor Man* 148). Women and other animal beings are both seen as objects that exist to fulfill male desire.

For Carol Adams, this view of human women and other animal beings has a common foundation in conceiving of woman human beings and other animal beings as usable, consumable, abusable. They exist to fulfill the desires of male human beings. Gilman had pointed this out a hundred years earlier. It is important to recognize this conceptual link in order to realize that it won't work to just intervene on a case-by-case basis. We need to get to the core attitude or habit that enables the abuse in the first place. As with research situations, where people turn the living beings into *things* to make it easier to perform various procedures, abusers also reduce living beings into things. Both require seeing a living being as something that exists not for their own purposes and desires, but to fulfill the purposes and desires of someone else. They exist to be used.

This view does not make for healthy or respectful relationships, and abusive relationships tend to perpetuate themselves in a cycle of violence. If we want to end abuse, we need to address the root causes at the same time that we help the individuals in front of us. A Pragmatist perspective requires us to acknowledge our fallibility and so to be careful about jumping to judgment of others. But it also requires us to promote the growth and well-being of ourselves and others. The pluralism of Pragmatism is not an anything goes permissiveness. Some relationships are not acceptable as they do not meet Alain Locke's criteria for behavior or beliefs we should tolerate–those that express tolerance, reciprocity, and parity. I do not have to tolerate those who would harm me; abuse is not a tolerable act.

PUPPY MILLS

One thing that contributes to humans viewing other animal beings as usable and expendable is that they are seen as easily (and cheaply) replaceable. One factor contributing to this view is the over-population of other animal beings considered to be pets. The very traits that make domestication possible also contribute to overpopulation. Dogs are relatively quick to mature, are disease resistant, exhibit high fertility and relative longevity (Masson 8). Because of this, there is a need to control their reproduction. Humans, however, exploit these traits in breeding for profit. This is especially a problem when there is no concern for the welfare and individuality of the dogs involved. They become means to an other's end. Puppy mills are not nice places. The facilities tend to be large and dirty, the dogs produce litter after litter and spend their lives in cages. There is "no love, no medical care, and no exercise." Estimates range from two to four million dogs being purchased from puppy mills each year. While there are fewer than one hundred USDA inspectors, there are over thirty-five hundred licensed breeders and eleven hundred dealers, transporters, and researchers. There are more than nine thousand facilities. If the inspectors do find violations, the operations just pay the fines as part of the cost of doing business. Some operations even get USDA rural development loans to *support* their operations (E. Williams 236–250).

Missouri has been making news recently as they consider action that would limit such operations. "Considered the puppy mill capital of America, Missouri hosts an estimated 3,000 puppy mills, far more than even well-known dog breeding states such as Iowa, Oklahoma, Pennsylvania, and Ohio" (Johnson 8). The rural nature of the state makes enforcement of existing laws difficult. And those existing laws aren't all that good in the first place. "'Here in Missouri, it's perfectly legal to confine dogs to tiny wire-floored cages for their entire lives,' says HSUS Missouri State director Barbara Schmitz, 'and the cage can be stacked one on top of the other so that waste streams down from one dog to the one's below'" (Johnson 8).

The breeding industry and groups like the Pet Industry Joint Advisory Council and the American Kennel Club (AKC) fight legislation that would control and monitor these operations. They spend millions of dollars fighting animal protection legislation as they see it as an infringement on breeder's rights (E. Williams 234). The Puppy Protection Acts of 2002 and 2003 were killed by the efforts of The American Kennel Club, the National Animal Interest Alliance, and the American Veterinary Medical Association (E. Williams 250). The AKC website encouraged its members to fight such bills. They were especially worried about provisions that would regulate "the frequency and age at which bitches are bred" and which would revoke "the license to breed and sell dogs of persons who commit three violations of the USDA's regulations over an eight year period." They are worried about putting breeders out of business. The Humane Society of the United States reports in their May/June 2009 *All Animals* magazine that "When The Indiana Legislature took up a bill to add modest requirements for exercise, shelter, and living conditions at puppy mills in the state, farming interests went on the warpath, complaining . . . that it was the first step to ending animal agriculture" ("Yays & Nays" 11). This continues with the debate about the current H.R. 835—known as the PUPS Act, for "Puppy Uniform Protection and Safety Act."

Similarly, when a dog breeder and dog show judge took a public stand against puppy mills, other breeders called him a traitor. The Humane

Society's July/August 2009 issue of *All Animals* tells the story of Ted Paul who, having been active in showing dogs for more than thirty years, testified in support of Oregon legislation that would create standards of basic care and limit the number of dogs a facility can produce for sale to pet stores and on the internet. Having bred and raised many champion dogs, he is not opposed to responsible breeding and is not trying to end the activities of responsible breeders. There is an important place for well-bred purebred dogs, but such breeders bear no resemblance to puppy mill operators who "are callous, ruthless animal abusers who will breed any two animals they think will sell. They are in it only for the money, and in their greed they treat animals as a cash crop deserving of no favors, just torture" (39). He thinks that puppy mills and backyard breeders are a big part of the pet overpopulation problem and he believes that joint action between groups like the HSUS and the AKC is necessary to "stop this animal carnage once and for all" (39).

Dogs can breed and survive in less than ideal conditions. However, dogs in puppy mills show signs of stress and depression (Masson 182). When groups like the HSUS and the ASPCA go to rescue dogs from one of these operations they find filth, injuries, and disease. They also find dogs with physical and psychological problems. Some of the common conditions include separation anxiety from early weaning, respiratory disease from bad living conditions, and congenital health problems from bad breeding. "Reports from undercover investigations and raids reveal a disturbing picture. . . . [D]ogs . . . had conditions such as canine herpes, kennel cough, parasites, and bacterial infections. The report included a pug-beagle mix puppy whose foot had been chewed off by his mother. 'That comes from having puppies in a stressful situation, and they don't know what they are doing, and they will just gnaw,' explained a rescuer. . . . 'We're seeing skin infections, urine burns on newborn puppies, dental problems, and sore feet from standing on wire'" (E. Anderson 183).

At the other end of production, the care the dogs receive in pet stores is not good. The people on staff are rarely well trained, nor do they have time to spend with the dogs. Moreover, when dogs are sold, most stores provide little education for the customer, much less advise on whether a particular dog is likely a good match for a particular person or family (E. Williams 246). This makes it less likely that a successful and respectful relationship will develop. The same goes for sales from many backyard breeders. This is not to say that all backyard breeders are uninformed or irresponsible, but it is a concern. There is less done to ensure that the dogs go to good homes when the primary motive is profit. Profit requires moving product and the dogs are the product.

In the past, most people who got dogs from a puppy mill probably had no idea what conditions the dogs had faced, nor did they have any idea of what they might continue to face. Now, however, with very public campaigns exposing the conditions at puppy mills, it is harder to assume that someone has no idea about the system to which they are contributing. But it still goes on as these operations supply large numbers of "cheap" dog beings. These dogs are bought online and from pet stores, often by people who have very little information about dogs and what is likely to come with adding a dog to their lives. These are not the people who are ready to take on the special needs many of these dogs have. As mentioned, some of these are physical needs that will require a great deal of time and money to address, if they can be addressed. Puppy mill puppies will also likely have behavior problems from premature weaning and lack of socialization. These require knowledge, time, and patience to deal with successfully. So, at this point, puppy mill puppies are most likely to end up in the homes least equipped to deal with their special needs. When these relationships break down, these same dogs are likely to be abandoned at shelters.

The American Veterinary Medical Association (AVMA) recognizes that the population of cats and dogs "currently exceeds the capacity of our society to care and provide homes for them as companion animals." They consider this a central welfare concern. They do not, however, support "regulations or legislation mandating spay/neuter of privately owned, non-shelter dogs and cats. Although spaying and neutering helps control dog and cat populations, mandatory approaches may contribute to pet owners avoiding licensing, rabies vaccination and veterinary care for their pets, and may have other unintended consequences" (avma.org).

We have too many dogs being born who are unlikely to find permanent, loving homes. The spillover from this problem, though, has been an attitude of intolerance toward any and all breeders. This is not really helpful, and is a primary reason why few of the responsible breeders are willing to support efforts to control or improve the conditions and monitoring of puppy mills. There is unnecessary animosity between animal advocates and dog breeders. Of course there are breeders who don't run puppy mills, but who nonetheless engage in unethical practices. My dog Nemesis's breeder is an example. Nemesis was going to be "destroyed" because she was not show quality. Not long after I got Nemesis I learned that the breeder had been suspended for undisclosed violations. She was fined for these violations and prohibited from breeding for two years. Of course, for every breeder caught and punished by the relevant breeding associations or the American Kennel Club, there are many who do not get caught or who have the political clout to get away with it. (This happens with horses and cats too.)

For a Pragmatist, though, the answer is not to lump all breeders together. The situation is complicated. Puppy mills and irresponsible small purebred breeders present different sets of problems. With careful consideration of the specific problems, one could create a situation in which the AKC and breed associations would help end puppy mill operations and take on greater enforcement of their own standards. Then one could move on to encourage an examination of some of the various breed standards and the practices that are required by these standards—tail docking, ear cropping, dewclaw removal. Again, though, for a Pragmatist it is not an all-or-nothing approach. There have already been some changes. These kinds of physical alterations are banned in the United Kingdom now and there is growing debate elsewhere. In the United States the AVMA opposes ear cropping and tail docking "when done for solely cosmetic purposes." They encourage "the elimination of ear cropping and tail docking from breed standards" (avma.org). I will discuss this more in the section on showing dogs. The point here is that taking an extreme stance on breeding has had the effect of alienating some of the dog's most natural allies. Some of these breeders would be very helpful in efforts to reduce abuse and abandonment. Further, if people who breed and compete with dogs learned to cooperate with people focused on animal welfare, rights, or liberation, they could also be allies in efforts to greatly limit (and perhaps end) the use of dogs in research.

Use in Research and Biomedical Context

Dogs have been used in a variety of research projects. Since they are covered by the Animal Welfare Act (while mice, rats, reptiles, and birds are not), there are requirements governing their use. Because of their status as pets there is often more public outcry if research involves dogs. Some think that dogs should be exempted from experimentation since so many are members of human households. Domestication results in animals with heightened sensitivities. Dogs are especially good at reading humans and have been bred and trained to have confidence in humans and to form a bond of sympathy. The research relationship betrays this bond and so is seen by many to be wrong (White 68).

The Family Pet Protection Act of 1996 and the Pet Safety and Protection Act of 1996 were passed in order to reduce the likelihood that pets will be used in such research. Prior to 1960, taking animals from pounds for use in research was common practice. Until recently, three states still mandated this practice—Utah, Minnesota, and Oklahoma. Utah just recently removed this mandate (*Animal Times*, Summer 2010 10). Seven additional states still allow the seizure of dogs and cats—Arizona, California, Colorado, Iowa, Michigan, South Dakota, Tennessee—and two more allow the seizure of dogs—Ohio and Wisconsin (banpound seizure.org). There are ten to twenty class B dealers who obtain around eighteen thousand dogs and cats for research through ads and auctions (E. Williams 186–187). Most people don't seem to like the idea of former pets being used in this way. "Buck's Bill" was introduced in 2007 to stop this practice, but it continues. Some of the excess dogs from puppy mills end up in research labs and many are bred specifically for research. There are eighty companies involved in such breeding (E. Williams 187–188). Marshall Farms, for example, is known for breeding (copyrighted) beagles for research (Greek 92). According to their own web site, "Marshall BioResources provides purpose bred research animals and related services for biomedical research. Within our federally regulated and inspected facilities in Upstate New York we maintain breeding colonies of beagles, mongrel/hound dogs, ferrets, and Gottingen Minipigs. Marshall Beagles are also raised at locations in Italy and China" (marshallbio.com). (You can't go beyond the first page of their web site without an authorized username and password.)

Dogs are used, for example, in research that examines diseases and conditions common to dogs. Vet schools and some animal hospitals keep dogs for the purpose of giving blood and colostrum. These dogs are given good care and are often adopted out after a certain period of time. However, they also use dogs to teach students how to perform surgeries. While at least half the vet schools house animals they use for multiple surgeries and then kill when the procedures are done, some are trying out alternatives. Some are starting to offer treatment and surgeries for shelter animals who need them. This gives the animal being a second chance at life and provides the students with valuable experience (MacAlpine 8). A similar kind of arrangement has also been made in order to teach students and bring care to animal beings on Indian reservations (Moxley 15–21).

Interestingly, when the AVMA lists their research priorities, pets only come in seventh on a list of eleven priorities—well behind several research priorities related to livestock. Even then, most of the reasons given for the research on pets are human centered. "Improved understanding of the human-animal bond indicates that companion animals contribute significantly to the quality of human life." They want to improve the lives of pets and their owners and they note that much research on pets has had secondary benefits in the area of human health. They say "[B]iomedical research has been enhanced by the use of animals as models of human disease" (avma.org).

There are numerous examples of research including dogs that is focused directly on human needs. Dogs have been shot, burned, and had their skulls crushed in order to study how to help humans. Ironically, dogs are used in research because they are easy to handle. In 2004, in the United States, sixty-five thousand dogs were used in toxicity tests, surgeries, dental experimentation, heart research, drug testing, and food testing. Most dogs used in research are kept alone in barrier cages and given little exercise. The same requirements are in place for keeping dogs and primates, but these are neither sufficient nor sufficiently enforced (E. Williams 183–84, 194).

The housing of dogs in labs usually prioritizes human preferences. They are set up for ease of cleaning and ease of access over the welfare of the animal being. Dogs should have places to hide, material to bed down with, and room to move. They need things to chew on and things with which to play. They also need social contact—other dogs and/or humans. Attention should be paid to how many dogs are housed in one area. Dogs in labs exhibit signs of stress by engaging in repetitive behaviors such as circling and pacing. These kinds of behaviors are reduced with social housing (Serpell, *Domestic Dog* 186, 191).[5]

Dogs in research facilities exhibit signs of stress and depression (Masson 182). The human beings working in research also often show

5. All of this can apply to breeding and boarding kennels as well as to research labs.

signs of stress and depression. To cope with the work, they often try to turn the animal being into a thing—a tool of research. "Animals must be de-animalized . . . in order to justify all the things that are done to them in the lab. This is one reason . . . that lab animal suppliers often don't use the term "animal" at all. The creatures whom they sell are "research models." Models are not animals, and they certainly are not *specific* animals" (E. Williams 221). This kind of distancing is harder for humans to do with dogs in part because humans are so tied to dogs. Many researchers go home to live with dogs and cats. This conflict can take a toll on all involved.

A Pragmatist would respond to these issues in some of the same ways discussed in the chapter on horses. There is a difference between research that improves the lives and health of dogs and research that is solely for human beings' benefit. The use of other animal beings as a research model for human beings' diseases and conditions can be problematic for several reasons. One, it may not work. There are differences among animal beings that can make it problematic to transfer results from one animal being to another. "Why do women who have had hysterectomies need to fight osteoporosis while neutered cats live longer, healthier lives? And why are humans not vaccinated for parvo and dogs for rubella" (Greek 15)? Despite our continuity, there are differences among animal beings that make simple substitution a problematic research model. This can be seen as a practical problem that has ethical implications. Examples abound: Chloramphenicol is not good for humans, dogs, or horses, but cats do well on it; dog testing on birth control pills suggested they would *decrease* clotting; the asthma drug Isuprel created no reaction in dogs, but proves toxic to humans in the same amount; the nausea drug Domperidone causes irregular heart beat in humans, but no such reaction can be reproduced in dogs; the arthritis medication Flosint caused several human deaths, but was well tolerated by dogs; an antidiarrheal, Clioquinol passed tests in dogs (and cats) but caused blindness and paralysis in humans; and the list goes on. The reverse is also often the case—drugs that proved harmful to dogs work well for humans: Tacromilus, an antirejection drug, did not do well when tested on dogs; corticosteroids have very different effects in human, dog, and cat beings. Turning to the more common drugs: Ibuprofen causes kidney failure in dogs; Benadryl works well in humans and dogs, but only in very different doses (humans needing much less) (Greek 62–73, 119).

Another issue is more directly an ethical concern. If the other animal beings used in research are enough like human beings to be a "useful test subjects," then they are enough like us to raise concerns about using them in this way. This argument is most often applied to the use of other primates in research, but it applies to all mammals for sure, and probably to many other animal beings. Dogs share a long history with humans and have intelligence specifically tuned to human perceptions and desires. They read us. As the previously mentioned study with hand-raised wolves and dogs shows, dogs are more attuned to humans than their nondomesticated counterpart. They are changed creatures and this has ethical implications. Is it okay to use such beings in the LD 50 test (Lethal Dose Fifty Percent)? The test requires that fifty percent of the animals being tested die as an indicator of the toxicity of the substance being tested (Greek 56). We need to look for approaches that are less wasteful of life.

Even if some research is justified, the nature of dogs also has implications for how they should be treated during research. For instance, a cancer treatment doesn't work in isolation from the whole context in which a person finds him or herself. With human beings the success or failure of any specific drug treatment interacts with the other forms of physical, social, and psychological support. If a human being with cancer is isolated and depressed, medical treatments that might otherwise be successful often fail. This can be true of dogs as well. So, when testing drugs on dogs they should be living in supportive environments. But, dogs (and other animal beings) in a lab are usually housed in less than ideal conditions and receive minimal social contact. They do not get adequate exercise or the stimulation of play. All of these can compromise the results of the research, not to mention the harm it does to the physical and mental well being of individual dogs.

The requirements for the treatment of dogs in a research facility are higher than for any creatures other than primates, mostly due to our attachment to them. Nevertheless, the care still can interfere with the possibility of good or reliable results. Again, this very fact points to the problem of using dogs this way at all and certainly for using them for research that doesn't benefit them or other species. Testing them for problems related to caffeine, cocaine, or nicotine addiction has few if any potential benefits for dogs. A bizarre example of such research was a 1987 test involving dogs and cigarette smoke. "Dogs with erections were forced to inhale cigarette smoke! Most of the dogs failed to maintain an erection after the smoke was inhaled. The researchers said this observation lent support to the human observation that smoking interfered with a man's ability to maintain an erection" (Greek 147). Enough said. There may be, however, justification for some research on the impact of second hand smoke on dogs' overall health given that many of them live with humans who smoke.

If there are questions about using dogs in research, what about more *trivial* uses? Some, who are willing to support limited use of animal beings—dogs included—in research that might improve the lives of human and other animal beings, are opposed to the use of these same animals for the more trivial interests of entertainment and competition. But I don't think it's that simple. When considered from the perspective of the dogs, the dogs stand to benefit more from certain aspects of entertainment and competition than they do from research. This position is in tension with a common compromise position that would continue to allow the use of pets in medical research, but disallow their use in entertainment and competition. A Pragmatist perspective helps us see just this kind of unexpected possibility. Rather than a simplistic "use is bad unless it saves lives" position, a Pragmatist must explore a more complex set of possibilities.

Use in Entertainment

Entertainment and competition with dogs often overlap, as do both of these with work, as I will note later. Dog fighting is an obvious example. As before, I will focus initially on those activities that involve some kind of show that people pay to see, and I will save for the competition section those activities that include a winner. I will say at the outset that dogs may suffer less than other animals used in these ways. This is because their long history with humans predisposes them to enjoy the training in which we engage them and many of the activities in which we ask them to participate.

For instance, circuses often include dogs riding horses and dog acts such as poodles jumping through rings. In movies, television shows, and commercials, we see dogs perform advanced obedience and agility. Most of this can be seen as a natural extension of the training in which dogs regularly engage. There are, of course, concerns about abusive training techniques and dangerous acts. There are also issues related to the hours the dogs are required to perform and the care the dogs receive. If these issues are addressed, however, these particular activities pose no unique problems unless one believes *all* training of dogs to be unethical. As mentioned before, this makes no sense from a Pragmatist perspective since it denies the human-dog relationship altogether.

As always, when the humans involved stand to gain money for the "entertainment value" of the dogs, there is a higher risk of abusive training techniques and overuse. But these are general issues of justice that apply to child actors and others as well. If trainers focus on breeds and individuals who actively enjoy the work, it is not clear such use is abusive or especially problematic from a Pragmatist perspective. This perspective does, of course, require that the human beings involved understand and respect the *natural* and *developmental* history of dogs in general as well as the *natural* and *developmental* history of specific breeds. It also requires one to pay attention to the *plurality* of individual dogs and recognize when a mismatch has occurred (*fallibilism*) and be willing to rethink (*experiment* with) the training and use of particular individuals. Again, money and publicity can often get in the way of the willingness to be flexible and respectful. To ensure the well being of dogs used in entertainment we need animal advocates. But these advocates also need to respect the nature and variety of dogs. Some enjoy the work. Hard and fixed rules are unlikely to be very helpful. The same can said for the dogs used in competition.

Use in Competition

Competition with dog beings is not a bad thing *if* they enjoy the activity and are treated respectfully. However, not all competitive relationships are respectful and some competition with dogs has had very negative side effects. Most of the negative effects are related to the development and promulgation of various breeds. To win competitions and maintain the various breeds, many resort to a limited breeding pool. Dogs can be said to suffer in many ways from domestication and much of this is connected to the human control of their breeding. While dogs exist as a result of transactive relationships with humans that include control of their breeding, it is not the case that humans need such highly differentiated and specialized dogs.

To start with, let's look at the breeds we have created. The great variety of dogs we have today is the result of thousands of years of intentional breeding. Some of this breeding was focused on improving a breed for a specific task such as hunting or herding. Some has focused on conformation and looks. The so-called working dogs have been the most recent group to be at risk of falling prey to breeding for cosmetic purposes. Cosmetic breeding has led to the most detrimental effects. This is the kind of thing that worried Gilman, as we saw in Chapter 3, when she described a dog as "(a) poor, wretched, little, artificial dog—alive, but only so by virtue of man's insolence . . ." ("When I Was a Witch" 25).

The results of this kind of breeding are highlighted at dog shows.

> [T]he shows are not without their critics. Though the dogs who compete at Westminster are beautiful and most are likely healthy, the rise of such spectacles—and judging measures that in some cases emphasize appearance over welfare—has been blamed for a host of genetic health problems facing scores of breeds today.
>
> Brachycephalic (or short-faced) breeds like bulldogs and pugs suffer from breathing problems; Great Danes and other large dogs from joint problems; long dogs like dachshunds and basset hounds from back problems; wrinkly-faced dogs like boxers and sharpeis from skin and eye problems. And due to prolific production to meet public demand, the most coveted dogs tend to have the most genetic disorders; Labrador retrievers, who've topped the AKC's popularity list for 19 years, are prone to around 50 inherited conditions. (Allan 17)

The focus on showing has resulted in breeds with congenital heart problems, blindness, hip dysplasia, turned in eyelids, backs that can't last the lifetime of the dog, noses that have to be cored, wrinkles that have to be cleaned (Serpell, *Domestic Dog* 181). Some breeds have been so altered that they cannot actually breed or give birth without human assistance. Moreover, the demand for "pure bred" dogs has resulted in puppy mills.

These mills not only partake in harmful breeding practices and so harm the genetic pool, they also abuse females by making them have litter after litter and abuse the puppies by weaning them too early and often keeping them in very crowded, filthy, and disease ridden conditions. The "excess" dogs who can be found at shelters are another byproduct of this kind of system. The Humane Society estimates that twenty-five percent of dogs in shelters are purebred dogs. (See the "Puppy Mill" section earlier in this chapter for more on this.)

Many humans breed and buy these purebred dogs so that they can compete in breed shows. Competing with dogs—showing, racing, hunting, herding—is not necessarily problematic in itself, but as with horses when human pride and profit get connected to the performance of the other animal beings, the potential for abuse is huge. Related to this are some of the surgical procedures performed on dogs to make them ready for the show ring. There are the controversial practices of cropping ears and docking tails. Originally justified to keep the tails of working dogs from getting caught in the brush or stepped on by stock animals, docking tails entails removing all or part of the tail. Probably started to add a more menacing look to dogs often used as guard dogs, cropping ears entails surgically cutting ears and bandaging them so they heal in an upright position. Some of the dogs who commonly have their tails docked include many kinds of terriers, many kinds of spaniels, Boxers, Schnauzers, Bouviers, Poodles, Corgis, Australian Shepherds, Weimaraners, and Dobermans. Some of the dogs who commonly have their ears cropped include Dobermans, Great Danes, Boxers, Pit bulls, and Miniature Pinchers.

In another realm of competition, racing dogs have their weight tightly controlled; they also may be given drugs and sometimes are raced injured (as are horses). Less obvious problems include the fact that animals used in racing and showing are often kept in kennels and not allowed to socialize and play—frustrating the very characteristics that made them a candidate for domestication in the first place. One of the common difficulties in adopting ex-race dogs is getting them properly socialized and helping them learn to play. This often applies to breeding and show dogs as well.

Any kind of training—for obedience, agility, or herding—may involve the use of "force." Properly done (and there are multiple sound approaches), such training does not rely on force, however, but rather works with the dog's nature and desires. Without good training many dogs become dominant and dangerous. They often end up being abused, ignored, dumped, or killed. Learning to live with each other is certainly one of the challenges dogs and humans must face. As mentioned, training is seen by some as a kind of positive bondage that allows for freedom.

While training methods differ, their primary purpose is to build communi-cation and create respect (Haraway, *Companion Species* 48). Good train-ing helps build respect and allows for happiness.

For the Pragmatist such training must be tailored to the breeds and the individuals. For instance, when I started herding sheep with Nemesis, I found a wonderful instructor to work with and we did well despite my inexperience. At a certain point, though, my instructor suggested I take some time to work with someone she knew who specialized in training Aussies. My instructor works mostly with border collies, though she has also worked with Aussies, Shelties, Bouviers, Australian cattle dogs, Belgian Tervurens, and others. She knows a lot about the differences among the breeds (as well as individual dogs) and had started us well. She did not approach Nemesis as a defective border collie, but as the individual Aussie she was. However, she knew she didn't know every-thing about how to encourage Nemesis to work to her full potential. She thought working with a different instructor for awhile might provide us some new techniques.

On the other hand, with Tao and Maeve, I did have an experience with an instructor who, while helpful, tended to approach the Aussies as if they were border collies and wasn't as able to adjust to the dog in front of her. Similarly, Tuffy and Pandora loved obedience work and a look was all that was needed to provide a correction. Nemesis, however, needed to see some greater purpose in the work and required firmer handling. She did not "turn on" to obedience work until she began to herd sheep. While I didn't show the dogs, Pandora clearly enjoyed showing off in her obedi-ence class. She probably would have enjoyed showing. Nemesis and I did once consider entering a herding trial. This meant changing our training to focus more on the elements of the test. She made it clear that she did not enjoy this increased pressure and we didn't continue. Of course, I could have been mistaken about either or both of these dogs. But I did my best to focus on and respect the dog in front of me. The point is, training for competition, and competition itself, is not inherently a prob-lem from the Pragmatist perspective. In fact, these can provide a way to respect a dog's abilities and desires and create a stronger relationship.

Abusive training or mismatching dogs and activities are problems to be addressed, but training itself is not. When any particular activity is currently practiced in a way that is problematic, dog racing for example, the response should not necessarily be to ban the activity. Done well, the

Figure 9. Nemesis herding sheep. A vet suggested Prozac as a way to manage her excess energy and help with her training when she was a puppy. Herding sheep instead, she found a reason to pay attention and listen. Herding provided a physical and mental challenge that respected her breed and individual personality.

various forms of competitive activities often provide a productive outlet for many dogs' natures and desires.

When the pressure to win in competition results in manipulating the very nature of the dog being in unhealthy ways, we need to respond amelioratively (that is, make it better). Physical alterations that serve cosmetic purposes only, and are physically harmful, are practices we should end. However, it is too simplistic and, in the end, unproductive, to take an all or nothing approach. Some breeds have opened their registries to bring in new genetic lines. Others use genetic screening to try to eliminate problematic conditions. There is still resistance, though. "In 2000, the AKC instituted a requirement that any male dog bred more than seven times would have to have a $40 DNA test. The policy inspired a boycott of AKC registration by breeders in Iowa and Missouri, two states where puppy mills thrive. The Iowa Pet Breeders Association urged members to register dogs through alternative organizations. . . ." (Allan 21). This kind of response may indicate that problematic breeding practices are profitable and so protected.

There are clearly many concerns about competition, and its related practices, that deserve our attention. We need to find a way to engage in open discussion and seriously consider the possibilities of changing. This requires a kind of respectful dialogue among a full range of humans interested in a variety of relations with dogs. I will address this more in the final chapter. Here I look at some specific examples of current practices in order to more fully understand the problems and possibilities.

DOG FIGHTING

Fighting dogs can be worth up to $10,000. The fighting industry is related to organized crime and involves drugs and gambling as well. So there is a lot of money at stake.

> Purses for a single fight range anywhere from several hundred dollars to tens of thousand of dollars, and up. (A recent raid in Georgia in 2004, which resulted in 123 arrests, was an event with a $50,000 pot.) Bets also include cars, property titles, weapons, drugs, jewelry, and other valuables. For many, dogfighting is a lucrative money making enterprise, but the price that the victims of the bloody sport must pay is simply too high to be ignored. (animallaw.info)

Dog fighting is a felony in all fifty states and the District of Columbia. Despite this, it has been gaining in popularity (E. Williams 327–328). "The Humane Society of the United States estimates that there are at least 40,000 dogfighters in America, though that number seems to underestimate the epidemic of street fighting in urban areas. In 2003, the city of Chicago alone recorded and responded to 1093 animal fighting complaints." It is also connected with other crimes.

> Dog fighters are violent criminals that engage in a whole host of peripheral criminal activities. Many are heavily involved in organized crime, racketeering, drug distribution, or gangs, and they arrange and attend the fights as a forum for gambling and drug trafficking. Within the last decade, enlightened law enforcement agencies and government officials have become cognizant of the clandestine culture of dog-fighting and its nexus with other crimes and community violence. (animallaw.info)

The recent conviction (and release after serving three years) of NFL player Michael Vick has brought a great deal of attention to this "sport."

The Humane Society is actually now working with Vick in order to reach out to young African American men in urban communities. Under no illusions that Vick has necessarily had a complete change of heart, the President of the Humane Society provides a response very much in line with Pragmatism. He says, "when we turn enemies into allies—like swords into plowshares—that's the essence of our work." He goes on to say, "It's about building new and better relationships with animals, and not treating people as if they are in a static state. It's about having kids today put down their break sticks and destroy their pit bull treadmills in favor of kindness and dog behavior training" (Pacelle 3). PETA's fall 2009 cover for *Animal Times* has a picture of "Sugar" Shane Mosley, who says, "I choose to fight—dogs don't." This is a very important point. This is not what these dogs are "meant to do." It does not actually follow from their natural and developmental history. Dogs do not naturally fight to the point of death or serious injury. That is a rare event. The Humane Society discusses Sean Moore's transformation about dog fighting in the July/August 2009 issue of *All Animals.* An African-American man from Chicago who saw his first dog fight when he was twelve, he is sorry for what happened to the dogs because of what he did. He especially remembers one dog—Butch. "After seeing hundreds of animals die over nearly 15 years, Moore tired of the suffering one day in 1997 when he was talked into one last fight with Butch, whom he had owned for just two years. "Even though my dog won that fight, I still had to put him down because he was severely injured—a puncture hole in his neck, a broken vein that couldn't be healed," he says. "That was it for me" (9).

The injuries and death involved in dog fighting are highly problematic. Among the dogs who do get rescued, only some can be rehabilitated to become pets. Many have to be put down because of their training. Those who do get new homes carry physical and psychological scars. There is also the issue of the "bait animals" used to train the dogs to fight. To train the dogs, the fighters use an apparatus "that looks like a carnival horse walker with several beams jetting out from a central rotating pole. The dogs are chained to one beam and another small animal like a cat, small dog, or rabbit, is harnessed to or hung from another beam. The dogs run in circles, chasing the bait. Once the exercise sessions are over, the dogs are usually rewarded with the bait they had been pursuing" (animallaw.info). Most animals used in training do not survive the experience. "The injuries inflicted and sustained by dogs participating in dogfights are frequently severe, even fatal. Dogs used in these events often die of blood loss, shock, dehydration, exhaustion, or infection . . . . Some owners train their dogs for fights using smaller animals such as cats, rabbits, or small dogs. These 'bait' animals are often stolen pets or animals obtained through 'free to good home' advertisements" (E. Anderson 195).

To complicate matters, the focus on dog fighting as the worst competitive use of dogs often comes with race and class overtones. Many white middle class people who will condemn dog fighting will have no problem with dog racing or showing. There are, to be sure, differences in the activities. The risk of injury and death for the dog is much higher in fighting. Nonetheless, Vicki Hearn had a point when she argued that the campaigns to ban fighting dogs are often thinly veiled attempts to also remove "those people" who have "those dogs." This is not to say that no critique of dog fighting can be made. It needs to be made, but it must be sensitive to the context in which these competitions occur. Any solution will need to address the issues of money, status, and power that currently are part of this activity.

As with all competitive and use activities we also have to address the idea that dogs are meant for the activity. Are these dogs *meant* to fight? The position I've presented as a Pragmatist position requires that we pay attention to and respect the nature of the dog beings and find ways they can express their desires and purposes. This position also suggests these desires and purposes can be enabled and enhanced with training. So why not transfer this to dog fighting?

The role as watch dog and protector is one of the oldest roles dogs have played in the human world. Through selective breeding we now have dogs who have more aggressive tendencies than other dogs. Don't they need to express this? With dogs, though, fighting is usually a last resort and, unless they are unusually aggressive, abused, or trained in certain ways, they do not fight to kill. They have lots of ways of winning. Human sponsored dog fights are set up to end with death or serious injuries that will likely disable one or more of the dogs. Most dogs need to be baited into the fight—it is not an expression of a natural desire or purpose. And as the cover of PETA's cover for *Animal Times* suggest, dogs don't have a choice. Certainly, some show more proclivity than others, but within a very narrow range.

Fighting has also resulted in stereotyping certain breeds, such as pit-bulls, in ways that make it hard to place them in good homes. Many cities, for example, have started to ban pitbulls. Again, this has race and class components. It is unfair to humans and dogs alike. Instead of dealing with the problems humans have created, we blame the dogs. It is mostly the dogs themselves who suffer—often being euthanized. To avoid seizure or euthanasia some dogs are kept hidden and so are more easily subject to abuse. Bans often have the opposite of the desired effect. Rather than focus on such inflexible responses, a Pragmatist response would focus on education about the history and nature of pitbulls and on helping to make changes in the breeding, training, and socialization of these dogs. This response would also need to address the education and socialization of those human beings who fight dogs.

DOG RACING

Like dog fighting, dog racing has ties to organized crime and to the world of betting. According to *Time Magazine*, January 22, 1965, there were thirty-two tracks in seven states. Today fifteen states have dog racing, and there are now forty six tracks. Despite this historical increase, there has been a recent decline.

> The sport reached its peak in 1992, when attendance approached 3.5 million and nearly $3.5 billion was bet on 16,827 races at more than 50 tracks. Since then, revenue has dropped by nearly 50 percent and 13 tracks have closed. Other forms of legalized gambling have been the major problem, but pressure from animal rights groups has also hurt.
>
> Idaho, Maine, North Carolina, Nevada, Vermont, Virginia, and Washington all passed legislative bans on dog racing during the 1990s. Tracks in Iowa, Rhode Island, and West Virginia now subsist primarily on revenues from slot machines. The industry has been pushing for legalized slot machines, video lottery terminals, and other types of gambling at tracks in other states, but so far without success. (gra-america.org)

In addition to the competition faced from other forms of gambling, the decline is also due to the exposure of the dark side of the racing industry (E. Williams 322). Animal rights, welfare, and liberation groups have focused attention on dog racing. As a result the Greyhound Racing

Association has posted responses to many of the concerns that have been raised. For example:

> **Remember:** Nobody forces Greyhounds to run. As anyone who raises them can tell you, that's impossible. Greyhounds are as opinionated and different from each other as we are – and if there was a way to make them run like we want them to, we would have figured it out long ago!
>
> Greyhounds aren't horses with riders on their backs telling them what to do. They are not African cheetahs running after gazelles because they are starving. Greyhounds are running for the sheer love of it!
>
> In all of history, what other dog has inspired people to build whole stadiums in its honor? What other dog is so treasured that we build wide-open spaces called racetracks so they can run as safely and as fast as they want to?
>
> Greyhound racetracks are soft and flat, much like playing on the beach. There are no stones for them to step on and hurt their feet, no clumps of grass or holes for them to trip over, and they are simply chasing a toy on the end of a stick. (gra-america.org)

These responses, however, do not assure everyone. Producing winning race dogs is about more than "chasing a toy on the end of a stick." Further, we know the lives of the dogs do not always end well. For example, in Alabama in 2002, the highly publicized discovery of a mass grave of former racing dogs, some buried alive, shocked the general public.

Nonetheless, a 1992 estimate tells us that 3.5 million people bet $3.5 billion dollars on dog races. Thirty thousand dogs are bred each year on fifteen hundred breeding farms just for racing. On the breeding farms, and at the track, the dogs are kenneled and offered no toys and no attention or love. Dogs in the racing industry show signs of stress and depression. It is cheaper to breed and race dogs than it is horses, so race dogs are seen as even more expendable than race horses. Injuries and death are common place. Dogs typically race until they are three or five and then are either killed or returned to a breeding farm to be used in another way (E. Williams 322–324).

Rescue groups have been working hard to place the "retired" or unwanted dogs. This is a double edged sword, though. If the dogs can be placed there is little incentive to limit breeding or provide better care for

the dogs in the racing industry (E.Williams 326). Again the Greyhound
Racing Association has a response:

> How many Greyhounds are registered each year in the U.S.?
>
> In 2003, a total of 26,277 pups were registered with the National
> Greyhound Association (NGA). Greyhounds must be registered with
> the NGA to race at any U.S. track. About 90 percent of all pups born
> are registered, factoring in pups lost from natural causes at birth or
> soon after.
>
> How do you justify breeding so many greyhounds each year when
> you know that thousands will have to be euthanized because they
> aren't fast enough to be successful competitors?
>
> Even if every greyhound were adopted after retirement, the
> animal rights movement would still oppose greyhound racing, because
> they oppose all animal use, no matter how humane or beneficial to
> society. If your concern is animal welfare, the industry is taking
> aggressive action on several fronts. Our goal is to reach a point where
> every healthy greyhound has a home to go to after retirement. We've
> dramatically reduced the number of dogs bred, and substantially
> increased the number of dogs adopted. In 1997, for example, we expect
> to breed fewer than 30,000 dogs, and adopt out more than 18,000.
> Thousands more will go back to the farm as breeding stock after their
> careers end. If animal rights groups really want to do something in the
> area of animal welfare, they should work constructively with the
> industry to maximize adoptions and secure a good home for every
> greyhound. That's our goal. (gra-america.org)

This dilemma of promoting adoption is one we face when dealing with
almost any animal issue. Should one focus on ending or changing the
larger practice or on taking care of the individuals in front of them?
Sometimes these tasks are at odds with each other. Pragmatists must find
a way through the dilemma to work on both. In dealing with racing dogs,
we need to acknowledge that years of specialized breeding has produced
dogs who love to run. This does need to be respected. However, we can
limit the numbers bred, require breeders to find retirement homes for
dogs they breed, and raise the standard and improve the enforcement of
treatment. The reality is that doing some of these things may have the
effect of ending the dog racing industry as it will be harder to make
money. However, that would simply be a by-product of demanding
respectful treatment for the dogs involved. Just banning racing may do

little to improve how most dogs are understood and treated. As the quote above indicates, the calls by animal advocates to end all use has done little to improve the actual lives of dogs. We need to consider ways to work together on behalf of the dogs.

As it is now, the fact that dogs are considered as even more expendable than horses has real consequences for them. I discussed the fate of failing and older race horses—often ending in breakdown and slaughter. The 2002 discovery of the mass grave of racing dogs grabbed the public's attention. Two to three thousand Florida racing dogs were shot and buried in a mass grave in Alabama. The Greyhound Protection League estimates that 20,000 racing dogs are killed each year. The lives of these dogs literally become worthless to their owners. Due to some of the public concern with the treatment of the dogs, along with the competition from other forms of gambling, dog racing seems to be in a decline. The *Las Vegas Sun* reported on the March 2010 convention of the American Greyhound Track Owners Association. Attendance at the convention has gone down as half of the tracks that were operating in the 1980s and 90s have closed—four in the last year alone.

> Track owners say they are doing their best to care for their dogs. Mistreating greyhounds isn't tolerated like it was decades ago, while the vast majority of dogs are adopted out after racing for a few years. "These are athletes. They live in air-conditioned buildings and are exercised frequently. They're on strict diets. They're massaged and given whirlpool baths," Richard Winning, vice president of Derby Lane, says. Still, even standard practices such as keeping dogs in cages, muzzling them and leading them out for exercise and back into their crates don't sit well with some people. (lasvegassun.com)

While it may be obvious to many that the practices of dog racing and dog fighting are problematic, what about the practice of the dog shows?

DOG SHOWS

Breed standards are mostly developed and enforced through the showing of dogs. This often results in breeders culling dogs who do not measure up to the breed standard. For example, Aussies who have too much white do not meet the breed standard and are more prone to deafness and heart problems. Breeders often kill such puppies. Some offer them for sale as pet quality dogs who must be neutered. As I mentioned, that is actually how I got Nemesis. When I heard from a friend that a breeder she knew was going to destroy one of her puppies because it had too much white I went to see her. It turned out it was not the case that she was largely white and so at risk for deafness or heart problems. She was simply not acceptable for the show ring. The white on her right hind leg went up an inch too far and her ruff, while technically correct, had the appearance of exceeding the standard as well. For this she was going to be "put to sleep."

Most breed standards focus on appearance rather than on intelligence or physical well-being. *This* is the central problem, not the existence of breeds or of the shows themselves. Conflating the issues, as many animal rights/welfare people do, is a problem itself and results in lost opportunities to improve the lives of other animal beings.

Breed books highlight the positive traits of particular breeds, but rarely acknowledge physical defects or bad traits that have emerged in the attempt to conform to breed standards (Coren 12–13). This can also contribute to less desirable breeding practices and the breeding of individual dogs who exhibit physical and social traits that result in offspring with exaggerated physical deformities and social and psychological problems. There are rules in place to discourage the breeding of "unsuitable" individuals, but profit often triumphs over ethics. If the breeders get caught in any violations, they pay the fines as part of doing business (E. Williams 244).

In addition to the risk of poor breeding practices, some breed standards also require physically altering dogs—removing dewclaws, cropping ears, and docking tails are the most common surgeries. While these are now outlawed in the United Kingdom, in the United States the AKC defends these practices while the AVMA opposes them (E. Williams 248). As I discussed in the section on puppy mills, there is room for discussion and change if approached Pragmatically. Any such reform will work best if the people most involved with particular breeds are involved in examining breed standards and practices. This does not mean they are the only ones who should be involved in such discussions. We would need veterinarians and other dog experts as we examine the history and purposes of the standards as they have evolved over time and the pain that may be involved for the dogs. Since many of the original alterations were connected to work the dog was doing in the past, they may not apply to dogs who are no longer engaged in such work. *The irony of show dogs who only compete in the conformation ring bearing a standard developed for working dogs is worth considering.* Also, as with horses, purely conformational showing can cause problems if breeders don't pay attention to how conformation impacts the health and well-being of the individual dogs. The same goes for judges who do not look at temperament or physical health.

Those individuals who win conformation titles do more of the breeding. This narrows the gene pool and increases the risk of congenital problems. There need to be more ways for dogs who are spayed and neutered to compete. Horse shows have conformation classes for geldings and their success can "prove" the worth of their breeding so the breeders can continue to profit from the sire or dam. Why not do the same with dogs? Neutered and spayed dogs should have more classes of their own. This would encourage more people to spay and neuter purebred dogs and still allow them to participate in conformation competitions. It need not be seen as a waste to spay or neuter a purebred dog. It need not be seen as wasted potential to not breed an exemplary individual.

I think it is important to defend purebred dogs given the current focus on eliminating them (though that should not entail denying or ignoring the serious issues related to their lives and well being). Some of those concerned about animal rights say that one should *never buy* a dog but *only* rescue dogs. For them, the only *excuse* for having a purebred dog is if you rescued that dog from a shelter or rescue group, and even then one might be looked at as suspect. My house has usually included a mix. I have bought some purebred Aussies from breeders. Two of these— Tuffy and Kira—I bought as puppies. A third—Pandora—was bought when she was over four months old. As I discuss below, her breeder had rejected her first home, but was getting desperate to get her placed and wanted her in a breeding kennel (I have never bred any dogs). Nemesis, also already mentioned, was about to be killed by her breeder. Freckles, who was originally my niece's dog, was being given away in a supermarket parking lot. Tao, is the mixed breed I found on an Aussie rescue site. I think there is room for all of these options.

The Pragmatist response is complicated, but includes paying attention to the household and what the dog will be doing. Since I have horses, the dogs go to the barn and on trail rides. Certain breeds are more naturally suited to this kind of environment and work. It actually shows respect for the dog's interests to get dogs who are inclined to this work. If I had a dog who chased horses, that dog would not be able to come with me to the barn. Similarly, my dogs can go to work with me, but if I had an aggressive or shy dog that would not be possible. If I lived in a different situation, or did different work, I might have different dogs. My brother, for instance, works outside in the mountains so he has a Husky. My mother, considering the possible future move to assisted living, recently searched for a small dog. That she ended up rescuing a purebred dog was an accidental by-product of other needs, but the match is a good one. There is nothing inherently wrong with the breeding of purebred dogs, just with the excesses of some breeders and some breeding practices.

Similarly, showing itself is not necessarily a problem, but the excesses and abuse that often accompany it are. For instance, many show dogs are kenneled most of their lives. They travel and show very frequently as the humans chase points for various titles. If they become breeding dogs after their show careers, this confinement is likely to continue. My dog Pandora was originally bought by an Aussie breeder. When her breeder went to drop her off, though, she found it was a breeding facility that kept the dogs kenneled. She took her back as she did not think this kind of life was good for a dog. While it is impossible to completely control how individuals choose to keep and handle the dogs with whom they live, if breed shows placed less emphasis on the purely cosmetic aspects of appearance, it would probably result in many more show dogs getting out to play and hike and herd.

HERDING AND AGILITY

Herding is a kind of competition that exercises the natural abilities of dogs. It can also be classified as work. There are many working stock dogs in the United States today. Many working dogs also enter competitions, and many more have never lived on a farm or ranch, but enter herding trials on a regular basis. In herding trials the focus is on an ability and skill, not looks. Agility is another activity that provides a great deal of physical and mental stimulation for dogs. It can be a wonderful outlet that helps dogs adjust to the demands of living in a home with human beings. This kind of activity helps the humans and dogs establish respectful working relationships and provides the dogs with an outlet for their energy and intelligence.

For certain dogs (breeds and individuals), this kind of activity is essential to healthy lives and successful relationships with humans. For others it is simply an added benefit. For others it might be an unwanted stress. Taking a Pragmatist perspective raises concerns about those who think doing agility is the cure for all dogs with behavioral issues. It is one of many possible outlets. Humans need to work with individual dogs to figure out what that individual needs and wants. The same goes for work.

There are issues of training techniques, of course, and the abuses that may occur when competition titles are on the line.[6] Once again, this takes us to the need to see dogs not as things to be used, but as beings to be respected.

USE IN WORK

Most pets have cognitive and emotional skills they want to exercise. They are happier when they can exercise self-control and enter into respectful and trusting relationships with humans and other animal beings. If the dog has a "job" this often does much to increase the trust and respect that can be built between human and dog (Haraway, *Companion Species* 38–39).

Since the relationship between humans and dogs began, we have used dogs. They have been, and still are, used for food. In some cultures they are seen as lazy and stupid—in much the same way most people in the United States conceive of cattle, sheep, and chickens. In others, however, dogs have been recognized, perhaps paradoxically, for their intelligence and put to work in a variety of ways. Some work is dangerous for a dog. For instance, dogs have been used in war, in police work, and as guard dogs. Hunting and herding dogs risk injury, but the work itself follows more naturally from their nature and is more an aid to humans. Presently we have search and rescue dogs, a variety of aid dogs, and dogs who

6. There are related issues pertaining to the sheep used in herding trial and training. Trials have regulations about the transport and care of the sheep, as well as how many runs they can do in a day. There are none of these regulations when it comes to training. I have found people who are very respectful of the needs of the sheep and won't let you begin training until you learn to read the sheep and know when they are stressed or tired. I have also found some, though, who ignore the sheep and only focus on the dogs.

search for drugs, explosives, and other illegal items. Most recently dogs are being trained to detect diseases. Dogs have long been used in entertainment as well. The job the majority of dogs get, however, is as companion to humans. Humans gain physical and psychological benefits from these relationships. So can the dogs, though little research has been done on the welfare of working dogs (Serpell, *Domestic Dogs* 194).

Search and rescue: Using dogs in search and rescue may go back to 980 when Swiss monks used Saint Bernards, but came into more common use in World War One when the Red Cross began using dogs to find wounded soldiers. There are now more than ninety teams on call. The Federal Emergency Management Agency (FEMA) uses rescue teams and cadaver dogs (E. Anderson 111–113). These dogs require a great deal of training and careful and sensitive handling.

Law enforcement: K-P officers have been in use since the 1940s and there are now at least three thousand teams in service. Most dogs become part of the handler's family. They may sniff out drugs and other contraband, locate explosives, or bring down criminals. They are used at airports, rail and bus stations, and at the country's borders. These dogs also require a great deal of training and careful handling. They also are at greater risk for injury and death (E. Anderson 109–111).

Therapy and Aid: Interacting with a dog can "reduce blood pressure, lower cholesterol, improve recovery from cardiovascular disease, increase exercise, forestall symptoms of Alzheimer's disease, and prevent acute health crises, such as seizures and panic attacks" (E. Anderson 121). Given this, they are used as part of "pet therapy" in nursing homes and hospitals, in prisons, as seizure and guide dogs, and as aid dogs. This kind of work also takes a great deal of specialized training and handling. These dogs also work long hours and the relationships with their handlers vary widely.

War: Dogs have been used in war much as search and rescue dogs are used. However, they have also been used as weapons. Given the cost of training these dogs, they are seen as the property of the military and spend more time in war zones than their various human handlers. When the war ends, they have been left behind. They are considered a piece of equipment. Individual soldiers have been fighting this perception and working to get the dogs sent home with their handlers (E. Anderson 113–117).

Other: Dogs are used in reading programs—kids read out loud to dogs without fear of judgment or embarrassment. "The Reading Education Assistance Dogs (R.E.A.D.) program improves children's reading and communication skills by employing a powerful method: reading to a dog. But not just any dog. R.E.A.D. dogs are registered therapy animals who volunteer with their owner/handlers as a team, going to schools, libraries and many other settings as reading companions for children" (therapyanimals.org).

They are also used in psycho-therapy. Just a quick search results in scholarly articles on the effects of animal assisted therapy on elderly schizophrenic patients, on the anxiety rates of hospitalized psychiatric patients, on loneliness in the elderly in long-term care facilities, and on depression in college students.

More recently some dogs have been trained to detect various kinds of cancers. "Ordinary household dogs with only a few weeks of basic "puppy training" learned to accurately distinguish between breath samples of lung- and breast-cancer patients and healthy subjects." And they are being used in the detections of bed bugs. A New York Times article notes: "Bedbug-sniffing dogs, adorable yet stunningly accurate—entomology researchers at the University of Florida report that well-trained dogs can detect a single live bug or egg with 96 percent accuracy—are the new and furry front line in an escalating and confounding domestic war" (Green).

Given all that dogs do for us, we owe them a great deal. This debt comes due in a very real way when we face their deaths. This is one of the most important times when we must do something for them.

Death

As do all the animal beings in our lives, dogs die. Unlike those who live with horses, almost every human who lives with dogs knows they will experience the death of the dog. They also know they may be asked to make decisions about life and death. Ironically, the use of dogs in research has resulted in advances in veterinary care. Advances in human medicine are also being transferred to veterinary care. Advanced diagnostic tools such as the MRI and CAT scan are available now, but they can be expensive. The same goes for treatments for cancer, for diabetes, for bone and ligament injuries, and for many diseases. This means humans increasingly face difficult decisions about disease, treatment, and death.

Better nutrition and health care allow more and more dogs to live longer lives. As with humans, though, age brings a range of potentially debilitating conditions—arthritis, deafness, vision loss, stroke, cancer. There is now an industry for pet health insurance to help people cope with the rising costs of pet health care. As significant advances make it more likely that a dog can successfully recover from various surgical procedures, the pressure for humans to provide such care increases. Procedures, often developed to help save a potentially profitable breeding dog, are now suggested for every "pet" dog as well.

These "advances" in medicine have some consequences. One, they increase the monetary cost of entering into a relationship with a dog as these procedures become the standard of care. Some rescue groups require adopters to pay a certain amount of money on life saving procedures. This was true when I adopted Tao. I had to agree to pay up to $2,000 on reasonable treatment for an injury or illness. Though it is important to find stable and committed homes for these dogs, I'm sure this rules out many potentially good homes for many dogs. It also limits the possibility of mutually transformative relationships between humans and dogs to those humans who already have a number of advantages. Dogs and humans both lose out when money is a barrier to these relationships.

Two, these advances can promote the idea that a longer life is always the best option. We see this with humans as they undergo debilitating treatments to buy a few months of life. This is being called into question with the introduction of "right to die" bills in a number of states. In the past, euthanasia for dogs was generally seen as a respectful option. I now see more guilt and hesitation as people try one treatment after another. They try to avoid death. Many veterinarians will say they will try any treatment as long as the dog gets to be a dog. For instance, I ended Tuffy's chemo therapy when it made it her too sick to show interest in the things she enjoyed. Philosopher John Lachs recounts such a decision in his piece "Questions of Life and Death." When a dog gave birth to a litter of puppies, he and his wife immediately provided care for a weak puppy the mother had rejected. He writes: "We were interfering in the operation of a process that was cruel perhaps but overwhelmingly natural." He goes on to suggest that we must realize that "[t]hese things just happen and the honest ones among us simply admit that from the moral point of view there is a mad contingency to the world—an element of sheer chance we can neither explain nor avoid" (163). He notes that at least with dogs "it is possible to raise the question of the desirability of interventions with some measure of objectivity" (164).

Individuals will differ, but it is important to respect the quality of life and quality of death from the perspective of the being experiencing it. Euthanasia can be the most respectful act one can perform—hard as it is. I have now been there for three dogs and two horses (one my own, one a friend's). While one of the dogs took longer than expected to respond to the drug, there was nothing painful or traumatic for the dogs or horses. Although I may ask myself if I waited too long or did it too early, these are the kinds of doubts that come with such responsibility. *Uncertainty is unavoidable, but not a reason to refuse to act.*

Aging can be a difficult process, and the line between providing supportive care and prolonging suffering is not always clear, nor something on which we all agree. To handle this part of the human-dog relationship, human beings need to think through the issues, and know their basic

Figure 10. Tuffy as a puppy. Her cancer raised questions about what kind and level of treatment was appropriate and how to handle her death. It is important to make sure the focus is on the health and happiness of the animal being, not just on the humans' hopes and desires.

position on what counts as a quality life for each individual dog. Knowing what one believes and why will help one make the decisions when the time comes. Ignoring the need to face death is irresponsible, and demonstrates a lack of respect for the beings with whom we have such intimate relationships. There is increasing recognition of the significance of the bond between people and their pets and the AVMA notes that the "grieving process following a pet's death is similar to that experienced by people who have lost a family member or close friend." They recognize "the benefits of pet loss support helplines and groups for pet owners, veterinarians, veterinary technicians" and others (avma.org). Counseling services for people facing end of life decisions would be a good idea as well.

Euthanasia to end suffering is very different from putting dogs down simply because they are no longer useful (can't work or breed anymore) or are seen as a nuisance. This kind of "euthanasia" views the dog as disposable, an object to be used and then discarded. That some people engage in this kind of euthanasia, however, is no reason to object to the practice when related to health and age. Similarly, that so many otherwise healthy dogs are destroyed in shelters each year is a separate concern. Regrettable as this is, it is no reason to hide from our ultimate act of respect and love for those dogs with whom we live. This is part of being together. We owe the dogs in our lives a painless and respectful death and we owe them enriched and interesting lives.

Given the need to enrich dogs' lives, there is no inherent problem in humans using dogs in ways that go with the dogs' natures—hunting, herding, searching, sniffing (Serpell, *Company of Animals* 141). But there are problems when humans rely on a master/slave relationship to get them to work (152). There are problems with overwork. But most relationships are not this way. Human and dog relationships can have practical elements, but they are not purely relationships of use.

> Long before animals were practical they were fascinating. Long before we wanted to eat them or ride them, we wanted to paint them and touch them. . . . We and other mammals have a common social biology that allows us to approach, interact, and relax in each other's company. The chemistry helped us earn the trust and dependence of animals, but we surrendered our independence in the bargain. . . . The humans and animals with the strongest social chemistry were attracted to each other. Once they began to interact in friendly ways,

that chemistry began to flow between them, creating an interspecies
culture based on cooperation and contentment. (Olmert 220–21)

Once we accept that we have been in transactional relationships with
dogs—altered as much as we have been doing the altering—many new
possibilities and responsibilities emerge for these long standing relationships. We are interdependent. Human health is improved by the presence of dogs; our hearts are opened by dogs; our loyalty and love is called
out by dogs. There are documented studies that show the effects dogs can
have on our physical and mental well-being. There are countless stories
of people confiding their hopes and fears to a dog—you may only need to
think of your own life to find an example. And there are plenty of stories
of people risking their lives to save the life of a dog, of the poor and homeless putting the needs of a dog companion before their own, of women
and children putting the safety of a beloved dog ahead of their own. We
share risks and possibilities.

FIVE

CATS

Respecting Playfulness and Personality

Of all God's creatures, there is only one that cannot be made slave of the lash. That one is the cat. If man could be crossed with the cat it would improve the man, but it would deteriorate the cat.

—Mark Twain

Beware of people who dislike cats.

—Irish proverb

Cats have a complicated history. They have been vilified as instruments of the devil, been blamed for the plague, and been considered in many superstitious beliefs as harbingers of bad luck. Yet, they are popular pets. In the United States in particular, cats have gone from being a witch's companion to being the most numerous pet. Nevertheless, their past still haunts them. Shelters report that it is harder to find homes for black cats. Cats are often targets of choice for those who want to torture other animal beings. In general, cats are seen as expendable and so not worth any investment of time or money. One can always just get another cat. However, the popularity of cats as pets indicates that this is beginning to change, as is the reputation of cat owners. While the "crazy cat lady" stereotype still exists and gains support from a few highly publicized cases of animal hoarding, it is not the norm. Further, many people are learning how to enrich the lives of the cats with whom they live. Learning about the nature of cat beings, human beings are starting to build indoor and outdoor habitats that respect a cat's desire to use vertical space, chase prey, and socialize. Long thought to be aloof or haughty, cats are now known to be very sociable and loving if humans approach them as such. Recent recognition of the social nature of cats complicates our understanding of the history of their domestication as well.

Keeping cats is not the same as domesticating them. "Domestication is a gradual and dynamic process, not a sudden event" (Serpell, "Domestication and History" 181). It often first includes capturing and keeping animals. It then moves to intentionally breeding them. For animal beings to be domesticated, humans need to control breeding. By this definition cats have only been domesticated about 150 years. Serpell notes that, "It might be better to see cats as drifting in and out of domestication" (181).

With that said, we have evidence of people living with cats as early as nine thousand years ago (Clutton-Brock, *Cats* 26), and there may be evidence for earlier dates. A recent find includes a burial site in Cyprus, dated at 7500 BC, with a cat skeleton. There is no evidence of wild cats in that area, so the hypothesis is that this was an imported domesticated cat (Bulliet 229). Most scientists assume domesticated cats probably spread by ship. They would have been as welcome on a ship as they were in the granaries. This relationship between human beings and cat beings was likely one of the first consciously chosen symbiotic cross-species relationships as cats helped humans with the control of creatures like mice and rats (Clutton-Brock, *Cats* 33, 90). Cats would have been attracted to human settlements as their prey were attracted to the growing stores of grain and refuse. Humans would have welcomed and even rewarded cats for their "pest" control services. Cats, habituated to human presence, would settle and reproduce in close proximity to humans. Though this did not yet involve domestication, it probably did allow humans to handle and tame young kittens who then could be "kept" and bred.

Some will argue that cats technically are still not domesticated. Cats are seen as solitary, nocturnal hunters—not prime candidates for domestication. Cats are, however, territorial and this can keep them close to humans who feed them. However, except for a few specialty breeds, cats' breeding is not greatly controlled by humans and there is little difference between "domestic" and wild cats (Liberg 133–134). They all share the same basic body plan, sensory apparatus, and hunting life. Some question whether they are sufficiently modified to be considered domesticated.

Others claim that by the second millennium BC cats were fully domesticated in Egypt (Clutton-Brock, *Cats* 33). It is thought this domestication began about 4,000 years ago (MacDonald 96). By the first millennium they are found in Europe and Asia. By 500 BC we begin to find many depictions of cats in art, suggesting that they were a common presence in the lives of humans. We know they were valued and held in high regard. Evidence of mummified cats indicates the high regard with which they were viewed in such cultures. It also appears they had work to do in the next life as there is evidence that some were bred specifically to be mummified. By 945 we have documentation that cats were worth more money than pigs, but less than greyhounds. They were primarily valued as hunters (Clutton-Brock, *Cats* 39–43).

Until recently it was thought that domesticated cats came from the European (*F. s. lybica*) and African (*F. s. cafra*) cat (Liberg 135). Recent genetic evidence, however, shows us that all domesticated cats are descended from cats first domesticated in the Middle East. In 2000, researchers Carlos A. Driscoll, Juliet Clutton-Brock, and Stephen O'Brien presented their findings in *Scientific American*. Based on DNA samples, they concluded that every domesticated cat in the world originates from one of five subspecies of wildcat found in the Middle East (*F. s. lybica*). The story, according to this article, goes as follows: 9,500 to 10,500 years ago humans began storing grain and attracting the mice cats hunt; 9,500 years ago there was a human cat double burial in Cyprus that suggests a special relationship between the two species; 3,700 years ago there were numerous artistic renderings of cats in Egypt; 2,900 years ago cat worship was strong in Egypt; 2,000 years ago cat remains and artistic renderings were present throughout Europe; 650 to 230 years ago we find descriptions of the Siamese breed in Thailand; by the 1800s most of the modern breeds developed in the British Isles were present; in 1871 the first cat show took place in London; and in 2006 the first hypoallergenic cat was created (Driscoll 72).

Today, while some cats clearly remain tied to humans, others seem to remain outside the realm of domestication. For example, the difference in colors of cats seems to depend on where they live. The majority are tabbies (Liberg 135–136). Some argue that temperament is often connected to coat color (Clutton-Brock, *Cats* 25). This implies that breed differences go deeper than the coat and demonstrates enough control of breeding for most to consider them to be domesticated. There are, however, many populations of feral cats. These are not technically wild cats, but domesticated cats who have reverted to a "wild" state. The breeding of these cats is not under any kind of recognized human control, so they

Figure 11. Cat history.

are no longer considered domesticated. Thirty-six to forty-one percent of all cats are considered feral. This contributes to cats' reputation as independent and "wild." Despite the disagreements about what counts as domestication and whether or not cats are domesticated, human and cat beings have clearly been in deeply transformative relationships for quite some time.

In spite of their complicated and uncertain history, cats have over-taken dogs as the most numerous companion animal being in the United States. Nonetheless, 17.4 percent of people say they dislike cats, while only 2.6 percent say they dislike dogs (Serpell, "Domestication and History" 190–191). This seems to be at least in part due to their perceived aloof and independent nature. While cats' reputation as independent and solitary is somewhat justified, they do share space. They know their family hunt-ing territory and will share space with humans. To have relationships that go beyond sharing space, kittens need early human handling (Clutton-Brock, *Cats* 16, 21). Kittens need to learn a lot from their mothers and this dependency can help them bond with humans who are present in their lives and help with their socialization and learning (Bateson, "Behavioural Development" 15). Evidence of their social nature starts with this fact.

As with all mammals, there is an interplay of genes and environment that affects the behavior and personality of individual cats (Bateson 19 and Mendl 55). While cats are usually considered solitary, they are very social when young and learn in a social setting. They learn by watching their mothers hunt, and experiments show they can learn to press a lever simply from watching their mother (Bateson 15). They have a relatively long dependency as they have a great deal to learn. This results in strong bonds. Some mothers and daughters live together and raise their litters together (Deag 25, 37). In a cat's development there are periods of plastic-ity, but also periods of stability of character (Mendl 57). Humans can take advantage of the period of plasticity to bond with kittens. Time spent handling them, feeding them, and vocalizing and playing with them are all very important to forming a relationship (Turner, "Human-Cat" 197). This is why building relationships with feral cats is very hard, but strong bonds can be more easily formed with the offspring of feral cats than with feral cats themselves.

Cats are often "kept" as an outdoor animal. People put out food and the cats come and go as they please. Some of these cats are truly feral cats; others are semi-socialized. With time and attention some are fully social-ized. For instance, we always had barn cats. They had a clear job to do—hunt mice and rats. Because my mother is allergic to cats she did not allow them in the house—except once. When I was about six, I was allowed to adopt a kitten of a feral cat living near my grandparent's house. She was a "wild" being. We needed to bond so it would not work to put her out with the barn cats right away. So, an exception was made and

I kept her in my room. I carried her everywhere (getting a few scratches for my trouble) and fed her in my lap. After a few months my mother insisted that she had to be put out with the other cats. We always remained very close, though she was not trusting of most people. She went on to have kittens of her own, all of whom were fully socialized and friendly with humans. She was always an excellent mother and hunter. When we made that move to the city that I mentioned before, the cats were left on the ranch. However, for some reason (never explained to me), that "wild" cat was given away to one of my father's co-workers. I will never forget the look of terror on her face as she was driven away. Since I knew she was happy living free, and did not easily bond with new people, I did everything I could to stop this from happening. But my arguments did not win the day. I felt that I had betrayed her.

While one cat was being treated as a thing that could simply be moved around at will, another cat benefited from this move. Sieglinda, who had never liked ranch life, did come with us. She was a big, long-haired, black cat who had originally been an indoor-only cat. She came to the ranch when her people moved and couldn't take her. She had very long hair and so, due to my mother's allergies, at our house she had to stay outside. On the ranch she did not socialize with the other cats. She hung out on the patio by herself. She had the privilege of being fed canned food—something not done for any other cat as they were expected to hunt. She was not happy with the change in her circumstances and would hiss and scratch anyone who came near her, even if that person was feeding her. Somehow it became my job to deal with her. Gradually we built a relationship. When we moved to the city she still had to stay outside, but my parents let me "spoil" her. She lived in the covered and partially fenced in area between the house and the garage—a semi-indoor environment. Feeling bad about the fact that I had to postpone getting my own dog, my parents let me buy her a cat house, special food, and lots of toys. Since my contact with other animal beings had been greatly diminished with this move, Sieglinda and I spent lots of time hanging out and playing. She no longer scratched or hissed at me, but she still lashed out at most other people. So we were left on our own to develop a special relationship. She seemed happy with her new circumstances, and she also became a great hunter of tree rats. These examples show that one can build relations with cats (even an older cat) with time, patience, and respect. In both cases time spent playing with the cats was very important.

More recently I lived with a friend who has a cat—Bunny. (Bunny has now been joined by Smokey.) Bunny was found out in the road. One night she hopped into my friend's car. Her history is unknown, but she does not act like a feral cat. At first she was "kept" primarily as an outdoor cat. This was necessitated by the landlord not wanting her in the house.[1] After an aggressive dog came to the neighborhood she disappeared. Fearing the worst, my friend conducted an intensive search that turned up nothing. Four months later, however, she was spotted near the house. She seemed happy to find her person and was clearly back at home. By this time the rental agreement had been changed to allow for animals and my three dogs were temporarily staying in the house. She seemed unimpressed by their presence and quickly became an indoor cat.

Bunny is an amazing cat who has proved herself quite capable of standing up to my dogs, including Tao who mostly sees her as a white squirrel. She won him over. And she and Maeve became good friends and playmates. They played chase, hide and seek, and tug of war. They also found time for snuggling. She has now taught Kira to respectfully play with a cat as well. However, this cat is now an indoor cat (something required by most shelters if one goes there to adopt a cat). What does this mean for her and the need to respect her individual personality and needs? She must be given outlets for instinctual activities as well as for her own individual desires. In this case it means a fair amount of play time and a good window. The addition of Smokey has given her more social contact. They play a lot, even though they have very different personalities. Smokey regularly brings toys to her human and asks to play. Bunny seeks out belly rubs. Both of these cats also regularly travel with their human rather than being left home alone. Bunny especially likes to look out the window of the car. Good relationships require humans to find ways to respect the preferences of various cats and to stimulate their intelligence.

Unfortunately many humans don't think of cats as being intelligent, or as having preferences or desires. Many "dog people" will deny that cats need or want much from us. For example, some point to the supposed solitary nature of cats to say, "[F]eeling compassion and committing

---

1. Many issues related to animal care and abandonment might be alleviated if more animal beings were allowed in rental housing.

Figure 12. Maeve and Bunny sleeping together. Maeve met Bunny when she was still a young dog and they developed a strong interspecies bond pretty much immediately. They played chase and wrestled, learning how to respect each others' different sizes through experience. Interspecies relations can be strong and need to be respected.

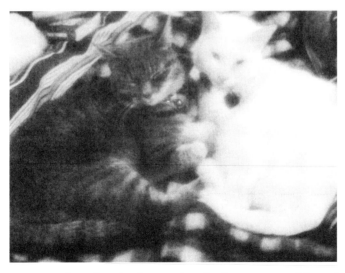

Figure 13. Bunny and Smokey sleeping together. Smokey was rescued from the streets and came to live with Bunny. At first, Bunny wasn't sure she wanted to share her home with another cat, but Smokey eventually won her over and now Bunny spends much of her time grooming Smokey and playing and sleeping with her. The company of other animal beings can be an important way to enrich the lives of pets—cats included.

compassionate acts make sense from an evolutionary point of view. Solitary animals—cats, for example—do not need to show compassion to survive, and examples of compassion among the big cats are scarce. On the other hand, humans and dogs are social animals, and all social animals must learn to get on with one another to survive" (Masson 95–96). While dogs are often thought to experience pity or sorrow, many humans deny that such a capacity exists in cats. This same logic argues that, "Dogs belong to a social species and therefore form friendships, while cats belong to a solitary species and do not" (Masson 136). People appeal to the fact that cats can revert to a feral state more easily than other domesticated animals as evidence that while they might live in proximity to humans they retain their independence. For example, Jeffrey Masson says, "It can scarcely be denied that cats only tolerate us, whereas dogs adore us" (139–140). This statement supports the idea that cats are often seen as not really domesticated since they remain more independent than most dogs. It is assumed that cats are not social and that therefore we do not understand each other the way humans and dogs do (Masson 7). At best the relationship is seen as interactive and not transactive.

Again such views cause problems for cats who are a part of human communities. For instance, cats are connected to pagan religions. From the 1300s to the 1500s, this connection endangered cats as they were considered to be symbols for Satan, were believed to be connected with witches, and were blamed for deaths (probably due to allergic reactions). By 1400 they were almost extinct in Europe (E. Anderson 8). In the eighteenth century cats were burned on bonfires during lent (Clutton-Brock 45–52). As Christianity turned against the female it also turned against women's companion cats. Black cats, especially, were tortured and killed (Serpell, "Domestication and History" 187–89). Today, bias still exists. In a letter from a reader of the *All Animals* newsletter, the Humane Society of the United States is taken to task for focusing so much more attention on dogs than on cats. Thanking them for an article on feral cats, she goes on to say, "It's extremely troubling to me that people in general do not value cats as much as they do dogs. Human neglect is to blame." Showcasing dogs is one of the factors that contributes to the devaluing of cats. Unfortunately, though, she doesn't stop there and continues playing into a divisive relationship by saying "I also think that those who own dogs want to possess. I want just company, so I have cats. I love freedom, so I have cats. I love elegance and cleanness, so I have cats" (*All Animals*, Summer 2008, 3). This kind of attitude—that cats and their people are better than dogs and their people—also contributes to the negative view many have of cats. There is no need to separate humans into "cat people" and "dog people." In fact, this simply supports the dualistic thinking that resulted in the human/animal separation in the first place. Instead, we need to learn to appreciate a variety of beings and a plurality of relationships.

It is the case that many people are drawn to cats by their playfulness, curiosity, and cleanliness (their willingness to use a litter box). Cat beings also provide emotional support for human beings (Turner 199–201). As with all domesticated animals, it seems that spending time with cats releases oxytocin in human and cat alike. This is one way we build a bond. Secondarily, we reap the health benefits. Allergies aside, petting a cat contributes to good heart health, reduction of stress, and peace of mind. "Compared to non-cat owners, those who lived with cats for at least one year showed significant cardiac and blood sugar-level improvements" (Olmert 161). Living with cats also has benefits for the social life of humans. The stereotype of reclusive cat owners turns out not to be the norm. People who live with cats generally have richer social lives with other humans than people who do not live with any other animal beings. The data from a study on heart disease found that "pets do not just substitute for human relationships; they complement and add to them, giving a special and unique dimension to human life" (Beck and Katcher 6).

So, despite persecution, cats have continued to grow in popularity. This popularity, however, does not protect them from all harm. I turn now to consider the current situatedness of cats living with humans and some potential ways to improve (ameliorate) that situatedness by getting to know and learning to respect cat beings for who they are.

Abuse and Neglect

Cats are the most commonly abused and abandoned of those animal beings considered pets. This is one reason that people who breed cats can be very particular about who gets their cats. Buying a cat may entail a home visit and the checking of references. Breeders want cats to have a stable home. One study found the 25 percent of cats stay a year or less in a home. Only a third of cats stay in one home for their entire life (Rochlitz 213). This lack of stability contributes to the death of many cats.

"In the 1970s, approximately 20 per cent of the total American cat population was euthanised in shelters. This dropped to 10 per cent in the 1980s and 5 per cent (5 million) in the 1990s. Nevertheless, euthanasia in shelters remains the leading cause of death of cats in the United States." A number of studies estimate that of the cats turned into shelters in the United States, 2.2 percent are reclaimed (this may be because some of the cats are feral), 23.4 percent are rehomed, 71.2 percent are killed. Most of those who are killed are healthy, adoptable cats (Rochlitz 210–211).

Part of the problem is a population problem. While one study found that 87 percent of female cats were spayed, this usually happened after they had had at least one litter of kittens. Cat owners are more likely than dog owners to cite cost as a reason to not spay or neuter. This may be because "Cat-owning households tend to have more cats than dog-owning households have dogs. . . ." It may also be connected to the perceived value of the animal. Many cats are free, and most are seen as having less value than a dog. It may also be connected to the idea that humans don't really own cats, and cats may not hang around very long anyway. Why invest financially or emotionally? However, there are low cost and free spaying and neutering services. We could also encourage non-surgical birth control in feral cat populations (Rochlitz 212). The AVMA recognized the problem of abandoned and feral cats as a "national tragedy of epidemic proportions" (avma.org).

To lower the death rate of cats we need to reduce the abandonment of cats. This requires educating people on "feline behavior, as well as the responsibilities of pet ownership." This would mean providing accurate information on allergies and health concerns, so that people don't get an animal being with whom they cannot live. This may also mean encouraging doctors to consider options besides getting rid of a cat. "In a survey of the American Academy of Allergists, over 40 per cent recommended the removal of animals in the presence of asthma and rhinitis, regardless of the cause, and even in the absence of pet allergy, 34 per cent of allergists still recommended the removal of pets" (Rochlitz 212–213).

It also means encouraging cat owners to provide veterinary care for their cats and to learn about feline behavior. Such knowledge could help humans resolve "problematic" cat behaviors. A study of cat owners who adopted cats from a shelter "found that those who kept their pets had fewer unreasonable expectations for pets' roles in their lives than those who returned their pets to shelters" (Rochlitz 213). We need to educate human beings about what to expect and how best to house, socialize, and interact with various cat beings.

Having evolved as a largely solitary hunter, the domestic cat does "not have as wide a behavioral repertoire for visual communication as, for example, the highly social, group-living dog, so assessment of their welfare may initially seem more difficult. . . . Cats are more likely to respond to poor conditions by becoming inactive and by inhibiting normal behaviors such as self-maintenance (feeding, grooming and elimination), exploration or play, than by actively showing abnormal behavior" (214). And, many behaviors that are seen by people as problematic are quite normal. Nighttime activity, for example, may disturb the sleep of humans but is normal for the cat. Attention to providing space for the cat can help with this as can vigorous play before bedtime. Scratching furniture and climbing curtains can be addressed by providing scratching posts and climbing structures. Marking territory is another common example of "misbehavior." If training and improving the cat's environment don't help with this, there may be a physical cause that needs to be addressed. Pragmatism calls on us to understand cat beings for who they are and work out ways to respect the natural inclinations and developmental stages of the cats with whom we live. There will be variation (*pluralism*) and we will get things wrong from time to time (*fallibilism*), but much can be gained from *experimenting* with different ways of living together.

For instance, welfare studies of cats tell us some things about what is needed to successfully and happily cohabit with cat beings. Bad examples of cohabitation are often very clear. Some cases of neglect are obvious. The public cases of cat hoarding show us neglected cats who are underfed, living in filth, infested with fleas, and covered in sores. Again, these are horrible instances of abuse and neglect, but less obvious are the conditions many more cats face in good and loving homes. Even well-intentioned humans can fail to fully respect the needs and desires of the cat beings with whom they live.

Cat welfare studies tell us that in order to respect the *natural* and *developmental* history of cats, good homes should respect the following needs: the need for space between the places cats rest, eat, and eliminate; the need for space to play and hide; and the need to have enough space for them to have time alone, especially if they live with other cats. Cats need to be able to climb as well as hide. This provides them secure places from which they can watch and assess their surroundings. No more than two cats should share a litter tray and it should be kept clean. Cats need comfortable bedding. They need surfaces to scratch and toys with which to play. Providing containers of grass can help with the elimination of fur balls. Food forages also provide important stimulation, so putting food in containers that make the cat work to extract the food can also be a good idea. Being exposed to visual, auditory, and olfactory stimulations is key, as is contact with humans. This contact needs to go beyond feeding and cleaning. Time needs to be set aside for petting and playing, and for paying attention to the individual preferences of various cats. While time outside can provide opportunities for exploration and predatory behavior, it also exposes cats to an increased risk for disease and injury. With some attention, cats can lead enriched lives indoors (Rochlitz 215–220).

Not all agree on whether cats should be allowed outside. But the reality is that outdoor cats, on average, live fewer than three years. The lifespan of indoor cats averages from fifteen to eighteen years (E. Anderson 147). One can build or buy outdoor enclosures that allow cats to safely explore an outdoor environment (though this does increase exposure to disease). Free roaming cats who go outdoors suffer and die from poisoning, traps, predation, disease, cars, and human abuse. They are also sometimes caught and used as bait animals to train dogs to fight (E. Anderson 194–195). Some are also concerned that outdoor cats overhunt various bird populations. It is estimated that roaming cats kill hundreds of millions birds, small mammals, reptiles, and amphibians each year (fws.gov/birds). This puts quite a stress on various ecosystems. Even well fed cats can put a great deal of pressure on local wildlife populations.

There is also the related, controversial, practice of declawing. To save birds some think cats should be declawed. Cats who are allowed outdoors, however, should not be declawed as their claws are a primary means of defense. Further, declawing itself is a controversial practice.

> Contrary to most people's understanding, declawing consists of amputating not just the claws, but the whole phalanx (up to the joint), including bones, ligaments, and tendons! To remove the claw, the bone, nerve, joint capsule, collateral ligaments, and the extensor and

flexor tendons must all be amputated. Thus declawing is not a "simple," single surgery but **10 separate**, painful amputations of the third phalanx up to the last joint of each toe. A graphic comparison in human terms would be the cutting off of a person's finger at the last joint of each finger. (declawing.com)

Declawing is not a universal practice. Some countries that ban declawing, or limit it to only medical emergencies, are: England, Scotland, Wales, Northern Ireland, Germany, Austria, Switzerland, Norway, Sweden, Netherlands, Denmark, Finland, Brazil, Australia, and New Zealand. In the United States, the AVMA only states that it should be a last resort, and suggests education of owners about the scratching behavior of cats. While declawing is banned in many countries, one survey found that 45 percent of cats in the United States are declawed. This may be related to there being more indoor-only cats in the United States, but this fact raises a whole host of issues. In addition to pain and physical vulnerability, declawing causes physical problems. After declawing, cats have difficulty keeping their muscular and skeletal systems strong and properly aligned. Even the Cat Fancier's Association, which defends classifying cats as property,

> perceives the declawing of cats (onychectomy) and the severing of digital tendons (tendonectomy) to be elective surgical procedures that are without benefit to the cat. Because of the discomfort associated with any surgery and potential future behavioral or physical effects, CFA disapproves of routine declawing or tendonectomy surgery in lieu of alternative solutions to prevent household damage. In certain situations, including high risk of injury or disease transmission to owners with bleeding disorders or compromised immune systems, declawing may be justified in order to maintain the cat-human bond. (cfa.org)

In most cases, increased socialization or creative responses to "destructive" behavior can resolve the conflict without resorting to surgery. We have more to consider than human convenience when it comes to living with cat beings. While some instances of harm to cats may be due to ignorance or a prioritizing of human convenience, many other instances are intentional.

Clear cases of cruelty are always a concern. These can range from neglect to outright abuse. Cats are dropped from buildings, lit on fire, intentionally run over, shot, kicked, thrown, and put in dryers. But equally of concern are the ways in which even well-meaning people may harm or frustrate the cats with whom they live. Cats are often kicked or thrown in response to them scratching a favorite piece of furniture or a person. They are put outside because they talk too much or wake up the humans during the night. They may also lose household privileges if stress or overcrowding cause them to stop using their litter box. Most of these "problems" result from human misunderstanding and frustration with aspects of cats' natural and developmental nature and/or misunderstanding personalities.

To address all of this we need to help people understand the cats with whom they live. The Humane Society provides examples of this in *All Animals* with articles in May/June 2009 ("The Cat's Meow"), September/October 2009 ("Life With My Cats"), and September/October 2010 ("The Dawn Patrol"). In "The Cat's Meow," Antoniades provides information describing the ways cats communicate and the range of moods one might experience with cats. She points out that "since domestic cats have spent thousands of years cultivating the meow to better communicate with their human friends, it's only fair that we listen" (39). In "The Dawn Patrol," Arna Cohen explains why cats are up at night and offers advice for mitigating the disturbance to human sleep patterns.

> Despite thousands of years of domestication, house cats don't operate on people time. Like their wild relatives, they're crepuscular: They sleep and play around the clock but are most active at dusk and dawn, when birds and small mammals—their natural prey—are most active. The typical pattern is hunt, eat, groom, sleep. Repeat, repeat, repeat. (38)

Humans disrupt this cycle with our attempts to get cats to follow our schedules. Being fed, the average house cat has little to do and becomes dependent on the humans in the home for entertainment. Providing enrichment in the form of toys, puzzles, and play time can help.[2] Playing right before bedtime can be especially helpful, along with a small meal. These solutions respect the *natural* and *developmental* history of cats, as Pragmatism suggests.

In "Life With My Cats" Melendez tells of the potentially "destructive" behavior cats can engage in, but explains how it looks from the

---

2. That less of this is done for cats than for dogs can easily be seen by perusing the aisles of a pet store or the pages of a pet supply catalog. There are far fewer cat toys.

cat's perspective. She then offers advice on how to engage cats so they don't do what one doesn't want them to do. Six to eight million pets end up in shelters each year—often because people don't like how they behave. The article suggests that "you have to think like a dog or cat. Thinking like a human will get you nowhere" (37). They point out that "all families and cats are different," but education is key to being able to adapt to what you face. This fits well with Pragmatism's commitment to *pluralism* and *experimentation.*

Ironically, much of what we have learned about cats' physical, social, and emotional needs comes from research studies done with cats. Some of these studies are non-invasive, but far from all. While we have learned a great deal from research, there are serious questions about using cats in such research in the first place.

Use in Research and Biomedical Contexts

Cats are used in research on conditions and diseases that affect cats. The Morris Animal Foundation solicits funds to support this kind of research. They point out that there is less money donated for research on cat health than for research on dogs. Nowhere on their web site, though, do they point out the tensions involved in using cats this way. Not all of this research is just to promote the health of cats. Some research focuses on developing allergen free cats. Some (including the AVMA and ASPCA) believe genetically modified cats might make "better" pets for humans.

As they do dogs and horses, vet schools and some animal hospitals keep some cats as blood donors. But that is far from the most common use. Cats are also commonly used in biology classes for students to learn dissection techniques and anatomy. For use in dissections, one can order cats that come in various sizes. Some are pregnant; some are not. It is easy to buy preserved cats for dissection; fifty to one hundred dollars will procure you a preserved skinned cat. Some use cats who have been euthanized at shelters and they justify their use of cats in a number of ways. Their anatomy is similar enough to humans to be useful, their organs are large enough for students to see, and "cats are plentiful and inexpensive enough so that each team of two students has the personal hands-on experience of the dissection" (biology.clc.uc.edu). One can also buy live cats for research. For example, live cats for research can be found for around $225 from Cedar River Laboratories (Greek 92).

Most cats used in research are used in research that is focused on human health. As before, we must raise the question about whether the animal model of research makes good sense for human health. Past research using cats to try to treat cholera could not even induce cholera in cats. In another case, cats did not reproduce the birth defects human subjects encountered with the use of thalidomide. As mentioned before, the antibiotic chloramphenical kills cats (and horses and humans), though dogs do well on it, and the antibiotic cleocin works well in cats but kills horses. Cats require double the dose of corticosteroids that dogs need, and cats suffer from diabetes if corticosteroids are overused while dogs suffer liver damage—neither really mirrors the effects in humans. Penicillin was delayed because the cat it was tested on died. Since aspirin causes blood abnormalities in cats, it probably would not have been approved if it had had to go through such animal testing. Just as do studies on dogs and horses, cat studies that attempt to induce atherosclerosis have not been successful. Stroke research has often failed to recognize circulatory differences among various animal beings. Cats can become hypertensive, but this generally results in eye problems, not strokes (Greek, 34, 45, 62–64, 73, 158–161, 170).

Today over 20,000 cats are used in research each year in the United States. This number is down from 74,259 reported in 1974 (ori.dhhs.gov). While strays are used in research, cats bred for this purpose are preferred. A government site notes:

> Most cats used in research are purpose bred, obtained from USDA licensed vendors; thus they are genetically selected for docility and even temperament. Also, of prime importance, the cats are from colonies specifically pathogen free for illnesses cats are susceptible to. This both increases the health status of the animals and cuts down on research variability. Feral cats are not useful behaviorally as research subjects; since they are not domesticated they will be very difficult to handle and highly stressed, again affecting research. Cats that have previously been pets may react adversely to a laboratory environment. (ori.dhhs.gov)

Note that it is the human-cat relationship that, ironically, makes domesticated cats "good subjects" for such research. But these same relationships can make them respond "adversely to the laboratory environment."

Despite being popular pets, though, there is less public protest about using cats in research than there is about using dogs, so the decline in their use is attributed to the difficulty cats present in handling when compared to animals like hamsters and gerbils. The claws of cats are referred to as their "weapons" in publications teaching proper cat handling in the lab. Nonetheless, cats are still used in neurological research: spinal cord injury, vision and hearing studies, and sleep research. We know a great deal about cat's neurological systems and so they are seen as important to such work. For spinal cord injury studies, cats have to be given the relevant injury; for vision studies kittens will often have one eye stitched closed; for sleep studies they are often given morphine. They are also used in research on Parkinson's disease, cancer, and genetic disorders. Colonies of cats are specifically bred with particular genetic disorders for research purposes. They have also been used in HIV/AIDS research, though the feline leukemia and feline immunodeficiency virus (FIV) differ from any human disease. Research indicates that FIV predates the domestication of cats and that it does not provide a good model for HIV.

Cats are relatively easy to use in research due in part to supply. Online materials for courses on handling lab animals point out that cats from companies that breed for labs are better in terms of health and known health history, but are not well socialized and therefore are harder to handle. They then note that cats taken from shelters or from ads in the newspaper have the disadvantage of having varied and unknown health histories, but they are well socialized and so easier to handle. In 2009 the American Veterinary Medical Association and the American Physiology Society both endorsed the increased use of random source dogs and cats. Without the use of such animals, they say, there will not be enough lab animals. Random source animals come from shelters and Class B dealers who collect the animals from ads in papers and on the internet. There is a similar statement from the American Society of Animal Laboratory Practitioners (aslap.org). So, someone may think their kittens are going to a loving home when in fact they are headed for a life in a lab. Ironically, domestication and socialization make them "better" lab animals, but the conditions in the labs rarely respect the specific needs that come with domestication and socialization.

Cats kept in labs have shown a need for positive social interactions with those who care for them, as well as for toys. They also need more space than most labs allow (Rochlitz 218–219). All that has been learned from welfare studies of cats (described in section on Abuse and Neglect) is generally ignored when it comes to housing cats in labs. The labs themselves acknowledge this in their guidelines for care.

The Animal Welfare Institute's Comfortable Quarters for Cats in Research Institutions presents an overview of laboratory cat husbandry. Housing for cats varies from single to group housing, usually constructed of stainless steel caging with food and water bowls usually attached to the cage. Cats need to be supplied with a litter box; they prefer some form of clay substrate to dig in and cover their urine and feces; this is normal behavior. The box should be placed away from the food and water dishes to avoid contamination. Cats prefer some sort of raised area for perching and sleeping, away from the food and litter box. Husbandry requirements will necessarily balance sanitation needs with cats' instinctual need for soft bedding of some sort, with areas for privacy. . . . Cats will form social hierarchies and are easily stressed with any changes, thus, moving cats in and out of groups is to be avoided and the housing goal should be one of stability. . . . Cats are idiosyncratic individuals who have a high curiosity index; thus enrichment should be part of their normal husbandry. . . . They can develop individual preferences and need variety in the diet. . . . They should be housed away from noisy species such as dogs, pigs or non-human primates. Many report that playing soft radio music lessens their sensitivity to noise and keeps them calmer for procedures. (ori.dhhs.gov)

The acknowledgement of the individual preferences and need for an enriched and social environment, while commendable, undercuts the idea that cats are good "subjects" for this kind of research.

These very acknowledgements, as with dogs, call into question the value of the research results that come from less than ideal housing and social situations for the cats. The social and psychological stress these cats experience may compromise their physical health. And, as with other animal beings, there are serious questions about using cats in research from which they do not stand to benefit. Using cats to study the effects of nicotine seems to reduce the cat to a tool in a way that is hard to justify (though there might be need to research the effects of secondhand smoke on cats). Humans don't *need* to ingest nicotine. I did not *need* to dissect a pregnant cat in high school science class. While there are honest disagreements about what constitutes human need, and human need *might* be used to justify some research with cats (and other animal and human beings), it clearly does not justify research that is related to cosmetic products or self-inflicted problems that result from things like smoking or drinking. These do not reflect human *needs*.

Nor does entertainment. But does use in entertainment provide something for cats?

Use in Entertainment

As with other animal beings, cats are used in movies and television. Rather than trying to get the cat to do something in particular there is usually more filming of what the cat is naturally doing. Their use seems to rely less on training than is the case with horses and dogs. Instead, they are lured by food and toys to try to induce the desired action. There are some cat trainers, though, who specialize in supplying cats for such purposes. They tend to promote the use of behaviorist models of modifying behavior, such as clicker training. Clicker training involves providing an immediate sign (the click) and a reward when the animal being produces the desired behavior. This kind of training is used to augment the communication between humans and many other beings—cats, dogs, and horses included. It does require some skill on the part of the human, but is an intriguing option.

Since many think it is difficult or impossible to "train" cats, they have not been subjected to the same array of techniques that horses and dogs face. Punishment does nothing to motivate a cat, for example. This may work in their favor as fewer humans even try to use cats, though it does have the negative effect of encouraging humans to see them as stupid, uncooperative, or defiant. These are traits that seem to anger some humans and to increase the rate of abuse cats experience. At present, however, the perception that cats are not trainable seems to be shifting slightly. This is good, but to rely on only behaviorist models like clicker training may underestimate what cats and humans can do together.

As we will see in the section on competition, there is an emerging interest in cat agility. Cats are not trained for agility in the way dogs are. They are lured through the course with food or toys. However, the activity increases the human cat interaction and provides mental and physical stimulation for the cat. A web site focused on helping with cat agility training says,

> Cats are very intelligent, and easily trainable! Practice for agility can be done around the house (over the bed, chair to chair, under the table, etc.) How young should you start cat agility? Taty Kalani

started Stardust at five weeks at home as you can see in this video (2.3Mb). — **Play with your cat every day!** Train with patience, respect and affection, because domestic cats are colony animals (not pack animals, like dogs are), and cats have a more cooperative nature than is customarily recognized. Take time to decode their communication and form a connection with your cat — you will both enjoy it. See pictures of Training at Home. — **Focusing on the beauty from within.** In Pictures of cats in action on the agility course, you can see how much they enoy it. — **Cat agility is fun for you AND your cat! (catagility.com)**

Cats' interest in and ability for such things has long been known to the few people who do run entertainment shows with cats. These exhibitions usually feature cats walking tight ropes, jumping through hoops, and leaping down from high perches. The "big cats" have been used in circus acts since they began so it is not a stretch to think that domesticated cats could participate as well. In "Cat Training Tips: Consider the Personality" the author tells us,

> Cat training can be difficult because each cat has a unique personality that they want respected, pretty much like us people. Unlike dogs who just want to please and are happy to follow orders when they understand them and see clear rewards, cats will not be so easily persuaded into doing something. There are things they like and things they don't like. Forcing them to do what they do not like does not work, ever.

Nonetheless, cats can participate in training. To illustrate the point the author points to an example of an act that uses domestic cats.

> Yury Kuklachev, one of the world's best cat trainers and the creator of the only cat theater in the world, Moscow Cats Theater, says that he never actually trains his cats. He just observes them, learns their personality and things they like to do, and then creates performance acts that incorporate the particular cat's natural preferences, be that running, climbing, jumping, or playing hide and seek. Mr. Kuklachev's cats, most of them former strays, perform amazing acts onstage, and you can tell they enjoy doing them.

She hopes other cat owners can come to adopt this approach in working with their own cats. Working with their personality is key.

I believe this is the key to cat training, as well as the reason why some people find it so difficult to train a cat: you can not order a cat around and expect them to obey just because you're the boss. If you want them to learn something, you should work with them and keep in mind their personality. (Lond)

While the Moscow Cats Theater show is an interesting example of a cat exhibition, controversy surrounds Kuklachev's training techniques, as is the case with all animal circus acts. I cannot personally judge his techniques without more direct evidence or experience. However, there will always be concerns about such exhibitions as well as with the source of the cats used in the exhibitions. For example, there are reports that cats' paws are burned to get them to jump and that they are kept under-fed so they will be motivated by food rewards. Further, while this site says he uses stray cats, he himself talks about using the offspring of his own cat. If he is breeding cats for this purpose, at a time when millions of cats die for being unwanted, there are issues to consider.

In contrast, Gregory Popocich's "Comedy Pet Theater" in Las Vegas does seem to get its cats from local shelters and then trains them for the act. They too say they work with the proclivities of the individual cats. Some prefer to climb, others prefer to jump. Working with individual personalities and inclinations, this show suggests that cats can be trained and that some seem to enjoy the process. Examples like these do promote the idea that humans and cats can work together and this message can do a great deal to change negative perceptions of cats.

This kind of education seems to be part of the motivation of another, more amateur example of a cat exhibition—"Samantha's Acro-Cats and Rock Cat's": "Chicago's only trained domestic cat show! Our fantastic felines will amuse and amaze your guests as they ride skateboards, ring bells, roll barrels, walk the high wire, climb ropes, push a shopping cart, jump through hoops, and even run a cat-size agility course." Another group of cats sing. Her web site says, "All of the animals live with Samantha and are trained through the use of positive rewards. Training is a beneficial and fun way to provide exercise and enrichment for our animals and tricks are based on the animals' own natural behavior so we are able to sneak in a little education as well" (amazinganimals.biz). On the available YouTube videos of some of her shows, it is clear the cats don't always perform as they are asked to perform. This actually seems to be part of what the audience most likes and appreciates. I cannot say how she responds to their "misbehavior" off the stage.[3]

Done respectfully, such shows can be a fun outlet for the natural behaviors of cats. Many will object that cats are just too different from dogs and horses and cannot gain anything from such use. However, there are counter examples. Just as with horses and dogs, not *all* cats will enjoy such activities, but many human beings may be denying cats an opportunity they would enjoy. As with all other animal beings used in this way, though, there can be concerns about training, travel, and confinement. Given their nature, cats may be especially susceptible to the stresses of these events as they tend to be territorial and so may not adjust to travel as well as many horses and dogs do. They like to roam, so long confinement can lead to behavior issues. These concerns would need to be addressed. And, obviously, abusive training techniques are highly problematic—burning paws to get them to jump off perches, using electric shock to get them to move, starving them so they are very motivated by food rewards are just a few examples. These same concerns apply to competition as well.

Use in Competition

The first cat show was in England in 1871 and their National Cat Club was established in 1887. For these shows, cats were first divided by color, then by breed (Clutton-Brock, *Cats* 61, 74). In the United States we have the Cat Fanciers' Association, founded in 1906.

> The first cat shows licensed by CFA were held during 1906 - one in Buffalo and one in Detroit. The first Annual Meeting was held in 1907 at Madison Square Garden. In 1909, CFA published the first Stud Book and Register in the *Cat Journal* magazine. Also in 1909, Volume I of the Stud Book was published in book form. On September 18, 1919, articles of incorporation were drawn up under the laws of the State of New York. CFA then entered a new and successful era, and the Association has grown steadily over the years. . . . (www.cfa.org)

---

3. There are some concerns with the fact that she also exhibits exotic animal beings and rents them out for parties.

As with other such organizations, the CFA is a public face for the promotion of purebred cats. It sets standards and rules for competitions and regulates cat shows. Their objectives also include "the promotion of interest of breeders and exhibitors of cats" and the "promotion of the welfare of cats and the improvement of their breed." These last two can come into conflict with each other. It is, however, also why they could be an ally for those interested in cat welfare. Regardless of the other stated objectives, though, it is clear that the main objective is the breeding and showing of cats.

Even with the attention of organizations like the CFA, there has been less artificial selection and restriction of cats' breeding than has occurred with dogs ((Liberg 120). So, there are not as many breeds of cats as there are different breeds of dogs, but they are on the increase. Twenty-eight different main breeds are listed. In all, the CFA recognizes at least sixty breeds. Some of the more popular breeds are the Siamese, Manx, Abyssinian, Angora, Persian, and the Russian Blue (Clutton-Brock, *Cats* 71–75, 64). Just as with horses and dogs, people point to differences in personality or temperament among the breeds. Here are just a few examples:

> Abyssinians aren't for those who want decorative cats to match the rust-colored carpet, or for those who want cats that enjoy being picked up and cuddled. Courageous, curious, and high-spirited, when restrained Abys tend to become struggling bundles of fur with more than the usual number of elbows; however, that's not to say that Abyssinians are aloof or standoffish. While Abyssinians will cheerfully entertain themselves, they are most happy when involved in every aspect of your life. They are particularly involved at dinnertime. In fact, you'll know it's dinnertime when small, furry, food-seeking missiles attach themselves to your legs!
>
> Breeders and fanciers report that Burmese are amusing, playful, and super-smart, the perfect interactive cats for home, office, shop— any place where people are in need of love and entertainment. . . . Devoted cats, Burmese are loyal and people-oriented.
>
> Breeders report temperament differences between males and females. The females are highly curious, active, and very emotionally involved with their owners. The altered males love their humans too, but are more placid. They like to lounge about, usually on top of whatever you're doing. They take life as it comes. The only issue about which they are passionately concerned is the selected cuisine and when it will be served.

The Manx's personality is probably the reason the breed has won such a strong following despite the physical difficulties and breeding challenges. Manx cats make great household companions. They are intelligent, active, and fun-loving cats that manage to express themselves very well without tails to swish around. Manx get along well with other pets (particularly dogs), and form strong bonds with their chosen humans. They enjoy a good game of fetch and are fascinated by water, but only on their terms, of course.

Determinedly social and very dependent upon their humans, Siamese crave active involvement in your life. Like Mary's little lamb, they want to follow wherever you may go. Siamese can be unpredictable in their behavior and can appear aloof and disinterested, but it's all an act. Siamese need to be treated with respect and patience and require lots of affection if they are to develop a close, caring relationship with their human companions. Siamese will pine if left too often alone. (animal.discovery.com)

Many people choose cats for looks, but many others choose on the basis of personality and activity level. As is becoming more common with dogs, there are questionnaires to help one select the kind of cat who will best fit a particular household. The ASPCA has nine categories of cats for adopters to consider. The "private investigator" stays out of the way, the "secret admirer" warms up slowly but is affectionate, the "love bug" likes lots of petting, the "executive" is busy checking things out but finds time for attention, the "sidekick" is "just plain good company," the "personal assistant" will help you type on your computer, the "MVP" can entertain herself but enjoys a scratch behind the ears, the "party animal" loves to play, and the "leader of the band" is always in the middle of things and is demonstrative (aspca.org). Humans need to consider how their own personalities and lives do and do not match with certain breeds and individuals—horses, dogs, or cats.

In addition to breed differences, there may be differences associated with coat color. There appear to be connections between coat color and personality and temperament. The gene for coat color is close to the gene for sensory organs like hearing, and there are established connections between coat color and problems with things like deafness (in dogs as well). The gene for coat color is also close to the gene that regulates dopamine, and so there may be connections to temperament and personality as well (Mendl 53). It is commonly thought to be the case. That said, breeding for color in horses, dogs, or cats can be very problematic in terms of other aspects of health. Similarly, choosing a cat (or horse or dog) on color alone is unwise.

First, as we increase the focus on pedigreed cats and specific traits, like color, we create an increased risk of health problems. There are, for example, concerns with the development of some of the features of the Sphynx, Scottish Fold, and the Muhchkin. Selection for exaggerated anatomical features, in particular head shape, is a concern. "Over the years, the show trend has been toward a flatter, more extreme facial type for the Persian. This troubles some fanciers, who feel the extreme face can be harmful to the breed. Reported problems include upper respiratory problems, weepy eyes, malocclusions, and birthing difficulties" (animal. discovery.com). The extremely short muzzle of some cats (and dogs) may be associated with sight and breathing problems. Excessive prolongation of the face and deep eye sockets can make eye infections more common and engender eyelid problems (Rochlitz 221).

The shortened tail of the Manx may be related to spinal problems.

> The Manx is one of the most challenging cats to breed because of the Manx gene. Homozygous Manx kittens (kittens that inherit the Manx gene from both parents) die in vivo early in their development. Since homozygous kittens comprise roughly one quarter of kittens conceived from Manx to Manx matings, Manx litters are generally small, averaging two, three, or four kittens. Even the heterozygous kittens (kittens that inherit the Manx gene from one parent) have a higher than average mortality rate, because the Manx gene can cause deformities such as spina bifida, fusions of the spine, and defects of the colon.

Similarly, breeding for the ears desired in the Scottish Fold can result in skeletal deformities.

> The Scottish Fold's folded ears are produced by a dominant gene that affects the cartilage of the ears, causing the ears to fold forward and downward, giving the head a rounded appearance. Since the gene is dominant, all Scottish Fold cats must have at least one folded ear parent to have folded ears themselves. When a Fold is bred to a straight-eared cat, approximately 50 percent of the kittens will have folded ears, although the number of Folds in any given litter can vary greatly. Breeding Fold to Fold increases the number of Fold kittens, but also greatly increases the chances of skeletal deformities. Homozygous Folds (Folds that inherit the folded ear gene from both

parents) are much more likely to develop congenital osteodystrophy, a genetic condition that causes crippling distortion and enlargement of the bones. (animal.discovery.com)

Obviously, the focus on appearance can have negative consequences for the cats (just as we saw with horses and dogs). While cat shows contribute to the demand for pedigreed cats there may be a shift in the making. Cat shows may not remain solely focused on appearance and pedigree in the future.

The Cat Fancier's Association started to add cat agility competitions to cat shows in 2004, though it seems to have had limited success (cfa.org). As with the cat exhibitions, some agility cats seem to enjoy performing and can be trained. Unlike dog agility, however, cat agility, as noted earlier, relies less on training than on luring the cats through the course with food or toys. Nonetheless it shows that there are previously unexplored activities in which human beings can engage with cat beings—to the benefit of both. As with horses and dogs, for this to be enjoyable for the cat, one has to choose the right cat for the right kind of activity. There are specific characteristics to look for in an agility cat. They must be outgoing, not scared or distracted by crowds, and they need to be naturally active and playful. (See the "Use in Entertainment" section for more on this.) This means one should pick an individual cat who is suited to agility rather than making the choice based solely on breed or appearance. The agility sections at cat shows are open to mixed breed cats. Here is a place that adopted strays can compete and excel. Nonetheless, the focus of cat shows remains on the pedigreed cat.

Because these cat shows focus on pedigreed cats, the CFA is very concerned to protect the rights of breeders. This is, in fact, the primary focus of their Legislative Group. This group

is charged with providing guidance to those individuals or member clubs who are opposing unreasonable animal control legislation in their geographic area. The committee members review and analyze proposals, offer opinions, and provide information to those working to overcome the pressure to limit and control the activities of pedigreed cat breeders as a way to end what has been termed "Pet Overpopulation." We continuously put forth a broader perspective, and this has led to our preference for the term, "cat and dog population surplus" since "pet" "overpopulation" implies that too much reproduction is the *sole* source of the problems which result in unnecessary euthanasia in shelters, and that people's pets are entirely responsible. Neither premise is correct. . . . Though we recognize that overpopulation is an important factor, **it is the uncontrolled matings of feral cats and the unplanned reproduction of free roaming pet cats** which need to be the focus. The numbers of cats of a recognizable breed found in shelters is negligible to extremely low in proportion to that of cats which are random bred, homeless, feral and/or unweaned kittens. (cfa.org)

As with dogs and horses, simply condemning all those human beings who breed and compete with cats fails to take into account the variety of ways humans can successfully and respectfully relate with cat beings. There is not just one acceptable way. To be sure, there are bad breeders and bad breeding practices. Abuses occur in the realm of competition, but this does not represent the majority of competitors. Most humans involved in these activities would actually be great allies in improving the general reputation and treatment of cats in the United States. They are passionate about cats and want them to be happy and to thrive. The statement from the CFA makes it clear that they do not currently see room to ally with others interested in animal rights or welfare. It is currently a war. This is due, at least in part, to a lack of openness and understanding on both sides. Extreme positions that resist all regulations on breeding and use, and extreme positions that suggest humans should have no relationship with cats, are equally problematic. But most cat (and other animal being) lovers fall somewhere between. It is important that we work out the middle ground as we are currently finding more ways cats can "work" for humans.

Use in Work

Of course, cats have worked as a means of rodent control since the start of the human-cat relationship. They continue to do so. The frequent offerings of dead animals to their human companions indicates that the cats understand their work as part of a cooperative relationship. However, the reputation of cats seems to have limited their use in the kind of work discussed earlier for horses and dogs. As we learn more about the nature of cats, though, and find more respectful and successful ways of working with them, this may change.

While dogs still dominate as the most commonly used therapy animal, cats are growing in popularity. Despite concerns about allergies, cats have the advantage of their small size. Nursing homes and hospitals have come to see the positive effects of using such animal beings. They reduce stress and often relieve depression among the patients, residents, and family members. Some suggest that Alzheimer's patients gain the specific benefit of having memories and emotions awakened. The purr of a cat seems to have a very calming effect on the mentally disturbed. With increased interest in this use of cats, some suggest that cats who engage in this kind of work should be declawed for the safety of the humans. This has major consequences for the cats as was noted earlier. This is an example of why it is important that we think through what living and working with cats means for the cats themselves, and that we work out respectful training and treatment.

Disease detection is another possible future line of work. While more has been done with dogs in this regard, cats have great senses as well and some seem to react to humans with various cancers. Famously, Oscar was a nursing home cat who was able to sense some kinds of metabolic changes in patients and curled up with them not long before they were going to die. These abilities may be put to work for humans in the future. Again, as our understanding of cats increases, more of their abilities may be seen as useful to humans. It is very important to work out the ethics of using cats in various ways so that we don't repeat some of the disrespect-ful approaches we have used with other animal beings such as horses and dogs. This understanding and respect also affects how humans live with cats and deal with their death.

Death

Cats tend to live longer than many dogs. However, some die early due to illness or disease. Others may be killed by predators or cars if they go outside. Unfortunately, I have experienced the death of many cats. Our barn cats, being outdoor cats, have been run over, burned in burn piles, killed by dogs, and died of disease. When we lived in Pennsylvania, rhino virus ran through the barn and I spent much of my time nursing sick cats. Putting medicine up the cats' noses did not always endear me to them, but somehow we remained friends. My dog Tuffy was also their friend and protector. She supervised the sick cats and my handling of them.

I received quite a glare from her when a cat objected to my medicating technique. She did not fight with other dogs, but she would take on any dog who dared to threaten her cats. When individual cats were sick and I brought them down from the barn and into the basement of the house, she would sleep there with them instead of on my bed. It was amazing to watch the development of such cross-species relationships. She seemed to share in the sorrow when one of the cats didn't make it.

Death is part of life. But how we handle death is important. As mentioned before, sometimes euthanasia is the most respectful and responsible choice. This choice is increasingly an option taken. However, since many cats are outdoors for a good part of their lives, many just disappear from their humans' homes. Some are found dead—perhaps hit by a car. This is a more likely occurrence for cats than for most other pets and adds an extra element of risk to humans' relationships with cats. However, it also means one can feel less directly responsible for the death. If death *happens*, it is often seen as unfortunate and sad, but not one's *choice*. But to be respectful of the lives of cats, sometimes we must face and make just this choice. An example that illustrates some of the issues involved with euthanasia can be seen with Sieglinda—the cat who moved with us to the city.

Sieglinda's death was different than the death of other animal beings in my life. With cats I had experienced mostly tragic and unexpected ends. There had been a few who had gotten old and disappeared. As Sieglinda got on in years, though, she got sick. One day she was to go to the vet for a check-up while I was in school. Instead, without telling me, my parents had arranged to have her euthanized. I found out when I got home. I again felt as if I had betrayed a very special friend. I believe it is my responsibility to be with loved ones when they die if I can. It is hard, but it is our responsibility. I wasn't there for Sieglinda. I'm not questioning that putting her down was the right thing to do, but I do not believe it is right to drop a friend off with the doctor to face this alone. I was there with Tuffy, Pandora, Nemesis, and Donald. Sieglinda deserved better.

She may have also deserved more in the way of diagnosis and treatment—I do not know since I was not involved in the discussion and decision. And here is another challenge of providing a good life and a good death for cats. Today we have medical options we have not had before. We can diagnose and treat many conditions and diseases, but at what cost to the cat? Increasingly, humans face difficult decisions about what treatments to try. Cats today live with diabetes, and other conditions, that require regular medical intervention. Balancing the welfare of the cat with the human desire to keep the cat alive can be tricky and is something that can only be approached in the context of a particular cat's life. However, what is known about cats' nature and desires should be used to guide these decisions about death as well as decisions about how best to live and work with cats. A human's desire not to "lose" a friend should not be the sole basis for decision-making. In mutually transformative (transactive) relationships, the interests of all parties need to be considered.

Pragmatist Response

While a minority of people choose cats by breed, most tend to choose cats based on color, coat, and size.[4] While this may provide some information, people should pay more attention directly to temperament and the natural and developmental history of cats in general (Turner, "Human-Cat Relationship" 200). This means they should also pay attention to the social and physical environments provided for the cat. There are consequences to the ways in which kittens and cats are handled. One needs to consider the level of confinement, the amount of mental stimulation and physical activity, and socialization with other beings (Mendl 58). The fact that so many cats are adopted means that many humans don't start to get to know the cats until they are already socialized. This may limit the potential for bonding unless the humans are willing to spend a lot of time with the cats. Most cats will bond more fully if they get lots of attention and time for interaction. It is also important to accept and respect their independence (Turner, "Human-Cat Relationship" 203–204). If people pay attention to these *natural* and *developmental* aspects of life with a cat they can create more successful pairings. More attention to the individual personalities (*pluralism*) of cats would have a similar result. Each cat's needs and desires need to be considered. This requires *experimentation* and the willingness to admit mistakes (*fallibilism*). All of this can improve (*ameliorate*) human-cat relationships.

We know that six to eight million cats and dogs are relinquished to shelters each year, and over half of these are killed. Many more are simply

---

4. Many people say they are chosen by the cats, rather than the other way around.

abandoned—let loose to fend for themselves. Some of the abandoned cats join the always present feral population of cats (Clutton-Brock, *Cats* 87). Others die of disease, injuries from fights, or are killed by cars or predators. This does not speak well of the human relationship with cats.

Another complicating factor, not yet really discussed, is that these other animal beings we consider to be pets are also considered to be property. Legally, we own them and are responsible for their actions. For many animal rights/animal welfare activists this is yet more evidence that we think of these animal beings as "things"—things that can be used as we please and discarded when we choose. In contrast, the Cat Fancier's Association actually defends cats' status as property. They think it offers them protection.

> The "guardian" issue has become prominent over the last few years and legislation to add this word to animal laws has now passed in several cities and the state of Rhode Island. The Cat Fanciers' Association, along with many other organizations, is concerned about the potential implications of this term in both animal related laws and in common usage. The "guardian" word as a replacement for owner is part of a campaign, led by In Defense of Animals, called "They Are Not Our Property - We Are Not Their Owners". IDA disavows the concept and language of animal ownership and seeks to "reconstruct the social and legal relationship between humans and animals". . . .
>
> At its October 3, 2003 meeting the CFA Board of Directors unanimously approved an official CFA position statement as follows:
>
> **I OWN my cat!! - CFA's statement concerning the "guardian" term:**
>
> "The Cat Fanciers' Association, Inc. strongly supports caring and responsible pet ownership. CFA upholds the traditional property rights of animal owners that provide the basis for their ability to make decisions about their animals' well-being, including health, reproduction and transfer to a new owner. Owned cats are valued family members. As legal property, they cannot be taken away from us except by constitutional due process. The term "guardian," whether inserted into animal laws or in common usage, contradicts this critical protective and personal relationship. CFA rejects the concept of animal "guardianship," which can be challenged or revoked, because of the potential legal and social ramifications that would negatively impact veterinarians,

animal rescuers, breeders and sellers of animals as well as pet owners." (cfa.org)

This is an interesting and important debate and it applies to all animal beings considered to be pets. As it stands, though, the animal rights and welfare groups are dug in at one extreme and the various breed and species associations are pushed to dig in at the other extreme from fear that admitting any agreement with the views expressed by animal rights and welfare groups will result in the end of their relationships with other animal beings. For the Pragmatist this kind of polarization is not helpful. Part of the problem is not letting the various animal beings have a status of their own. We try to force them into pre-existing categories that do not do justice to their specific place in the human world.

I do not try to settle this issue here. In the conclusion to this book, though, I will sketch out how Pragmatism can help in approaching the points of tension that exist between those who live, compete, and work with pets, and those who seek to work for the rights, welfare, or liberation of all animal beings.

Here it is enough to say that a Pragmatist examination of the relationships between human beings and cat beings shows that there is a much closer relationship between us than many assume. It also reveals that human beings have not always respected this relationship as they should. Cats have been seen as more disposable than other pets; their supposed solitary nature and independence have been used to relieve humans of responsibility and have also been one reason many humans have contempt for cats. These assumptions result in missed opportunities to develop human-cat relationships fully. Humans assume you can't expect much from a relationship with a cat, so they do not put in the same kind of petting and play time with cats as they do with many other animal beings. If humans don't enter the relationship fully, cats won't either. However, there are plenty of examples of great human-cat relationships that show the potential of such relationships. One needs to know the species, the breed, and the individual in order to find a good match of personalities, interests, and abilities.

CONCLUSION: MAKING THINGS BETTER

So far I have examined a variety of relationships between human beings and some other animal beings commonly considered as pets. I have examined some practices and activities that can be harmful for these other animal beings. This harm is very real and very possible for individual horses, dogs, and cats. They have some legal protections, but they are ultimately dependent on the good will of the humans with whom they are involved. Even if we strengthen the legal protections for them, human good will remains the defining framework of their lives. So, I have tried to argue for a change in attitude that makes it more likely that horses, dogs, and cats will encounter humans who understand them and work to make their lives good and fulfilling.

I have used American Pragmatism to frame the discussion because it begins by trying to understand other beings as they are. It calls on us to examine their natural and developmental histories at the same time that it recognizes that transactive relations with human beings have affected both human and other animal beings. It further calls on us to use our critical capacities to examine past and current experimentation with ways of living together. It also helps us realize that there is no one size fits all solution given the plurality of beings and situations, and it warns us to be cautious about providing all or nothing approaches because we are fallible creatures who are usually mistaken in one way or another. Further, Pragmatists believe that any "solution" generates a new host of problems to address. Making relations better is, and will continue to be, an ongoing task with new and emerging conditions. So the role of the ethicist is not to provide rules or mandate specific action. Rather, her role is to set out the things to consider, guide that consideration with good information and careful thinking, and help people move to thoughtful action in the hope of improving human relations with the other animal beings we call pets. The ethicist can also help identify possible coalitions of groups who, despite real differences, share some common goals and commitments. By getting beneath the differences to see some commonalities, ethicists can help people work across their differences for the good of other animal beings.

For each of the relationships examined here to be successful, we need to make it possible for human and other animal beings to express their unique personalities. These relationships require that human beings get out of their own heads and observe and respect the individual animal beings in their lives. It does not mean human beings do nothing, however. These relationships are not about somehow leaving horses, dogs, and cats alone just to be themselves. Who they are is partly experienced in being beings who live with humans. They are not "wild" and we all need to learn to navigate this mixed-species world.

For instance, Tao—the border collie mix—required some assistance to make the move from seeing Bunny the cat as squirrel to seeing her as possible friend. To do this simply by force or domination does not usually work well and fails to honor the dog. Thinking about who he is and how he sees the world, though, allows for negotiation. In this case the dog, the cat, and the humans all had to make some adjustments. Working with Tao's nature need not entail that he express *all* of his desires, e.g. chasing and catching the cat. Similarly Donald and Hank were recently in living conditions that were great for Donald, but not so good for Hank. Donald was out in a pasture with two mares, but Hank did not have the turnout he is used to. Consequently, I spent more time at the barn so that he could be out in the ring and would get more exercise and mental stimulation. I also provided extra enrichment toys. This situation would not have been acceptable to me for the long term, but in the short term we all adjusted and accommodated. In fact, given that Donald was thirty at the time, I felt I owed him this time and experience. But it would have been wrong not to see the situation as a problem for Hank.

Further, having Donald in the pasture did put him at increased risk for developing laminitis—a painful and often crippling hoof condition. Morgans are more prone than many other breeds to developing this condition and being out on pasture grass can be a contributing factor. Having carefully managed his time on grass his whole life, I reasoned in this case that the risk was lower due to the fact that his worn teeth limited his ability to graze. I also decided that it was more important that he live and enjoy life rather than live longer. I will never know what role that year on pasture played in the fact that Donald did develop laminitis at the age of thirty-two (it could be that it would have happened no matter what I did), but for me it was more important to help him live an interesting and fulfilling life at his advanced age. I also owed him a quick and painless death once the diagnosis was made.

Similarly, it recently became clear that as Tao aged he was no longer the play partner Maeve desired. So I began considering looking for a young dog or puppy. My rational and selfish side kept me from acting. My life makes sense with two dogs since they come to my (small) office, ride in my (small) car, and since most motels that allow pets have a two pet limit. Another dog would complicate my life. A puppy would ruin the household peace. But I knew deep down it needed to happen. Still, I did not actively look. But, when a lost Aussie "just happened" to wander into my yard, and it turned out she had three-week old puppies at home, my rational side was overcome. At eight weeks old, Kira joined our household and she and Maeve are best friends. This is another example of humans needing to sometimes put the interests of the other animal beings in their lives ahead of their own. Compromise is a part of all successful relationships, but so is respect for individual needs and differences.

It is the fact that these other animal beings use intelligence, have emotions, express a purposive nature, and value particular things that allows us to form these amazing relationships in the first place. These same traits, however, mean that humans have more responsibility in how we care for and live with pets. Pets are not merely appendages, but living, feeling, thinking, valuing creatures whose interests must be considered and respected. For many this includes training and competition activities,

Figure 14. Kira, the puppy who joined the household to be a friend and playmate for Maeve. This is an example of putting the interests and desires of a dog before the interests and desires of a human. Maeve needed the company of a younger dog and in this case that was a more important consideration than concerns about the increased work and inconvenience of life with three rather than two dogs.

Figure 15. Tao and Bunny sharing a couch. This level of companionship came as the result of working with the individual dog and cat. Tao's background is not known, but he likes to chase small mammals. When he needed to live with Bunny, his desire to chase cats could not be given an outlet. With time and training, he learned to not just live with Bunny, but seemed to come to like her.

or time spent in entertainment and work. To remove these could be cruel and would limit the opportunities for these beings to express themselves.[1] This does not, however, justify the abuse that often takes place in such contexts.

What I have tried to sketch here is a Pragmatist approach to some of the most common issues and concerns related to developing reflective, ethical, and responsible relationships among human and other animal beings. This position is rooted in the fact that human beings are a kind of animal being and that all animal beings share a great deal in common. Following Peirce's point that animal beings exist in a continuum without sharp and definitive breaks, we need to learn to see the things we share and the ways in which we differ from one another. There is, however, no human exceptionalism. For instance, human and other animal beings may communicate differently, but that does not justify the claim that other animal beings do not communicate. While human use of language makes some things possible for our species—transmission of information over multiple generations or the expression of complex concepts and relations—the same faculty is accompanied by many inabilities. For instance, most human beings are not as good as most other animal beings at sensory awareness of our surroundings. Each species of creature has developed an array of abilities and skills that enable them to successfully transact with the environment in which they live.

Part of that environment for other animal beings is, and has been, the presence of human beings; part of that environment for human beings is, and has been, the presence of other animal beings. Humans have always been in relations with animal others and we have influenced each other's development along the way. This influence is more pronounced between human beings and those other animal beings who have become domesticated, but it holds for all animal beings. Taking this *naturalism* seriously requires that human beings pay attention to how other animal beings negotiate their worlds, and we need to learn to relate to these beings from within that context. A certain amount of anthropomorphism makes sense

1. This also raises questions about spaying, neutering, and confinement. These do limit the ability of these beings to fully experience their nature in certain ways. However, they allow other kinds of freedoms. In a mixed-species world, there are compromises that are necessary for the well-being and safety of the pet animals and their human companions. If handled well, the other animal beings won't notice any loss. But this requires putting effort into fulfilling any frustrated needs or desires.

in developing these relations as human and other animal beings have so much in common. However, we must also respect the differences.

This takes us to the call to respect *pluralism* so clearly found in the work of James and others. This entails not assuming everyone else is just like me—other animal beings are not just like each other or just like human beings. To have respectful relationships across species, humans need to inquire into the different needs, interests, and abilities of other species—especially those domesticated species with whom we share our lives. If a dog is going to share our house, we must ask what temperature is healthiest for the dog; what food suits a dog's nutritional and digestive needs; what are the dog's needs for attention, exercise, and mental stimulation? Much of this can be addressed by *experimentally* studying dog beings. The same is true of horse and cat beings.

Learning to respect the pluralism is further complicated by the fact that human and animal beings are all *developmental* beings. For all of us, our needs, interests, and abilities change over time. This applies to the developmental history of each species, breed, and individual. Human beings are not the same creatures they were when they first started living with horses, dogs, and cats. We have been transformed over time, in part by these very relationships. Our various relationships with other animal beings have enabled us to travel across the globe and to survive in a variety of climates. Perhaps the release of oxytocin these relationships induce has helped us be more social and peaceable than we otherwise would have been.

Similarly, these animal beings who live with us have been altered during the many years of domestication. They have experienced physical and temperamental changes. Some of these changes actually threaten the well being of these animal beings, though, and we need to think about this seriously. For instance, some breeds of dogs cannot copulate and/or give birth without human assistance. What does this mean for their future development? Some horse breeds are very susceptible to specific genetic conditions because of the ways horses have been selectively bred. What does this mean for their well-being and future development? Some cats have spinal issues as a result of intentional breeding practices. What does this mean for their future development? What do all of these practices mean for future human development as well?

To address these issues and concerns we turn to the *experimentation* suggested by Pragmatism. As live creatures seeking to find better ways to live within the environment in which we find ourselves, most animals experiment to one degree or another. It is a part of learning to negotiate the world. Human beings carry this further in the degree of manipulation and control we exercise over ourselves and the environment in which we find ourselves. Some of the results of such experimentation seem to improve the lives and possibilities of various animal beings, some seem to harm them, and others seem to outstrip our ability to judge their value and effect. In connection with our relationship with other animal beings—pets in particular—Charlotte Perkins Gilman offers a cautionary view. In some cases human experimentation with other beings has been abusive, excessive, and damaging to their well being as individuals and as species.

The whole history of domestication has been a series of experiments. From the human point of view, some failed, some succeeded. Success was determined by moving from living in proximity with other animal beings, to taming some, to controlling their breeding in order to achieve desired characteristics. However, much of this "success" also caused harm—genetic flaws and diseases have been present in most "pure bred" animal beings. Advances in technology may help in controlling potential harm through genetic screening and gene manipulation. As we create a hypoallergenic cat, though, we need to ask if we are respecting the natural and developmental history of cats, as well as the pluralism of cats as a whole. It is not "unnatural" from a Pragmatist perspective to engage in such technological experimentation, but we do need to be careful about narrowing our vision and narrowing the ways in which a cat can be a cat.

Caution is especially warranted because the Pragmatists take human *fallibility* as a given. We have, at best, partial and imperfect understandings of how things work and we are often mistaken. Certainty is not possible, and seeking it can be dangerous. This means that as we manipulate genes to create a hypoallergenic cat, it is highly probable that we will also create other unexpected and surprising outcomes. Just as breeding dogs and cats for specific colors has often resulted in increased instances of blindness and deafness, manipulating them in new ways will likely continue to lead to unanticipated and unexpected effects. Caution is warranted. However, it does not make sense to pretend we could somehow halt all manipulation and interaction among species. Further, to take absolutistic positions that call for the outright banning or requiring of any particular practice fails to respect the call for *experimentation* or the recognition of *fallibilism*. This applies to breeding practices, to training techniques, and to various forms of "use" of other animal beings by human beings.

Given all of this, Pragmatist experimentation regarding human relationships with those animal beings commonly considered to be pets in the United States provides no absolute answers, nor does it suggest specific policies to be enacted. Instead it seeks to get individual human beings (such as pet "owners," breeders, trainers), and various groups of human beings (such as HSUS, ASPCA, AKC, CFA, USEF, AVMA, PETA) to consider different ways of thinking about the various relationships among human and other animal beings. This *thinking differently* will have ramifications for what is seen as morally acceptable but it won't always result in full agreement or clear and certain policies. Instead it will suggest an approach to understanding and improving these relationships that is rooted in humility, caution, and respect. A model for this effort can be found in the work of another American Pragmatist—Jane Addams.

Addams was the first American women to receive the Noble Peace Prize, largely for her work related to women and peace. However, she is probably best known for her work at Chicago's Hull House which she founded in 1889—a settlement house in a poverty stricken neighborhood of recent immigrants. She ran the settlement house with the intention of working with others to define and address pressing problems such as poverty, child labor, political corruption, sanitation, sweatshop labor, and more. Even though women did not have the right to vote during most of Addams' life, she was politically active. But she did not think changing laws would be enough to change people's lives. She also worked to change attitudes and habits.

Addams was both a theorist and a practitioner of Pragmatism. This meant she did not arrive in the neighborhood with all the answers or with the idea that there was just one approach to any of the many problems faced by the people in the neighborhood. Instead she remained a *pluralist* in her approach to problem solving and she talked with the people to identify their problems and priorities; she worked with them and *experimented* with approaches to help improve the situation. She recognized the *fallibilism* of all her experiments and was willing to re-think and revise the approaches they were trying according to the results they engendered. Her focus was not on being right but on improving the lives of the people with whom she worked. This brings us to the final point of Pragmatism that I wish to discuss—its focus on *amelioration*.

To ameliorate a situation is to work to make it better. It is not about finding a perfect or final solution, which is not possible, but is about seeking improvement. This focus on amelioration often meant that Addams had to make compromises. Humility, caution, and respect contribute to the possibility of amelioration. One must respect others—even those with whom one disagrees. Addams modeled this in an exceptional manner. If one has no respect for those with whom she is negotiating, little progress is likely. Further, being a fallibilist, Addams remained open to the possibility that she was mistaken. So she was cautious in forming opinions. She was open to being persuaded even as she sought to persuade others.

This kind of humility requires a great deal of courage—especially when done in the public realm. For instance, she was a pacifist who opposed the U.S. entry into World War One. She vehemently opposed the new draft legislation that was enacted at the time, especially since it had no exceptions for conscientious objectors. She fought the law and helped those jailed for failing to comply. At the same time, some wanted Hull House to be a place for people to register for the draft. Addams did not stop this from happening even as she worked to change the larger issues. Some faulted her for this openness and willingness to compromise, but I think it is exactly the approach needed when taking on complex and emotionally laden public problems (Seigfried).

This is exactly the approach we need if we are to ameliorate successfully the situation pets face today. Instead of the us versus them attitude that has resulted from some of the more extreme positions taken on animal issues—by PETA and CFA for example—if we care about animal beings we need to find ways to work together. Ethicists could help members of these groups see some of their common commitments and help them work together on those issues instead of always working against each other. Further, within this context of cooperation, conversations about their real differences could take place in a respectful manner that allowed for real listening and consideration of the views. They would likely remain opposed to each other on a number of key concerns, but such interaction would transform the nature of their interactions and could make possible many cooperative ventures that would directly benefit other animal beings.

Similarly, in the context of research, Animal Care and Use Committees exist. But without the presence of an effective animal advocate these have had minimal success in really improving the lives of animal beings. I know, for example, that at my own institution no one who has expressed ethical concerns about using other animal beings in research is considered for the committee. I believe this is a defensive reaction to many who hold the extreme non-use position that has come out of fields like philosophy. This leaves the animal beings used in research even more vulnerable to harm. If animal advocates were at the table, engaged in informed and respectful dialogue with researchers, much could possibly be done to improve the lives of these animal beings and further limit the number used. This won't happen if fear and defensiveness keep people apart.

To make amelioration possible we need to heed Alain Locke's call for a critical relativism and we need to

> reach a position where we can recognize relativism as a safer and saner approach to the objectives of practical unity. What is achieved through relativistic rapprochement is, of course, somewhat different from the goal of the absolutists. It is a fluid and functional unity rather than a fixed and irrevocable one, and its vital norms are equivalence and reciprocity rather than identity or complete agreement. But when we consider the odds against a complete community of culture for mankind, and the unlikelihood of any all-inclusive orthodoxy of human values, one is prepared to accept or even to prefer an attainable concord of understanding and cooperation as over against an unattainable unanimity of institutional beliefs. ("Cultural Relativism" 71)

This means leaving extreme and absolute positions behind in order to focus on common concerns and ameliorative approaches. Currently, the Humane Society of the United States tends to work in this way and might provide a model with which we can start.

Animal rights groups who have ruled out the option of animal welfare are not especially helpful when it comes to coalition building or enacting concrete change. For the Pragmatist the absolutist mentality is a serious issue that prevents us from addressing the concrete problems we face. As Locke said:

> We know, of course, that we cannot get tolerance from a fanatic or reciprocity from a fundamentalist of any stripe, religious, philosophical, cultural, political or ideological. But what is often overlooked is

that we cannot, soundly and safely at least, preach liberalism and at the same time abet and condone bigotry, condemn uniformitarianism and placate orthodoxy, promote tolerance and harbor the seeds of intolerance. I suggest that our duty to democracy on the plane of ideas, especially in time of crises, is the analysis of just this problem and some consideration of its possible solution. ("Pluralism and Intellectual Democracy" 57)

We need to get beyond the desire for simple and absolute answers or solutions. We need to see the absolutistic tendencies in our own commitments and loyalties. Pragmatism is helpful here. For instance, while Pragmatism will not be able to identify and create rules to end all abuse and neglect, it can provide a more nuanced understanding of what counts as abuse and neglect, can assess what the interests are from the point of view of the being experiencing abuse and neglect, and can suggest a variety of responses to try out.

This approach suggests, for example, great caution in keeping as pets any non-domesticated animal beings. Exotic pets, such as reptiles and birds, have not adjusted their needs and behaviors over years of domestication. Some of these animal beings may be tame, but their needs can be very difficult to meet in a household with humans. Further, these beings are not the orphaned young being taken in to help them survive. Instead, they are usually the young who have been stolen from their homes for the sole purpose of being sold as pets. Similarly, chimpanzees and big cats also represent kinds of animal beings who do not make good pets. Their size and nature do not fit mixed-species communities. While we have affected each other at a distance, we have not evolved to cohabit and it is unlikely we will.[2] Only a small number of animal beings seem readily adapted to the conditions of domestication and we need to respect that.

We also need to respect the reality of domestication, though. Given that reality, Pragmatism will not call for the end of all other animal beings participating in entertainment, competition, or work arenas. But it will suggest guidelines and limits for such activities. Such guidelines will

2. There are also concerns connected to the procurement and housing of the exotic animals who are part of the pet trade. Mortality rates are very high, both for the animal beings who are captured and for those who are left behind in disrupted communities.

always be provisional and under review—never perfected. Increasing the number of rules and the severity of the punishments is only a band-aid on a very large wound. The abuses that can take place in these activities are the result of the attitudes that some human beings have toward other animal beings. Punishments are unlikely to change the attitudes. Some abuse is the result of ignorance and so education would be a more appropriate response in those cases. However, the larger project here, for which the Pragmatist view is important, is a shift in our ontological perspective. *We have to re-think the human relationship with the rest of the world. In this particular case, I'm calling for a re-thinking of our connections, interactions, and relations with those animal beings with whom we most intimately share our lives—pets.*

If humility, caution, and respect guide the re-thinking, I am hopeful that humans can engage in even more fulfilling relations with horses, dogs, and cats. To flip from an extreme of domestication and exploitation—these beings are here for humans to use in any way they please—to an extreme of non-interference and separation—these beings should just be left alone and no longer bred or kept with humans—is not helpful. Neither extreme is descriptively accurate nor warranted by our long experience with each other. Things are not all right, but we are clearly involved with each other and no simple "break up" will solve our problem. In some instances we need to develop entirely new ways of relating with each other; in others we simply need to pay more attention to, and respect, the needs, interests, and abilities of these "others" in our lives. This will enrich the experiences for all involved.

One important step in this effort would be to have some kind of mediation among the competing animal groups. Philosophers could help with this work. Ethicists on hospital boards often do the work of helping involved parties identify, work out, and articulate their various commitments and values. They could perform a similar function around the issues discussed here. The role of the philosopher on this account is not to provide *the* answer or *the* theory, but to help all involved explain and consider a variety of options in an open, tolerant, and respectful manner. Such work will expand philosophers' experience with other human and animal beings and help make their work less abstract and more helpful. Such work will also enable various groups to get a fair hearing; everyone involved must really listen to make such a process productive. It could make real cooperation on behalf of various animal beings a more common reality.

This Pragmatist "position" may seem to some like common sense, but it is a view that is hard to find in the current work on or about human relations with other animal beings. In other words, while it may be common sensical, it is still not a very common outlook. It is hard to work with a framework of fallibility, uncertainty, and tolerance and at the same time remain committed to improving the world. Taken seriously the Pragmatist approach stands to change a great deal about how we live with the other animal beings we call pets.

If taken seriously, the Pragmatist approach also has obvious consequences for our relationships with other domesticated animal beings—those many beings considered to be farm animals—and nondomesticated animal beings—those many beings considered to be "wild." In the next phase of this project, I will consider how human beings do and should relate to other domesticated animal beings—cattle, sheep, goats, pigs, turkeys, chickens, and fish. As with pets, complete separation and non-use does not really make sense. But this does not justify the domination and exploitation that most contemporary farm animals face in the United States. The next part of my project is based on field research with farmers and examines how they view the human relationship with the rest of nature—animal and nonanimal. The basic Pragmatist framework provided here is used to examine the various approaches these farmers take to raising, housing, slaughtering, and consuming these animal beings. It also involves an examination of how consumers' beliefs limit and expand the possibilities for farmers and other animal beings.

I think there are some relevant differences in the human relationships with those animal beings we classify as pets and those we classify as farm animals, but in the end I think the differences in how we should understand and treat these two kinds of animal beings are very small. Here the work of the ecofeminist philosopher Val Plumwood is most helpful. She appeals to John Dewey, among others, to argue for a more inclusive approach to decision making. She argues, echoing Peirce, to include the perspective of nature and other animal beings as part of the continuum in which human beings exist. She points out that we have separated domesticated animal beings into "pet" and "meat" animals. The middle ground of a familiar animal with whom we participate in use and economic relations is lost. There is no room left for integrating the economic and the affective. This divide has the consequence that

> in real life, non-privileged animals assigned to the 'meat' side of this dualistic hierarchy die to make meat for the pets of people who think of themselves unproblematically as animal lovers—kangaroos, dolphins, penguins, anonymous and rare marine animals in yearly billions are slaughtered at some remove to feed the cats and dogs whose own deaths as meat would be unthinkable to their owners. (163)

Even more ironically, she notes, many of these animal lovers are vegans or vegetarians themselves. But, not only do they breed and keep carnivorous animal beings, they often (especially in the case of outdoor cats) let them loose in places where they disrupt ecosystems and kill free-living animals (163).

None of us—omnivore, vegetarian, flexitarian, or vegan—should be blind to the fact that the deaths of other beings support our own lives and the lives of the pets we love. There are good vegetarian dog foods available, for example, and this might be a good choice for many dogs. Feeding such a food, or practicing a vegan or vegetarian diet oneself, does not eliminate the suffering and consumption of other animals beings, though. Many insects and mammals die in the process of farming grains, vegetables, and fruit, not to mention the exploitation of human labor and health that is involved. Such a choice may greatly decrease one's complicity, but does not eliminate it. "While many people are seeking alternatives to foods that may harm their pets, some have an added motive: avoidance of foods that harm other animals and the environment. Most products on the mainstream market include ingredients from polluting factory farms that subject animals to intensive confinement, deprive them of basic needs such as fresh air and sunlight, and pump them with hormones and antibiotics to promote unnaturally fast growth" (Cohen, "No Dilemma" 39).

We both enrich and complicate our lives when we live in mixed-species communities. Our responsibilities for the well-being of ourselves and those animals beings with whom we live involve us in the death and use of other life. Most often this is done in a blind and self-serving way and thus results in the pet/meat divide mentioned above. As Plumwood notes:

> Just how aggressive this can be and how little space it leaves for the other can be seen from the way animals are treated in the name of rational agriculture, with chickens and calves held in conditions so

cramped that in a comparable human case they would clearly be considered torture. Its logic of the One and the Other tends through incorporation and instrumentalism to represent the Other of nature entirely in monological terms of human needs, as involving replaceable and interchangeable units answering to these needs, and hence to treat nature as an infinitely manipulable and inexhaustible resource. (119)

This approach needs to be replaced with an approach that respects life in the ways this Pragmatist account has suggested for pets. "This alternative line of thought would make potentially ethically available forms of use that respect animals as both individuals and as community members, in terms of respect or reverence for species life, and would aim to rethink farming as a non-commodity and species-egalitarian form, rather than to completely reject farming..." (Plumwood 156). This means, quite literally, knowing your meat in much the same way many of us know our pets.

If you have been persuaded by any of the Pragmatist suggestions addressed in this book, I encourage you to think about the possible implications this change in attitude might have not only for human-pet relations but for other relationships humans have with other animal beings. Even if your main interest and concern is with pets, remember that most of our pets eat the flesh of other animal beings (not to mention herding sheep with dogs or cutting cattle with horses). It would be sadly ironic indeed if our respect for the animal beings we love was based on the exploitation of more distant animal beings. The Pragmatist call for humility, caution, and respect has the potential to shake up many human habits. It can take us on the next stage of "our journey towards a non-oppressive form of the mixed-community and a liveable future respectfully shared with animals" (Plumwood 166).

Bibliography

Adams, Carol J. *Neither Man Nor Beast* (New York: Continuum, 1995).

Adams, Carol J., and Jospehine Donovan. *Beyond Animal Rights: A Feminist Caring Ethic for the Treatment of Animals* (New York: Continuum, 2000).

———. *The Feminist Care Tradition in Animal Ethics* (New York: Columbia University Press, 2007).

Allan, Carrie. "The Long Way Home: The HSUS Partners with Equine Expert Pat Parelli to promote Humane Training Methods and Change the Lives of Rescued Horses," *All Animals*, July/August 2009, 15–19.

———. "The Purebred Paradox: Is the Quest for the 'Perfect' Dog Driving a Genetic Health Crisis?" *All Animals*, May/June 2010, 17–23.

———. "Rescued from Squalor," *All Animals*, July/August 2010, 26–33.

All Animals. "Letters to the Editor," Summer 2007, 12.

———. "Stopping the Slaughter," Summer 2008, 3.

Anderson, Douglas R. "Peirce's Horse," in *Animal Pragmatism: Rethinking Human-Nonhuman Relations*, eds. Erin McKenna and Andrew Light (Indianapolis: Indiana University Press, 2004), 86–94.

Anderson, Elizabeth. *The Powerful Bond Between Pets and People: Our Boundless Connections to Companion Animals* (London: Praeger, 2008).

Animal Times. "Cover," Vol. 24, No. 3, Fall 2009.

———. "Race to Save Thoroughbreds from Slaughter," Vol. 24, No. 3, Fall 2009, 12–13.

———. "Utah Bans Pound Seizure," Summer 2010, 10.

Antoniades, Katina. "The Cat's Meow: Understanding Your Feline Friend," *All Animals*, May/June 2009, 38–39.

Balzar, John. "A Brave Voice Against Puppy Mills," *All Animals*, July/August 2009, 38–39.

Bateson, Patrick. "Behavioural Development in the Cat," in *The Domestic Cat: The Biology and Its Behavior*, eds. Dennis C. Turner and Patrick G. Bates (Cambridge: Cambridge University Press, 2000), 9–22.

Beck, Alan, and Aaron Katcher. *Between Pets and People: The Importance of Animal Companionship*, Revised Edition (West Lafayette, Ind.: Purdue University Press, 1996).

Benton, Ted. *Natural Relations: Ecology, Animal Rights, and Social Justice* (London: Verso, 1993).

Borchardt, John K. "New Findings About Equine Domestication," *Equus*, Issue 384, September 2009, 14.

Bowan, A. N., ed. *Animals and People Sharing the World* (Hanover, N.H.: University Press of New England, 1988).

"Breaking the Chain," *All Animals*, Spring 2007, 9.

Budiansky, Stephen. *If a Lion Could Talk* (New York: The Free Press, 1998).

———. *The Nature of Horses* (New York: The Free Press, 1997).

———. *The Truth About Dogs* (New York: Viking Press, 2000).

Bulliet, Richard W. *Hunters, Herders, and Hamburgers: The Past and Future of Human-Animal Relationships* (New York: Columbia University Press, 2005).

Callicott, J. Baird. "Animal Liberation and Environmental Ethics: Back Together Again," in *The Animal Rights/Environmental Ethics Debate: The Environmental Perspective*, ed. Eugene Hargrove (New York: State University of New York Press, 1992), 249–61.

———. "Animal Liberations: A Triangular Affair," in *The Animal Rights/Environmental Ethics Debate: The Environmental Perspective*, ed. Eugene Hargrove (New York: State University of New York Press, 1992), 37–70.

Clutton-Brock, Juliett. *A Natural History of Domesticated Mammals* (Cambridge: Cambridge University Press, 1999).

———. *Cats: Ancient and Modern* (Cambridge, Mass.: Harvard University Press, 1993).

Cohen, Arna. "The Dawn Patrol," *All Animals*, September/October 2010, 38–39.

———. "No Dilemma for These Omnivores: A Meat-Free Diet May be the Right Choice For Your Canine Friend," *All Animals*, March/April 2010, 38–39.

Coren, Stanley. *The Intelligence of Dogs: A Guide to the Thoughts, Emotions, and Inner Lives of Our Canine Companions* (New York: Bantam Books, 1994).

Daston, Lorraine, and Gregg Mitman, eds. *Thinking With Animals: New Perspectives on Anthropomorphism* (New York: Columbia University Press, 2005).

Deag, John M., Aubrey Manning, and Candace E. Lawrence. "Influencing the Mother–Kitten Relationship," in *The Domestic Cat: The Biology and Its Behavior*, eds. Dennis C. Turner and Patrick G. Bates (Cambridge: Cambridge University Press, 2000), 23–46.

Dewey, John. *Democracy and Education*, in *John Dewey: Middle Works, Vol. 9: 1916*, ed. Jo Ann Boydston (Carbondale: Southern Illinois University Press, 1989).

———. "The Ethics of Animal Experimentation," in *John Dewey: Later Works, Vol. 2: 1925–1927*, ed. Jo Ann Boydston (Carbondale: Southern Illinois University Press, 1989), 98–103.

———. *Human Nature and Conduct*, in *John Dewey: Middle Works, Vol. 14: 1922*, ed. Jo Ann Boydston (Carbondale: Southern Illinois University Press, 1989).

———. *Knowing and the Known*, in *John Dewey: Later Works, Vol. 16: 1949–1952*, ed. Jo Ann Boydston (Carbondale: Southern Illinois University Press, 1989), 1–294.

———. "Modern Philosophy," in *John Dewey: Later Works, Vol. 16: 1949–1952*, ed. Jo Ann Boydston (Carbondale: Southern Illinois University Press, 1989), 407–19.

———. "Note on 'What Is It to Be a Linguistic Sign of Name,'" in *John Dewey: Later Works, Vol. 16: 1949–1952*, ed. Jo Ann Boydston (Carbondale: Southern Illinois University Press, 1989), 468–74.

———. *The Public and Its Problems*, in *John Dewey: Later Works, Vol. 2: 1925–1927*, ed. Jo Ann Boydston (Carbondale: Southern Illinois University Press, 1989), 235–372.

———. *Reconstruction in Philosophy*, in *John Dewey: Middle Works, Vol. 12: 1920*, ed. Jo Ann Boydston (Carbondale: Southern Illinois University Press, 1989), 77–201.

Driscoll, Carlos A., Juliet Clutton-Brock, and Stephen O'Brien. "The Evolution of House Cats," *Scientific American*, June 2000, 68–75.

"FEI General Regulations," 23rd edition, 1 January 2009, updated 1 January 2010, found at fei.org.

Ferraby, John. *All Things Made New: Comprehensive Outline of the Baha'i Faith* (Wilmette, Ill.: Baha'i Publishing Trust, 1963).

Francione, Gary L. *Animals as Persons: Essays on the Abolition of Animal Exploitation* (New York: Columbia University Press, 2008).

Franklin, Julian H. *Animal Rights and Moral Philosophy* (New York: Columbia University Press, 2005).

Fudge, Erica. *Animal* (London: Reaktion Books, 2002).

Gilman, Charlotte Perkins. *Herland*, with an introduction by Ann J. Lane (New York: Pantheon Books, 1979).

———. *His Religion and Hers* (Westport, Conn.: Hyperion Press, 1923).

———. *The Living of Charlotte Perkins Gilman*, with an introduction by Ann J. Lane (Madison: University of Wisconsin Press, 1935).

———. *The Man-Made World* (New York: Charlton Company, 1911).

———. *Moving the Mountain* (New York: Charlton Company, 1911).

———. "Our Brains and What Ails Them," in *Charlotte Perkins Gilman: A Non-fiction Reader* (New York: Columbia University Press, 1991, 219–33.

———. "When I Was a Witch," in *The Charlotte Perkins Gilman Reader* (New York: Pantheon Books, 1980), 21–31.

Green, Penelope. "A New Breed of Guard Dog Attack Bedbugs," *New York Times*, March 10, 2010.

Greek, C. Ray, and Jean Swingle Greek. *Sacred Cows and Golden Geese: The Human Cost of Experiments on Animals* (New York: Continuum, 2000).

Haraway, Donna. *The Companion Species Manifesto: Dogs, People, and Significant Otherness* (Chicago: Prickly Paradigm Press, 2003).

———. *When Species Meet* (Minneapolis: University of Minnesota Press, 2008).

Hargrove, Eugene C., ed. *The Animal Rights/Environmental Ethics Debate: The Environmental Perspective* (New York: State University of New York Press, 1992).

Harris, Leonard. "Introduction," in *The Philosophy of Alain Locke*, ed. Leonard Harris (Philadelphia: Temple University Press, 1989), 3–27.

Hens, Kristien. "Ethical Responsibilities Towards Dogs: An Inquiry into the Dog-Human Relationship," in *The Journal of Agricultural and Environmental Ethics* 22:3–14, 2009.

Hettinger, James. "Wheels of Injustice," *All Animals*, March/April 2010, 12.

"High Volume Breeders Report—Report to AKC Board of Directors," November 12, 2002, found at akc.org.

Huddleston, John. *The Earth Is But One Country* (London: Baha'i Publishing Trust, 1976).

Ingold Tim, ed. *What Is an Animal?* (London: Unwin-Hyman, 1988).

James, William. "On a Certain Blindness in Human Beings," in *The Writings of William James*, ed. John J. McDermott (Chicago: University of Chicago Press, 1977), 629–45.

———. *Pragmatism* (Indianapolis, Ind.: Hackett Publishing Co., 1981).

———. *Principles of Psychology* (New York: Dover Publications, Inc., 1918).

Johnson, Ruthanne. "Signatures of Change: Groundbreaking Ballot Measure Would Help Dogs in Missouri's Puppy Mills," *All Animals*, July/August 2010, 7–9.

Kaminer, Michael. "Foreclosures: Left Behind," *All Animals*, Summer 2008, 6–7.

Katcher, Aaron, and Allen Beck. *Between Pets and People* (West Lafayette, Ind.: Purdue University Press, 1996).

Krikstan, Catherine. "Mounted Police Face Cutback," *Equus*, Issue 382, July 2009, 69.

Lachs, John. "Questions of Life and Death," in *The Relevance of Philosophy to Life* (Nashville: Vanderbilt University Press, 1995), 163–69.

Lawrence, Elizabeth A. "Horses in Society," in *Animals and People Sharing the World*, ed. Andrew N. Rowan (Hanover, N.H.: University Press of New England, 1988), 96–112.

Lee, Keekok. *Zoos: A Philosophical Tour* (New York: Palgrave, 2005).

Liberg, Olaf, Mikael Sandell, Dominique Potter, and Eugenia Natoli. "Density, Spatial Organization and Reproductive Tactics in the Domestic Cat and Other Felids," in *The Domestic Cat: The Biology and Its Behavior*, eds. Dennis C. Turner and Patrick G. Bates (Cambridge: Cambridge University Press, 2000), 119–48.

Locke, Alain. "Cultural Relativisim and Ideological Peace," in *The Philosophy of Alain Locke*, ed. Leonard Harris (Philadelphia: Temple University Press, 1989), 67–78.

———. "Pluralism and Ideological Peace," in *The Philosophy of Alain Locke*, ed. Leonard Harris (Philadelphia: Temple University Press, 1989), 95–102.

———. "Pluralism and Intellectual Democracy," in *The Philosophy of Alain Locke*, ed. Leonard Harris (Philadelphia: Temple University Press, 1989), 51–66.

Lond, Laura. "Cat Training Tips: Consider the Personality," February 19, 2008, http://voices.yahoo.com.

MacAlpine, Andy. "First, Do No Harm," *All Animals*, September/October 2009, 8–9.

Macdonald, David W., Nuboyuki Yamaguchi, and Gillian Kerby. "Group Living in the Domestic Cat: Its Sociobiology and Epidemiology," in *The Domestic Cat: The Biology and Its Behavior*, eds. Dennis C. Turner and Patrick G. Bates (Cambridge: Cambridge University Press, 2000), 95–118.

Malkin, Nina. "American Tragedy: The Horrors of Horse Slaughter and the Fight to Protect Our National Treasures," *All Animals*, Spring 2007, 19–20.

Manning, Aubrey, and James Serpell, eds. *Animals and Human Society: Changing Perspectives* (London: Routledge Press, 1994).

Masson, Jeffrey Moussaieff. *Dogs Never Lie About Love: Reflection on the Emotional World of Dogs* (New York: Crown Publishers, 1997).

McDermott, John J. "Experience Grows by Its Edges: A Phenomenology of Relations in an American Philosophical Vein," in *The Drama of Possibility: Experience as Philosophy of Culture*, ed. Douglas R. Anderson (New York: Fordham University Press, 2007), 372–89.

McKenna, Erin, and Andrew Light, eds. *Animal Pragmatism: Rethinking Human–Nonhuman Relations* (Indianapolis: Indiana University Press, 2004).

Melendez, Michele. "Life with My Cats: A Love–Hate Story," *All Animals*, September/October 2009, 36–37.

Mendl, Michael, and Robert Harcourt. "Individuality in the Domestic Cat: Origins, Development, and Stability," in *The Domestic Cat: The Biology and Its Behavior*, eds. Dennis C. Turner and Patrick G. Bates (Cambridge: Cambridge University Press, 2000), 47–64.

Merchant, Carolyn. *Earthcare: Women and the Environment* (New York: Routledge, 1995).

Midgley, Mary. "The Mixed Community," in *The Animal Rights/Environmental Ethics Debate: The Environmental Perspective* (New York: State University of New York Press, 1992), 211–26.

———. "The Significance of Species," in *The Animal Rights/Environmental Ethics Debate: The Environmental Perspective* (New York: State University of New York Press, 1992), 121–36.

Mitchell, Sandra D. "Anthropomorphism and Cross-Species Modeling," in *Thinking With Animals*, eds. Lorraine Daston and Gregg Mitman (New York: Columbia University Press, 2005), 100–18.

Morton, Eugene S., and Jake Page. *Animal Talk* (New York: Random House, 1992).

Moxley, Angela. "A Mission of Hope and Healing," *All Animals*, November/December 2009, 15–21.

Nussbaum, Martha. *Frontiers of Justice: Disability, Nationality, Species Membership* (Cambrige, Mass.: Harvard University Press, 2000).

Nussbaum, Martha, and Carl Sunstein. *Animal Rights: Current Debates and New Directions* (Oxford: Oxford University Press, 2005).

Olmert, Meg Daley. *Made for Each Other: The Biology of the Human–Animal Bond* (Cambridge, Mass.: Da Capo Press, 2009).

Oliver, Kelly. *Animal Lessons: How They Teach Us to Be Human* (New York: Columbia University Press, 2009).

Pacelle, Wayne. "President's Note," *All Animals*, July/August 2009, 3.

Pearson, Karl. *The Grammar of Science* (New York: Charles Scribner's Sons, 1892).

Peirce, Charles Saunders. *The Collected Papers* (Thoemmes Contiuum, 1998).

———. "The Doctrine of Chances," in *The Essential Peirce: Selected Philosophical Writings, Volume I (1867–1893)*, 142–54.

Peterson, Anna L. *Being Human: Ethics, Environment, and Our Place in the World* (Berkeley: University of California Press, 2001).

Plumwood, Val. *Environmental Culture: The Ecological Crisis of Reason* (London: Routledge, 2002).

Podberscek, A. L., E. Paul, and J. A. Serpell. *Companion Animals and Us* (Cambridge: Cambridge University Press, 2000).

Price, Steven D. "On Patrol with the NYPD," *Equus*, Issue 398, November 2010, 45–48.

"Puppy Mills: Seeing Is Believing," *All Animals*, May/June 2009, 9–10.

"Race to Save Thoroughbreds from Slaughter," *Animal Times*, Vol. 24, No. 3, Fall 2009, 12–13.

Rachels, James. *Created From Animals: The Moral Implications of Darwinism* (Oxford: Oxford University Press, 1990).

Regan, Tom. *The Case for Animal Rights: Updates with a New Preface* (Berkeley: University of California Press, 2004).

———. "Foreword," in *Animal Rights: A Historical Anthology*, eds. Andrew Linzey and Paul Barry Clark (New York: Columbia University Press, 1990).

———. "The Struggle for Animal Rights," in *Animal Rights: A Historical Anthology*, eds. Andrew Linzey and Paul Barry Clark (New York: Columbia University Press, 1990), 176–86.

Rochlitz, Irene. "Feline Welfare Issues," in *The Domestic Cat: The Biology and Its Behavior*, eds. Dennis C. Turner and Patrick G. Bates (Cambridge: Cambridge University Press, 2000), 207–26.

Rodberseck, Anthony L., Elizabeth S. Paul, and James A. Serpell. *Companion Animals and Us: Exploring Relationships between People and Pets* (Cambridge: Cambridge University Press, 2000).

Rollins, Bernard E. *Animal Rights and Human Morality*, third edition (Amherst, N.Y.: Prometheus Books, 2006).

———. *The Unheeded Cry: Animal Consciousness, Animal Pain, and Science*, Expanded Edition (Ames: Iowa State University Press, 1998).

Rowan, Andrew N., ed. *Animals and People Sharing the World* (Hanover, N.H.: University Press of New England, 1988).

Sabloff, Annabelle. *Reordering the Natural World* (Toronto: University of Toronto Press, 2001).

Scott, John Paul, and John L. Fuller. *Dog Behavior: The Genetic Basis* (Chicago: University of Chicago Press, 1965).

Seigfried, Charlene Haddock. "The Courage of One's Convictions or the Conviction of One's Courage? Jane Addams's Principled Compromises," in *Jane Addams and the Practice of Democracy*, eds. Wendy Chmielewski, Marilyn Fischer, and Carol Nackenoff (Urbana: University of Illinois Press, 2009), 40–62.

Serpell, James, ed. *The Domestic Dog: Its Evolution, Behavior, and Interaction with People* (Cambridge: Cambridge University Press, 1995).

———. "Domestication and History of the Cat," in *The Domestic Cat: The Biology and Its Behavior*, eds. Dennis C. Turner and Patrick G. Bates (Cambridge: Cambridge University Press, 2000), 179–92.

———. *In the Company of Animals: A Study of Human-Animal Relationships* (New York: Basil Blackwell, 1986).

———. "People in Disguise: Anthropomorphism and the Human-Pet Relationship," in *Thinking with Animals: New Perspectives on Anthropomorphism* (New York: Columbia University Press, 2005), 121–36.

Sharp, Micahel. "Sore Winners: Horses Suffer Extreme Pain for the Sake of a Prize," *All Animals*, November/December 2010, 8–9.

Shephard, Paul. *The Others: How Animals Made Us Human* (Washington, D.C.: Island Press, 1996).

Singer, Peter. *Animal Liberation* (New York: HarperCollins, 2002).

Spiegel, Marjorie. *The Dreaded Comparison: Human and Animal Slavery* (New York: Mirror Books, 1996).

Steiner, Gary. *Animals and the Moral Community: Mental Life, Moral Status, and Kinship* (New York: Columbia University Press, 2008).

Taylor, Paul W. "The Ethics of Respect for Nature," in *The Animal Rights/Environmental Ethics Debate: The Environmental Perspective* (New York: State University of New York Press, 1992), 95–120.

Tester, Keith. *Animals and Society: The Humanity of Animal Rights* (London: Routledge, 1991).

———. *Man and the Natural World* (London: Allen Lane, 1983).

Thomas, Elizabeth Marshall. *The Hidden Life of Dogs* (New York: Houghton Mifflin, 1993).

———. *The Tribe of the Tiger: Cats and Their Culture* (New York: Simon & Schuster, 1994).

Thompson, Lynn, "Rescue Groups Save Race Horses from Slaughterhouse," *Seattle Times*, November 9, 2010.

Turner, Dennis C. "The Human–Cat Relationship," in *The Domestic Cat: The Biology and Its Behavior*, eds. Dennis C. Turner and Patrick G. Bates (Cambridge: Cambridge University Press, 2000), 193–206.

Turner, Dennis C., and Patrick G. Bates, eds. *The Domestic Cat: The Biology and Its Behavior* (Cambridge: Cambridge University Press, 2000).

White, Paul S. "The Experimental Animal in Victorian Britain," *Thinking With Animals: New Perspectives on Anthropomorphism* (New York: Columbia University Press, 2005), 59–82.

Williams, Erin E., and Margo Demello. *Why Animals Matter: The Case for Animal Protection* (Amherst, N.Y.: Prometheus Books, 2007).

Williams, Jennifer. "When Your Horse Needs a Buddy," *Equus*, Issue 377, February 2009, 45–48.

"Yays & Nays," *All Animals*, May/June 2009, 11.

Zeuner, Frederick E. *A History of Domesticated Animals* (New York: Harper & Row, 1963).

http://www.24thstate.com
http://www.akc.org
http://www.amazinganimals.biz
http://animal.discovery.com
http://www.animallaw.info
http://www.aspca.org
http://www.avma.org
http://www.banpoundseizure.org
http://biology.clc.uc.edu
http://www.catagility.com
http://www.cfa.org
http://www.declawing.com
http://www.defendingdog.com
http://www.fei.org
http://www.fws.gov/birds
http://www.gra-america.org
http://www.humanesociety.org
http://www.idausa.org
http://www.immunize.org
http://www.lasvegassun.com
http://www.marshallbio.com
http://inside movies.ew.com
http://www.newscientist.com
http://newyorktimes.com
http://ori.dhhs.gov
http://www.peta.org
http://www.psychiatrictimes.com
http://seattletimes.nwsource.com
http://www.therapyanimals.org
http://www.ttouch.com
http://www.vgl.ucdavis.edu
http://white Arabian.tripod.com

Index